THE MAKING
OF A SENATOR
DAN QUAYLE

THE MAKING OF A SENATOR

DAN QUAYLE

Richard F. Fenno, Jr.
University of Rochester

PRESS

A Division of Congressional Quarterly Inc.
1414 22nd Street N.W., Washington, D.C. 20037

Cover photo: Joe Houston

Printed in the United States of America

Third Printing

Library of Congress Cataloging-in-Publication Data

Fenno, Richard F., 1926-
    The making of a senator.

    Includes bibliographies and index.
    1. Quayle, Dan, 1947-   2. Vice-Presidential candidates—United States—Biography. 3. Legislators—United States—Biography. 4. United States. Congress. Senate—Biography. I. Title.
E840.8.Q28F46 1989   328.73′092′4 [B]   88-37588
ISBN 0-87187-511-X
ISBN 0-87187-506-3 (pbk.)

Contents

Preface

When this book was written, in 1987, Dan Quayle was a United States senator, little known beyond his home state of Indiana. As the book goes to press, in 1988, Dan Quayle is about to become the vice president of the United States. During the recent presidential campaign, he received as much attention as any vice presidential candidate in this century. And yet, for all of that publicity, he remains, still, "a United States senator, little known beyond his home state of Indiana." Little known, that is, *as a senator*. The media avalanche that landed on him between August and November 1988 covered every available inch of his precongressional career—but not his career in the Senate. In breadth and depth, in intensity and impact, far more attention fell on Dan Quayle's private life than on his public life. This pattern was, perhaps, the media's own contribution to what has been widely called a disappointing and unedifying campaign. In any event, lasting assessments of our public political figures require, in the end, a concentration on their public political careers. In the case of the new vice president, what follows may help us to begin.

This little book is a segment of a much larger research project on the United States Senate. In May 1978 I began the project by observing, at first hand, a campaign for the Democratic Senate nomination in New Jersey. Between 1978 and 1986 I travelled in the Senate campaigns of seventeen individuals—some incumbents (nine), some not (eight); some Democrats (eleven), some Republicans (six); some winners (eleven), some losers (six). My intention was to approach the Senate by way of its members, and to approach its members by way of their election campaigns. For those who won, my intention was to watch over their subsequent political performance, and to conclude by observing their reelection efforts six years later. The plan worked for the nine successful candidates—five elected in 1978 and four elected in 1980. For each of these senators, I hoped to present a six-year slice of a political career. And through the variety of those careers, I hoped to present an enriched picture of the Senate itself.

One of the nine was Dan Quayle. I went to Indiana in September 1980 to travel with him as he first campaigned for the Senate. And I returned to accompany him in his home state three times—in 1982, 1985, and 1986. I spent the academic year 1981-1982 in Washington observing his senatorial activity—among that of others. The most interesting and important of Quayle's activities that year was his work on job training legislation. My observations eventually focused on that activity. Quayle came to represent, in institutional terms, a subcommittee chairman at work. But my larger focus was on his six-year term and on the relation of his job training activities to his political career during that period.

My research ended with his reelection in November 1986; my case study of Quayle was completed in the summer of 1987. When he was chosen as the Republican nominee for vice president one year later, a finished 253-page manuscript lay in my desk drawer. Completed case studies for two other senators rested beside it. They were to have remained there until the other sections of the book were finished. In the face of an explosion of interest in Dan Quayle, I decided to publish the section on the senator from Indiana. It remains, as it was intended, a book primarily for students of political science. With the exception of routine copy editing, it appears here as it was written in 1986-1987. Except for an epilogue, nothing has been altered or added. In sum, the publication of the manuscript has been affected by the nomination of Dan Quayle, but the descriptions and the judgments have not. The timing has been changed, but not the text.

A guiding question in my senatorial research has been this: what is the relationship between what senators do in their home states and what they do in Washington? Or, what is the relationship between *campaigning*, which is done mostly at home, and *governing*, which is done mostly in Washington? I have watched senators engage in both these activities, in both settings, over one complete electoral cycle. My notion is that an intensive period of campaigning is followed by an intensive period of governing, which is followed, in turn, by another intensive period of campaigning. I have come to think of this six-year cycle—*campaigning-to-governing-to-campaigning*—as the "master sequence" of every senator's political life. And I have sought answers to my original question by tracing the activities of some senators along this path. Dan Quayle is one of them.

The book applies the design of the larger project to describe a segment of one senator's career as he moves across one electoral cycle, from 1980 to 1986—from campaigning to governing to campaigning again. Readers can also discern, in this case study, certain activities that provide intermediate linkages and contexts within the master sequence. For example, special attention is paid to the relevance of an individual's *interpretation of his election* in linking campaigning to governing near the front end of the sequence, and to the relevance of an individual's *explanation of his legislative activity* in linking governing to campaigning at the back end of the sequence. Within the governing phase, special attention is paid to the newcomer's *early adjustment* to the Senate and to the *succession of decision-making contexts* within which legislative decision making takes place. Throughout the book, as in the larger research project, special emphasis is placed on the effects—both political and personal—of changing contexts and developmental sequences. The notion of "seasons" in the chapter headings is meant to suggest the rhythms and the regularities of political careers.

My vantage point has been the view "over the shoulder" of Senator Quayle and his staff. My perspective has been their perspective. I have not tried to watch or talk to other relevant actors in the events described herein—although I have come across some of them in the normal course of my research. And I have relied, at several points, on the accounts and judgments of interested political reporters—the media scorekeepers.

My personal debts, therefore, are obvious. First, to Dan Quayle, without whose cooperation there would have been no study. I have often argued that from a scholarly standpoint there are only two kinds of politicians—good interviews and bad interviews. Dan Quayle was "a good interview"—accessible and forthcoming, informative and interested.

Next, I thank the members of his staff, whom I have described collectively as "the Quayle enterprise." I am especially indebted to Robert Guttman, the key staff person in the job training story, whose knowledge and friendship were crucial to my education. Among those who smoothed my path and helped with my research, I thank, first of all, Cynthia Ferneau, and also Tom Duesterberg, Myrna Dugan, Rich Galen, Peter Lincoln, Barbara McLennan, Les Novitsky, Lester Rosen, Larry Smith, Jim Wolfe. In Indiana my chief benefactors were Ron Breymier, Frank Gulledge, Mary Moses, Ralph Van Natta, Greg Zoeller.

For preparing the manuscript, from interview notes to finished copy, my thanks go to Janice Brown. For checking it, I thank my wife, Nancy. For promoting, editing, and handling the production, my debt is to Joanne Daniels, John Moore, and Kerry Kern.

Finally I thank the Russell Sage Foundation, under whose auspices, and with whose financial support, the larger research project was undertaken.

Seasons of Campaigning and Adjustment

THE SUBCOMMITTEE CHAIRMAN: AMBITION AND OPPORTUNITY

If there is any uncontested generalization about the operation of the United States Senate, it is that the policy-making work of the body is done in its committees. This generalization can be qualified or embroidered, but the committee-based division of labor stands as one of the few defining characteristics of the institution. If there is an uncontested corollary, it is that the Senate is a distinctively nonhierarchical, decentralized, policy-making organization. Each committee is given a policy jurisdiction and, within that prescribed domain, the committee acts for the Senate, as the dominant agenda setter and decision maker. If there is a second uncontested corollary, it is that the largest share of each committee's policy-making work is done in its subcommittees. In 1982 the Senate's 20 committees were subdivided into 102 subcommittees. So numerous were they that every member of the majority party chaired at least one committee or subcommittee. And, for each of those senators, the leadership of his or her subcommittee consumed—or, better perhaps, could consume—a substantial part of his or her legislative life. Senate subcommittees provide a major conjunction of legislative policy making and senatorial careers. The story of this book is the story of one such conjunction.

It is a conjunction that produced the most important new piece of social legislation in the Ninety-seventh Congress and gave definition to the career of an otherwise unknown U.S. senator. The committee was the Senate Committee on Labor and Human Resources—with broad jurisdiction in matters of health, education, labor, and public welfare. The subcommittee involved was its Subcommittee on Employment and

1

Productivity. The policy-making activity was the production of the Job Training Partnership Act of 1982 (JTPA). The senator was Dan Quayle, a Republican from Indiana.

The conjunction of the senator and the subject matter was purely accidental. Nothing in Quayle's previous experience would have led anyone to expect him to be especially interested in—much less influential in—this area of public policy. No person in the network of job training policy makers could have foreseen the Republican take-over of the Senate in 1980—much less that their interests would be put in the care of an unknown freshman senator. On the subject-matter side, there was the fortuitous opening of what John Kingdon has called "a policy window," a special set of circumstances that thrust job training onto the Senate agenda.[1] On the personal side, there was the ambition of a new young senator to make a mark for himself somehow in some part of the Senate's work. Once he had positioned himself on a committee and on a subcommittee, the subject of job training fell into his legislative lap.

So one large question becomes: given the circumstances under which he began, what did Senator Quayle make of his opportunity— first, in producing legislation and, second, in capitalizing on his legislative accomplishment? Since most of the capitalizing took place at home, the story gives us an uncommon perspective on the Washington/home relationship. It gives us an unusually clear look at the second link in the campaigning-governing-campaigning sequence. By watching the senator over a six-year cycle, we are in a position to as-sess the impact of his governing activity in Washington on his campaigning activity in Indiana. And this impact, "back home again in Indiana," is given special prominence in our six-year slice of Dan Quayle's career.

THE POLITICAL CAREER
OF DAN QUAYLE: 1976-1980

When he was elected to the Senate, Dan Quayle was thirty-three years old. He had served two terms in the U.S. House of Representatives, where he had been its second-youngest member. He had held no other public office nor tried for any. He had no legislative success to his credit. He was not well known in Washington or Indiana. He was not without ambition or philosophy, nor was he, obviously, without political talent. But he was insufficiently experienced and insufficiently accomplished to provide any clear idea of what kind of senator he might be. His public record did, however, contain essential clues.

SELF-CONFIDENCE

First, there were the circumstances of his two electoral successes. In 1976, at the age of twenty-nine and without a shred of electoral experience, he took on a congressional race almost no one believed he could win. He ran against a sixteen-year incumbent. And he won. Four years later, in 1980, he took on a Senate race very few people thought he could win. He ran against an eighteen-year incumbent, and he won. These actions revealed a degree of self-confidence that has shaped his political behavior throughout his career.

In 1976 Quayle seized an unexpected and uninviting opportunity to run for Congress. In the abstract, it was not an appealing prospect. Indeed, all the obvious, experienced candidates had declined to run, and it was late in the game when the party leadership turned to Quayle. "Ed Roush was a very popular congressman," Quayle recalled.

> He had beaten Ross Adair and been in for sixteen years. All the big guns in the district had tried to beat him and failed—two well-known state senators for example. Nobody was anxious to run against him. Ernie Williams was the editor of the *Fort Wayne Sentinel* and a good friend of mine. One day he said to [the Republican county chairman], "Instead of running someone from Fort Wayne every year and losing, why don't you give young Dan Quayle down in Huntington a chance?"

At that time, "young Dan Quayle" was a newspaperman-lawyer, who had worked for about a year as associate publisher of the family-owned *Huntington Herald-Press*. It was part of a chain of newspapers published by his grandfather, and it was run by his father. It was a job he had inherited; he had no track record as a newsman; and he had not practiced law.

Growing up in the publishing business had given him early exposure to politics and had nourished an interest. "Because of my family," he said, "the interest [in politics] has always been there. The publishing business and politics are compatible—the people you see, the functions you go to." While attending law school at night, he held several appointive jobs in state agencies—including one in the governor's office. It was there, he said, that he first became interested in electoral politics.

> In college . . . I was never involved in student government. I didn't run for student body president. But when I worked in the governor's office, I looked around and thought, "This is fun." That's when I first thought about going into politics. I thought about moving back to Huntington and running for state representative. I had my eye on an incumbent Democrat

who had been in office for a while. But I never thought about running for Congress.

So, there had already been stirrings of political ambition when the Allen County Republican chairman asked him in March of 1976 to be the Republican candidate for Congress. "I told him," Quayle recalled,

> that I was thinking of running for state representative, but that I was not ready to run for Congress. I told him he should ask other more qualified people. He said, "I've asked them all and no one wants to run." I told him that I couldn't give him a decision, that I would think it over. But I told him that I wouldn't even consider it unless they guaranteed me that I'd have no primary opposition and unless they would raise money for me.

The chairman agreed.

Quayle's conditions indicated that behind his willingness to take the gamble, there lay some calculation. He believed he could win. But his optimism was not widely shared. The Republican National Committee "targeted" two other Republican challengers in Indiana to receive financial help—but not Dan Quayle.[2] He was thought to be "an underdog and least likely to win for the Republican party."[3] When he checked with his father about leaving the paper he got a similar message. "He told me to go ahead but that I couldn't win," said Quayle. "He said that he'd been trying to defeat Roush for fifteen years and it couldn't be done. I said, 'We'll see.' I was a twenty-nine-year-old kid that nobody took seriously."

It was not just the well-known advantages of incumbency that made Quayle's success seem so unlikely. It was also that Quayle, by conventional standards of political science, was not a "quality challenger."[4] He was without experience or recognition. A Fort Wayne political reporter said that

> Quayle came out of nowhere to run against Ed Roush.... No one knew who he was. No one knew what he had been doing.... I know he had never been in politics. I had been around politicians in Fort Wayne for years; and I had never heard of him.

When "the little-known Quayle" was announcing his candidacy, another reporter recalled, "the local press ran out of his Fort Wayne press conference to cover a breaking police story."[5] "He started the campaign as a nobody," said this reporter.[6]

Six years later, in Fort Wayne, during a discussion of Indiana politics with his closest advisers, the young senator said,

> You've characterized the others by what they did before they got into politics. [Gov. Otis] Bowen was a country doctor. [Sen.

Richard] Lugar was a Rhodes Scholar. What are we going to say about me before I got into politics—that I was a newspaperman?

One of his friends said, "No, we'll call you Dan Quayle, student." Another chipped in, "How about Dan Quayle, father?" And amid general hilarity, another said, "After all, you were only twenty-nine; we'll just say you never did anything else." It was close to the truth. He was a candidate without credentials.

In 1976, and ever since, local scorekeepers have labelled Quayle's election "an upset," "an upset victory," "a stunning upset," "a huge upset victory," and "nothing short of remarkable." [7] Obviously, Quayle needed to run a good campaign and had to be a good campaigner to win. In the summer, Republican polls showed him trailing Roush by 27 percent to 61 percent, with 12 percent undecided.[8] On election day he won by 54 percent. We shall discuss his campaigns shortly. For now, we shall think of this first adventure as a triumph of self-confidence.

Much the same conclusion can be drawn from his Senate victory over Birch Bayh in 1980. Quayle entered that race, too, after the party's only preferred candidate, and the Democrats' only feared candidate— Gov. Otis Bowen—declined to run. Quayle began the race, again, as a decided "underdog," and as someone who—on the record—"is going to have to prove that he's a heavyweight." [9] One of the best-known Republican party consultants declined to bid on his campaign because he thought Quayle had no chance. As before, he enjoyed little recognition in his prospective constituency; he was "hardly known outside the Fourth District." [10] And in the summer before the election he was, once again, running well behind the incumbent—by sixteen points—in the polls.[11]

There were, however, differences between 1976 and 1980. His two terms in the House gave him a set of prima facie legitimizing credentials he had not had before. He had proven his campaigning abilities with a 2-1 reelection victory in 1978; and that victory put him into the senatorial spotlight.[12] Also, in 1980, Quayle was eager to move to the Senate and he did not have to be asked. Instead, he acted in ways that created his own opportunity.

"Right after my election in 1978," he recalled later,

> I went to see Governor Bowen to ask him if he would have any objections if I started talking to people on an "if-not-Bowen,-then-Quayle" basis. The governor told me I could go ahead. He said he hadn't made up his mind. But the way he said it led me to believe he was not going to run. . . . He was sixty-three. His wife was very ill. I never thought he would run. . . . So I started moving around the state. My assistant in the district could

> handle things there; so I went to a lot of Lincoln Day dinners in 1979, to Rotary clubs, and to Kiwanis. I talked about the Senate. People were shocked; they thought Bowen was going to run. And, anyway, what was this unknown congressman doing talking about a Senate race. Well, in early May [May 8] Bowen announced he was not going to run. I had $20,000 left over from my congressional campaign and we transferred it to a Senate Committee. We had a campaign going by May 14, 1979.

The governor felt that "I had not waited my turn," Quayle said. In his declination statement, the governor reportedly "listed over a dozen potential candidates." [13] But none of them materialized.

When asked during his announcement of his Senate candidacy, in Huntington, whether his task was not a daunting one, Quayle replied in terms of 1976.

> I can remember when we started out in 1976 ... the name recognition of Dan Quayle outside Huntington was about 1 percent and in some parts of the Fourth District it was zero. A lot of people warned me that I was running against a tough incumbent, and it was true. But we won.... In 1980 we're starting out again in Huntington. We have a long hill to climb, but I'm confident we can do it. [14]

Given the race he had undertaken against Roush and the race he was undertaking against Bayh, Dan Quayle fits David Rohde's definition of the risk taker who leaves the House for the Senate. [15] To his Fourth District constituents, he spoke of that risk.

> Certainly, giving up my congressional seat to run for the Senate is a risk. But it's a risk I'd like to take. If I thought it was improbable or impossible that I'd succeed, I wouldn't make the venture. [16]

Behind the acceptance of risk lay a good deal of confidence about his ability to win.

And behind his risk-acceptant behavior, once again, probably lay a good bit of calculation. He was not a compulsive gambler. "To someone from the outside," said a long-time political associate, "he may seem like a risk taker. But he doesn't do anything unless he thinks he can win. Other people may not think he can win; but he does. He's a calculating risk taker." During a 1986 conversation about his career, I asked the senator if he thought of himself as a risk taker. "No," he answered.

> It's more a matter of self-confidence. I have complete confidence that whatever I want to do, I can do. I am confident that things will turn out right for me. And they always have.... In

my race against Roush and in my Senate race, I was the only person who believed that I could do it. I surprised everyone but myself.

Doubtless, each added success had made an added contribution to this attitude. Doubtless, too, he had led a favored—if not charmed—life. But the point to be made is this, that the little-known and little-accomplished young man who entered the Senate in 1981 was an especially successful and an especially self-confident politician. And therein lies an important clue to his behavior as a senator.

CONSERVATISM

Quayle's pre-1980 record disclosed another basic clue to his later behavior—his conservatism. Summarizing his 1976 race, a local scorekeeper wrote,

> In classic small town Midwestern Republican style, Congressman-elect Quayle . . . called for a limited government, an end to deficit spending and a stop to the Federal bureaucracy's "cancerous" growth.

Summarizing his first-term voting record, the local newspaper said that

> Quayle's approach to economics is almost a pure form of laissez faire—keep the government out and let the natural interplay of supply and demand set prices in the market place.[17]

Calling him "the established conservative," another reporter summarized his 1978 campaign,

> Quayle campaigned in 1976 on a "less is better" platform: less government, less spending, less taxation. He has seen little cause to change that approach for this campaign. . . . The majority of his constituents, he says, are most concerned over high taxes, excessive government spending and too much government interference in their day to day lives.[18]

The core of his conservatism was a deep antipathy to government bureaucracy.

When I asked him, later, about that antipathy, he described it as rooted in a business that is "deeply cynical about government." "You have to go way back to the way I was brought up," he said.

> You don't get these values overnight or from some book you read somewhere. You have to go back to my background in the newspaper business. People in the newspaper business hate the government. They distrust the government. It is the last unregulated business; it is almost immune from regulation. It is

> deeply ingrained in them that the government should keep
> hands off, that government cannot do any good, that it only
> brings trouble. That distrust is deeply ingrained in me.

His attack on governmental bureaucracy was the foundation stone of
both the congressional campaigns and of the Senate campaign of 1980.

By all the standard scoring systems, his two-term voting record in
the House reflected strong conservatism and an equally strong Republican party loyalty. In the years 1977-1980 his support scores on issues
important to the conservative Americans for Constitutional Action were
96 percent, 81, 91, 90; and his agreement with the U.S. Chamber of
Commerce stood at 88 percent, 76, 88, 73. On the other hand his support
levels, over the four years, on issues important to the liberal Americans
for Democratic Action stood at 15 percent, 15, 11, 0; his agreement
ratings on AFL-CIO scores were 10 percent, 11, 16, 13. By these
measures, Quayle's conservatism was unmistakable. So was his support
for Republican party policies. On votes where a majority of House
Republicans were opposed to a majority of House Democrats, Quayle
voted against his party majority only 10 percent of the time in 1977 and
13 percent, 9 percent, and 8 percent in succeeding years. He can be
described, in general, as an orthodox conservative Republican.

There is, however, an element of Dan Quayle's conservatism that is
not captured by roll-call votes or aggregate numbers. From the beginning of his congressional service, he expressed some restlessness in the
harness of fixed positions and an open mind in exploring new approaches to old problems. There was a willingness—almost an eagerness—to lean occasionally against the accepted position of conservatives.
"He doesn't like to be taken for granted," said one of his House staffers.
Quayle spoke of it as another derivative of his newspaper background.
"In the newspaper business, one thing you try to avoid is being
stereotyped," he said.

> And independence is the thing everybody strives for. Some-
> times you have to go against community opinion. You can't be
> afraid to do that and still do your job. It's the same thing here. I
> don't mind going against the crowd when I think it is right.

Within his fundamental conservatism, there is contained an activism of
thought and approach that can lead to pragmatic rather than ideological
behavior. Since it is an attitude related more to means than to ends, we
might think of it as an instrumental independence.

In the earliest part of his career, this independent stance was most
noticeable in his relations with the well-organized "movement conservatives." Two months after his election to the House, he was given a featured role at the Conservative Political Action Conference sponsored by

Ronald Reagan's Conservative Political Union. The union and the other staunchly conservative groups participating in the conference had given strong support to Quayle's election campaign. They were touting him as "a bright new conservative light" and a future leader.[19] In advertisements for the conference placed in conservative publications, he was pictured with Reagan and thirteen other prominent national conservative leaders. He went eagerly to the meeting. But in talking about it he described himself as "a creative conservative" and a "creative or progressive conservative"; and he said he would take "independent" positions on "Reaganite" policy matters. He described himself as looking for "new approaches," "new leadership," and a "new image" for the party.[20] He seemed not to want to be put in pigeonholes or taken for granted.

A few months later he was arguing that Republicans needed to develop "positive progressive attitudes" to deal with people's problems. A local reporter wrote, "He said he never was aware of the kinds of difficulties people have until he became a member of Congress and learned from his constituent case load what some people have to deal with." [21] At the end of the year, he was at pains to point out that "I really don't associate myself with the far right of the party." He was describing himself as "somewhere between a moderate and a conservative," and as "a moderating influence on the far right groups." [22] This stance was not reflected in his votes. It was reflected rather in his approach, in a willingness to entertain the other side of the question and to discuss modifications. It was perhaps his newspaperman's sensitivity to civil liberties that produced this open-mindedness, this preference for independence of thought. "On the major issues—the Panama Canal, abortion and farming," wrote one scorekeeper at the end of his first year, "Quayle has walked the fence, leaning to the right, but not quite falling." [23] In a period when conservatism was gaining ideological intensity and organized expression, Dan Quayle's votes were correctly conservative, but he was much less of a true believer than the movement conservatives would have liked.[24]

STYLE

Much has been written about the "new breed" of politicians who came to the House of Representatives in the mid-1970s. They were young and they represented a new generation; they rode in on personal candidacies and they were not devoted to party; they were electorally self-sufficient and they applied themselves to servicing their constituents; they were comfortable with the media and they wanted open politics; they matured in an era of change and they wanted institutional reform; they were issue-oriented activists and they wanted a piece of the congressional action. It was the big Democratic class of Watergate babies that drew most of the attention.[25] But incoming Republicans exhibited the same profile. Dan Quayle was one of them and, in matters of style, very much a politician of his times.

While it was his self-confidence that launched his 1976 campaign, it was his abilities as a campaigner that produced the ultimate victory. Not that he was a miracle worker. For one thing, the electoral history of the Fourth District showed it to be, despite the long incumbency, a marginal district. For another thing, the local Republicans and the national conservatives raised more than $100,000 for his campaign.[26] But his personal attributes as a campaigner proved formidable.

To begin with, he was young and he was handsome. He was often described (and still is) as a Robert Redford look-alike.[27] A party leader instrumental in choosing Quayle to run said to me in 1982, "I told the fellas that I thought he could win because every woman in the district would want to make love to him. You may not want to put that in your book. But that's the fact." Local commentators typically described him as: "young, handsome, and outgoing" or "young, handsome, articulate" or "good looking, articulate, energetic" or "young and personable" or "good looking and easy to talk to." [28] "Dan winces at the suggestion that he won the election because of his good looks," wrote one reporter, "which is a suggestion he hears all the time." [29] Doubtless it was a huge asset. But so, too, were the other personal characteristics mentioned: "outgoing," "energetic," "articulate," "personable." A key party leader summed up his 1976 candidacy: "Dan was a natural. He not only has good looks, but his forthrightness and ability in speaking out on the issues appealed to the conservative nature of the district." [30] The sum total of these characteristics gave him an exemplary media presence. "The Fort Wayne media market covers about 70 percent of my District," he said later. "That was the only reason I could win in 1976—with the media." He had not been a self-starter; but his candidacy was based on some potent personal strengths.

A derivative of those strengths was Quayle's ability to attract the primary constituency so important to new-breed campaigns. His organization was, by all accounts, a prototypical volunteer group. He had solid support from the Republican organization—to which went "some credit" from observers. But the major emphasis of the media scorekeepers was on the campaign work of the "volunteers." "Quayle set up his own grass roots organization in the wards and the precincts," wrote one reporter. "He hit the coffee klatch circuit, enlisting the legwork of many housewives and young people who, like him, were new to politics." [31] He campaigned at eighteen county fairs and in thirty-two parades.[32]

His Democratic opponent, Ed Roush, attributed his defeat to his being "out-organized" by Quayle's volunteers. Accounts of the campaign flow emphasized that the incumbent "underestimated" Quayle, was "over confident," was "complacent," [33] and that the Quayle campaign developed very strongly at the end. "Roush didn't take me seriously till the last ten days," said Quayle. "And then it was too late." His campaign "started building up steam," "gained terrific momentum in the waning weeks," "caught [Roush] off guard and brought defeat." [34] Quayle's campaign style was, in sum, heavily grounded in his personal attractiveness, his youthful energy, and his volunteer organization.

Once in Congress, he exhibited a similarly prototypical style to superintend his constituency relations. In several ways that contrasted with his predecessors but imitated his House colleagues, he set out to create binding personal ties to his constituents. He went home often to the district—every week for "the first few months" and every other week afterwards.[35] He leased a mobile congressional office van and toured the district with his staff searching out opportunities to help his constituents.[36] He inaugurated a series of "town meetings" to meet with constituents to discuss issues.[37] He established an open-phone-line policy, taking calls directly from his constituents and returning all missed calls personally.[38] He declined to accept a pay raise and put the money instead into a fund to bring high school students to Washington.[39] He held "frequent district news conferences." [40]

As he settled into the job in Washington, he kept up a rhetorical barrage disparaging life "out there" and denigrating the politicians who work there. "The atmosphere [in Washington] is intoxicating," he would say. "It can be a problem if you let it go to your head. That's one reason I'm going to insist on getting back to the district and getting out of the intoxicating atmosphere." [41] "I'm awed by the lack of real dynamism [in the House]," he said. "To be quite blunt about it I'm not impressed with the overall caliber of members of the House." [42] Or, "If there is one thing Congress is efficient at doing, it's taking care of themselves." [43] Or, "It seems we're off more than we're in . . . I guess the only thing to do during all these breaks is to go on junkets." [44] It was not a flattering portrait of Congress.

Even more, Quayle went on the legislative attack against institutional provisions. His first legislative action was to introduce a constitutional amendment limiting representatives and senators to twelve years of service. The proposal was a major platform plank in each of his first three elections. "There are a number of young congressmen, myself included," he explained, "who are critics of the old ways and we'd like terms limited to twelve years or so. That would guarantee a constant infusion of new blood." [45] "We need to restore the citizen-legislator concept of representative government," he argued, to make members "less enamored of self-perpetuating pork barrels and more responsive to the needs of the people they represent." [46] One of his most heralded legislative accomplishments of his first term was his activity ("almost singlehanded," as he put it) in preventing House approval of a congressional pay raise.[47] Seventy-five percent of his colleagues, he said, could not make as much money in the private sector as they made in Congress.[48] It was a common tactic among members of his generation to run for Congress by running against Congress; and he seemed to have excelled at it.[49] Typically, too, this anti-Washington stance helped cement his relations with his constituents.

By all accounts, this devotion to constituency cultivation was not matched by a devotion to legislative work. In the words of one staffer, "He covered his district well because he liked being with people. But his legislative record was undistinguished to say the least." By his feet as well as his mouth, he demonstrated a lack of attachment to the institution of which he was a part. Among staffers and scorekeepers alike, his devotion to his workaday duties was suspect. "People called him 'wet head' because he was always coming out of the [House] gym," said a top campaigner. "His attendance record was lousy.... They didn't know where he was a lot of the time. He'd be in the gym or he'd sneak off to play golf and they'd have to call all around to find him." A Washington staffer said, "He would miss meetings, miss votes. He'd meet [Rep. Tom] Railsback who would say, 'Let's play golf,' and off they'd go."

His otherwise insignificant 1980 primary opponent saw it as Quayle's major point of vulnerability. "The only issue he used against me," said Quayle, "was my attendance record. He claimed I missed 270 votes and said I was not doing my job. I spoke at twenty-three Lincoln Day dinners and every time I came to town there would be an ad in the paper criticizing my attendance record." Quayle protested that "my record was well above average ... 90 percent the first two years and 85 percent overall." But he admitted that the charge "took away an election issue I was planning to use against Birch Bayh—his attendance record." During that election, a Washington scorekeeper reported that Quayle had missed ten of fourteen Small Business Committee meetings during one period of time and forty of sixty-one meetings of the Foreign Affairs Committee during another.[50] His lack of attentiveness to legislative work dominated his reputation in the House. In the words of two Indiana colleagues there, "He has not, it's fair to say, had a very prodigious legislative record.... The most positive thing you can say is that this was his game plan—not to tackle controversy." And, "He's personable, he's handsome, he's fun to be around, and he's about a quarter of an inch deep." [51] It was hardly a complimentary reputation for a legislator.

OBSERVATIONS AND REFLECTIONS:
INDIANA, SEPTEMBER 1980

I met Dan Quayle when I joined his Senate campaign for two and a half days in late September. He was locked in a very tight race. But the mood was distinctly upbeat. "We started May 14 last year," he said, "and have moved in a straight line ever since. At one point, we were 30 points down. One of Bayh's polls had us 40 points down. In August we were 8 points down; and now we are 4 points down. There is another poll, done by a sociologist, that has us 4 points up. I'd rather be 4 points down. We are right on target." We campaigned, in typically farflung senatorial style, from the bottom to the top of the state, from Evansville to South Bend, in Vincennes, Terre Haute, Indianapolis, and Elkhart in between. I watched him in a number of settings, from a plant gate to a country club, from a fund raiser to press conferences, and in meetings with realtors, broadcasters, Jaycees, ministers, Christian educators, labor unions, students, and dentists.

He struck me as a remarkably handsome kid, but more kid even than handsome. As a campaigner, he was a natural—vigorous (but not polished) in speech, attentive in personal contact, open in dialogue and undaunted by potentially unfriendly audiences. "All you have to do," said the staffer who was with him most often, "is turn him loose in an alien environment and collect him at the other end and he will have converted everyone in the place." At the end of my visit I asked him where, among the events I had attended, he felt most comfortable. He singled out the dentists (at the country club) and the realtors ("They're our natural constituency")—both of which I would have expected. But he gave first billing to the Alcoa plant gate—which I would not have expected. "I'm very comfortable at factory gates," he explained. "Some Republicans aren't but I am. I like it. I was very comfortable, too, with the dentists and the realtors." Then he added, "Actually, it's easier to say where I was uncomfortable. . . . With a few exceptions, I'm comfortable with all kinds of people. I believe that in almost everyone you meet you can find a friend." He campaigns in that unguarded, outgoing, optimistic spirit—like a kid.

He seems particularly effective at one-on-one campaigning. He likes to touch the person he talks with; he looks at each one directly and brightens as he does so; he uses a lot of body language to convey surprise, or interest or enthusiasm or dismay. With men he has a habit of shaking hands while punching them on the arm or clapping them on the shoulder with his left hand. If he is talking to two people at once, he often places one hand on the shoulder of each person as they converse.

With women, he has the habit of clasping their right hand in both of his as he listens. Among women he knows, he will put an arm around them. But he does not kiss them. Given his attractiveness, I was struck by the easygoing way he approaches women, without the slightest intimation of sexuality. And he never talks about women as such in private—never joining in, for example, when the subject absorbs the conversation of his young male staffers. A staffer told me, "He's good with women, like the Congressman (B) in your book *Home Style.*" [52] But the two men could not be more different. Congressman B flaunts and exploits his good looks, conveying the message that his appeal to women is a major key to his success. Quayle carries his good looks as a silent asset, conveying the message that the keys to his success must lie elsewhere. In his absence of self-consciousness about them, he is, indeed, "good with women."

There is a very straightforward quality about his strategic thinking, too. The first thing he said to me when we met was:

> You've come to a very interesting race, between liberal and conservative, between the old and the new. I'm a new-breed Republican, like [Budget Director] David Stockman or [Maine Senator] Bill Cohen. It's a classic confrontation in a very important state. Indiana is a rural state, but it is also a major industrial state—more industrial than most people think. . . . It's a bellwether state. Birch Bayh and I differ on almost everything. We'll have a campaign and then we'll see what the people want.

Later, he expressed, in the same matter-of-fact tone, his respect for his opponent's political skills. "He's tough," said Quayle.

> He's good on the stump. He's a better campaigner even than I am. He can get by with less sleep than I can. He doesn't represent the thinking of Indiana. . . . But he's a survivor. He comes home and says "aw shucks" and "golly" and talks about Shirkeyville and gets reelected. He's tough.

Quayle was a first-rate campaigner; but he never believed that he won his 1980 election—as he did believe in 1976—because he was a better campaigner than his opponent.

Shortly before my arrival, Quayle and Bayh had debated. And the upbeat mood of the campaign was in large measure due to the perception that Quayle had done well in his confrontation with a formidable opponent. "Our goal was to hold our own," said one staffer. "You have no idea how much we worried about it. We took five days from campaigning to prepare. We even had a plan to counteract the bad publicity if Dan flopped." When it was over, however, the Quayle campaigners declared victory and had a victory celebration. "In every campaign, there is a psychological moment when the campaign really takes off," Quayle generalized,

> People get excited and start to work harder. It happened with the debate. People start calling and asking if they can help. You get more attention. It helps the candidate, the staff, and the workers. The campaign gets a big kick.

Outside the campaign, too, he said,

> The reaction has been favorable. The only criticism has come from dyed-in-the-wool Republicans who said I didn't hit him hard enough. They'll vote for us anyway.... The people we want are the independents and the soft Democrats. And these people have been telling us that Bayh came across as cocky and arrogant.

The debate, apparently, had helped him in several respects.

A couple of years later, listening to him meet with his closest advisers, I learned that they had not wanted their candidate to agree to that 1980 debate. Recalled one adviser, "To a man, we were against it. We thought you would lose." And another said, "We thought Bayh would ... dance you around, make you look silly." Quayle said,

> I didn't know you were telling them I wouldn't debate, so I went ahead and agreed. It was one time we didn't coordinate and discuss something. But I didn't feel there was any problem debating Birch Bayh. It's an advantage to any challenger. And I was for it anyway. You know me. I just go plunging ahead.

It was one more example of Dan Quayle's self-confidence, one more instance in his career, where he "surprised everyone but myself."

Dan Quayle did not campaign in 1980 primarily as an attractive candidate—though he certainly was. He campaigned primarily as a conservative—as the agent of an orthodox conservative philosophy. He also campaigned as the agent of a political party that espoused conservative principles, that had been out of power too long, and that would bring new leadership to a country in trouble. He presented himself as part of "a new generation of leadership" as a leader "for the 1980s and for the twenty-first century." Beneath this all-purpose theme, he campaigned against the status quo. His targets were essentially the same as those of his earlier races—too much government, too much spending, too many taxes. He advocated cutbacks in the bureaucracy, reductions in spending, indexation of tax rates, the Kemp-Roth tax cut, and a larger defense budget. On the social side, he advocated prayer in the public schools and tuition tax credits for private schools, and he opposed all federal funding of abortions. His strongest supporters were philosophical soul mates more than the personally attached volunteers of his House campaigns. "As far as a cadre of volunteers who thought Dan Quayle was the greatest thing since toast," said a top campaign staffer, "we didn't have any of that. It was ideology." Quayle's views were indistinguishable from those of his party's standard bearer, Ronald Reagan.

There was one exception—the twelve-year limit on years of service in Congress. He gave this proposal top billing in his "issues" list in his literature. To the Jaycees in Elkhart, he described it as "a reform for the 1980s that I've been pushing since 1976, . . . one I want to push as a member of the United States Senate." "I believe adamantly in a limit on the number of terms you can serve," he told a union group in Evansville, ". . .Then you ought to retire and come back and live under all those wonderful laws you passed." Congress, he told all his audiences, was the creator and the protector of the federal bureaucracy. And largely because its members were out of touch. "Once they get there and once they're there for a long time," he told the Jaycees,

> they become Washington people rather than people from Indiana. They move out there . . . they send their kids to school out there, they breathe the air out there, they drink the water out there, they become part of the Washington buddy system.

It was a continuation of his long-standing attacks on Congress—not just as a Democratic Congress, but as an institution. He brought the Jaycees to their feet, for example, with his "incentives" proposal to "freeze all congressional salaries till they get inflation below 5 percent." He did not yet think of himself as part of the government.

He pressed his conservative, antibureaucracy theme everywhere. "Middle-income people are overburdened with taxes and regulation and government," he told Pfizer executives in Terre Haute.

> I'm as compassionate as anyone for the poor and downtrodden, but let's think of a little relief for the working people of this country. . . . The majority in Washington believe we need a big government. Wherever there's a problem, throw money at it and the problem will go away. I think creating bureaucracy creates the problems.

"If you elect a Democratic Congress, you'll get business as usual," he said to a broadcasters group in Vincennes.

> Senator Bayh's party has been in control for thirty-seven years. Now it's time for a new generation to take control of the government. . . . We need to say, "No new laws shall be passed." Let's go look at the ones we have on the books and get rid of some we have. [applause]

"We are going to have to have government that is compassionate, but let's get the government off our back and out of our pocket books," he said to dentists in Warrick.

> Since 1962, when Senator Bayh was elected, Congress has created 399 new bureaus, agencies, and commissions. How many do you think your senior senator voted against? Not one.... In 1962 Birch Bayh said to [Sen.] Homer Capehart, "Eighteen years is too long for a United States senator to serve." For once in my life, I agree with Birch Bayh. [applause]

The problem of "creating more and more bureaucracy," he told a convention of Christian educators,

> couldn't be demonstrated any more vividly than the creation of the new cabinet-level Department of Education.... [applause] We should be searching for ways the federal government can begin to reduce and consolidate and limit the size of the federal government, and the number-one department I will start with is that new Department of Education. [applause]

He said that "the difference between me and my opponent" was that he wanted to "get the IRS off the backs of the private Christian schools, trying to put them out of existence." And he advocated tuition tax credits for all parents sending children to such schools.

Behind the sweeping antigovernment rhetoric and the blanket appeals for support, there was evidence of what we earlier called an instrumental independence—an openness to argument, a wariness of inflexibility, a pragmatism in the implementation of his ideas. To the Pfizer executives, he declared his devotion to free enterprise but defended his vote for the government's loan to Chrysler. "I had to balance," he said,

> what was written in the economics books about the free enterprise system and the real situation that there would have been thousands and thousands of people [in Indiana] out of work. When I had to vote, I voted for the workers. I wish that Chrysler hadn't come. But they did.

In view of the publicity given in 1980 to the support of conservative candidates such as Dan Quayle by "the religious New Right," his arms-length discussion of their causes was noteworthy.[53] In his talks to two Christian groups, his central theme was a sympathetic but general one. "Let me just say as one Christian to another," he said to the educators' group, "it's time for the Christians of this country to come out of the closet and come to the polling booth and make the country work again." "One of the reasons we have problems," he told a meeting of fundamentalist ministers, "is the lackadaisical and removed attitude people like yourself have had. Finally people are saying, 'Hey, we've got to do something.' . . . What's dangerous is when Christians do not speak out on the issues of interest to you—abortion . . . prayer in schools." He did not match the emotionalism or the extremism of either audience. As we drove along a staffer noticed a billboard picturing a baby. "Look at that sign," he said. [The sign said: "If you kill her now it's murder. Three months ago it was abortion."] Quayle commented, "We've told those people to tone it down. They are just hurting their own cause when they go to extremes. I hope they don't call Birch Bayh a murderer. It doesn't help their cause to call him a murderer." In our trip post-mortem, he named his two meetings with Christian groups as the only ones where he felt uncomfortable. "They always ask you questions about your religion, and to me that's a very personal matter."

In my own notes after the trip, I wrote, "Conservatives may be embarrassed by their extreme supporters and may be much more moderate than their extreme supporters. . . . If you go to Indiana thinking you will find a Republican Senate candidate who is an apostle of the New Right, you will not find it." On economic and social issues, therefore, he presented himself as a solid conservative. But he did not present himself as an ideologue or an extremist. He would not, I believed, be particularly difficult for others to work with in the Senate.

Indeed, in discussing his move from House to Senate, he spoke vaguely of his desire for accomplishment in the Senate. "I was very bored in the House," he said.

> It's an awful job—especially being a Republican there. You can't get anything done. I couldn't be satisfied just taking care of my district and getting reelected. If I had not run for the Senate, I would have run for one more term and then I would have looked around for something else. I might have gotten out of politics. But I didn't want to stay in the House. Ever since I was elected, I thought about the Senate if anything came up. So you could say I had my eyes set on the Senate for a long time.

His progressive ambition seemed born of a desire to move to a place where he could get something done. He said, too, he had been encouraged by his understanding of House-Senate differences. "The House is more informal," he reported.

> You can get a bunch of guys and go down to the gym and play basketball. You can't do that in the Senate. I'll miss the informality of the House. But in the Senate you can work with the guys—the top twenty guys anyway—to get something done. I'll like that about the Senate.

In November, he was propelled into that body by a plurality of 166,000 votes and a victory percentage of 54.

THE ELECTORAL INTERPRETATION

Two weeks after the election, we talked in Washington. His post-mortems echoed his preelection thoughts. His interpretation of the election was quite predictable. "You had a classic contest between two philosophies," said Quayle, "and the people want a conservative philosophy." That had been Quayle's interpretation of the campaign and it was his interpretation of the result. He remained unstinting in his respect for his opponent. "It was a tough campaign. He's a fighter.... He is as good a campaigner as there is anywhere in the United States." This prowess was not, however, sufficient to overcome a context unfavorable to Bayh's liberalism. "His big problem was the times and the economy," Quayle explained.

> We stuck to one theme—that 300,000 people were without jobs and that Birch Bayh was to blame. Our polls showed that people blamed the Democratic Congress for the economy, but that they didn't blame Birch Bayh. They wouldn't take that second step. My style was to blame the whole Democratic Congress for the economy, not just one senator. After all, you can't blame one person. But when our polls showed that people were not making the connection, I changed. I said, "Birch Bayh and Jimmy Carter *cause* inflation. Birch Bayh and Jimmy Carter *cause* unemployment." I wanted people to blame Birch Bayh.... He was done in by the times and the economy. He would have had to have swum upstream to ever be elected senator in 1980. The state we were in was too much—even for a candidate like Birch Bayh.

Given this electoral interpretation, we would expect that the conservative themes he had struck on the campaign trail would soon be readied for application to national policy making.

During our mid-November conversation, there was evidence that movement conservatives were opting for a different electoral interpretation—one that elevated their importance to the outcome. After the Senate races of 1978 and 1980, there was a good deal of debate over the electoral potency of the newly activated New Right. These ardent conservatives claimed credit for a number of victories and were claiming credit for that of Dan Quayle. "We've been in a pissing match with NCPAC [National Conservative Political Action Committee] for the last week," said one staffer in November.

Dan went on the "Today" show and said he didn't think NCPAC had anything to do with his victory. He said our polls showed that NCPAC and the Moral Majority had a net negative effect of about 4 points on our vote. They got mad, went on TV, and blasted Quayle.

Not too surprisingly, the defeated candidate agreed with the winner. "The Repressive Right claims powers that it does not have," said Birch Bayh. "It claims credit for defeating . . . me . . . but the Repressive Right had less to do with my defeat than 18 percent unemployment among Indiana autoworkers and outrageous interest rates." [54]

That this economic interpretation of what happened was going to guide the new senator's future activity became clearer still when we discussed his Senate committee preferences.

I know one committee I don't want—Judiciary. They are going to be dealing with all those issues like abortion, busing, voting rights, prayers. I'm not interested in those issues, and I want to stay as far away from them as I can.

He would, of course, have to deal with them. But he kept the same kind of distance in 1980 that he had kept in 1976 between himself and the hard right wing of his party. "Conservatives have very different ideas than the New Right about where we ought to go," he said. "Some of the New Right people really want to turn the clock back . . . on affirmative action and all the civil rights gains. There's no way they're going to do that. We won't let them."

On the positive side of his committee preferences, he was undecided. But, again, his thoughts echoed a theme I had heard on the campaign trail—a desire to get something done. There was nothing in his House record to indicate any particular subject matter interest. And so he was thinking broadly about committees. "When I see you again, I'll have a surer idea of what I'm doing, with the committees and all," he concluded.

Appropriations would be good. But there's no creativity there. You can't get down to the ground level and build like you can on Finance or Energy. You can cut, but you can't innovate. I want to specialize, but I also want to save myself to go where the action is. My golly, you can do that in the Senate—with 100 people. Appropriations would be good in that way because it covers everything—every area. Still, the creativity thing bothers me. And I have to be realistic too. Maybe I couldn't get Appropriations or Finance. As you can see, I'm still sloshing these things around in my mind.

His season of adjustment lay ahead.

EARLY ADJUSTMENT AND ACCOMPLISHMENT: 1981

At the conclusion of my September campaign visit, after reflecting that "he is not an ideologue," I had written about Dan Quayle,

> A better description is that he's just a kid—or so he seems to me. I wonder what gives a kid of thirty-three the confidence to go around his state calling for "a new leadership for the 1980s and the twenty-first century." What can he possibly know about the 1980s and the twenty-first century? He's just a kid. Maybe the answer is that once you decide to run for the office you simply adopt a posture of confidence and worry about doing something afterward.... All this raises an interesting challenge for D.Q. Can he grow? I would guess that if there is a personal side to it, that's it. If he makes it, will he grow?

It remained my central question after he had "made it."

Implicitly, the question was raised by others, too. That is, they began their evaluations of him by giving him no credit for past experience or accomplishment. Under the title "The Charmed Life of Indiana's Golden Boy," the author of Washington's first scorekeeping effort, in January, described the new Indiana senator this way: "Strawberry blond hair. Blue eyes. Cute. The golden boy ... [whose] life ... seems nothing less than charmed ... [to whom] everything came easily ... [who was] a lazy and ineffectual congressman.... But [who] as a candidate, is a dream." [55] A knowledgeable staffer for Indiana's other senator called him, similarly, in 1981, "a package-the-candidate kind of candidate, a good looking playboy." In the eyes of others, Dan Quayle began his Senate service at ground zero in terms of past achievement and without much compensatory future promise.

When I dropped in to say hello in March, I found him caught in a burgeoning scandal that had the potential for confirming his "playboy" image and ending his "charmed life." One week earlier, a story had broken that Quayle, two House colleagues, and three other men, on a golfing weekend in Florida, had shared a cottage with a female Washington lobbyist, who later posed nude for *Playboy*. "Congressmen Shared House with Female Lobbyist," read the March 7 front-page *Washington Post* headline. Pictures of the lobbyist, Paula Parkinson, Thomas Evans, R-Del., Tom Railsback, R-Ill., and Quayle were on page two. "U.S. Will Probe Allegations of Hill Vote Trading for Sex," read the *Post* headline the day I arrived a week later. "Last Friday the dam broke," said his press secretary. "Between 10 A.M. and 5 P.M. I had sixty-three calls from the press.... We have had only seven letters from the constituency in one week. But in Washington everyone wants to be Bob Woodward." Now, however, the story had finally made page one in

Fort Wayne. And Quayle, claiming total innocence in what appeared to be someone else's relationship, was wondering how to cope.

When we talked, he displayed the same open, straightforward manner he had shown on the campaign trail. "I'll bet you didn't think you were going to find anything like this," he exclaimed when we met.

> It's the damnedest thing. I don't know that woman at all. It's the others that will be in trouble. But my name is connected with it. You always think that something like this might happen, but when it does, it's hard to figure out what to do. My gut instinct is to go back to Indiana, hold a press conference, let people see me, and tell everything I know. But others say, "That will make you the focal point. Why should you do that when you don't even know the woman—not down there or up here?" Our first strategy was to say, "It isn't serious. It will pass over, snicker, snicker." But this week it's in the papers back home. Last week it wasn't. I'm going to check with some of my newspaper friends, to ask them what I should do. But all my instincts tell me to go back there. You picked a beauty for your book!

He let me sit there while he phoned one of his closest Indiana advisers to discuss his options. He did not go home. The advice of others that "we can wait to see what happens and we have plenty of time to deal with it gradually" prevailed. The story proved to be, as his press secretary put it, "a magnesium flare." It blazed briefly and died out. It had no lasting repercussions for Quayle. But it was not an auspicious public beginning. And beginnings, in the legislature, are not soon forgotten.

Out of the public glare, however, he was undergoing his "adjustment from" the House and his "adjustment to" the Senate. And he talked about its institutional and operational aspects. Institutionally, he was making a typical House member's adjustment. "I miss the informality of the House," he said.

> I miss my peer group. There aren't many senators under thirty-five with children under six. There are no basketball games. People don't get together in groups on the floor and tell stories. The House is so big you naturally break into groups and cliques. There are no groups or cliques here. It's more individualistic. The Senate is a club, but it is one big club. In the House, you have little clubs.

In March, Quayle was still sneaking over to the House in the late afternoon to play basketball. His comments about formality and group life were prototypical House member reactions. So was his reluctance to give up his contacts in the more comfortable body.

He was also making the adjustment from campaigning to governing. And the one, he said, had had an effect on the other. "One thing I learned from the campaign, was the importance of attendance," he offered.

> I never thought of it as very important. But it is a point of vulnerability. I didn't like it that they were able to use it against me. Not so much as compared to Birch Bayh, because he didn't take attendance very seriously either. In fact his was worse than mine. But because people talked about it. I'll be more attuned to it than I was before. I always thought 90 percent was tops, more than you needed. Now I'll shoot higher.

To the degree that he followed this resolve, he would be on the way toward reversing his legislative reputation. And his staffers, at least, professed to find exactly this happening during the early adjustment period. "He's getting the feel for the place and digging into his work," a staffer who had watched him in both chambers said in March.

> Over in the House, when he saw the first ray of sunshine, he'd be out on the golf course. But he's not doing that. He's had an incredible amount of information pushed at him and he's trying to absorb it. He's attending all his meetings. He hasn't missed a vote. Except for one week of vacation at Thanksgiving, he's been in the office every day. . . . His mind is working and he's getting more interested in things than when he was in the House. When we were campaigning . . . I don't think we knew what kind of senator we were foisting on the people of Indiana. . . . Frankly, we wondered whether he would take to the Senate once he got there. But he has. I think we're going to have us a senator.

If this assessment was correct, it constituted the beginnings of an important turnaround.

If there was ever to be a legislative turnaround, the most likely arenas would be his committees. So his choice of committees would be an important aspect of his adjustment. As it turned out, he had become a member of the Armed Services, Labor and Human Resources, and Budget Committees. I asked him how that had come about. He explained his first two choices.

> You literally sit around in a room with a sheet of paper in front of you and pick committees in order of seniority. Foreign Relations had no vacancies. It would have been my first choice. My next choice was Finance. [Three other senators] took it before me, so I missed it. I said, "Armed Services." It covers some of the same problems as Foreign Relations. . . .

On the second round, I wanted Governmental Affairs. But I sat there watching, and I saw that I could be third ranking on Labor and Human Resources. I noticed everyone was shying away from it. I didn't have any interest in it, to tell you the truth. I hadn't even thought of it. But if I were third ranking, and Bob Stafford retired next year, I could be second ranking— assuming Orrin Hatch is reelected. So I said to myself right there, "Why not take it? There are a lot of important policies there—education, employment, labor." I took it on the spot.

In view of the well-known reluctance of Republicans to seek membership on a committee that puts them in a no-win situation with organized labor and organized educational groups, Quayle's second committee pick represents one more demonstration of his fundamental self-confidence and his resultant willingness to take calculated risks when an opportunity presents itself. His snap judgment also gives evidence of an instinct for power and a desire to make a mark in the new institution. In all these ways—had anyone cared—the selection of Labor and Human Resources was far more predictive of his career in the Senate than anything he had done in the House. Furthermore, it became, as we shall see, the arena in which he did engineer his most sig- nificant first-term legislative accomplishment.

For his earliest period of adjustment, however, membership on the Armed Services Committee was probably more important for him. At least, it provided him with a formative opportunity to "get something done" in the Senate. In the late summer and early fall of his first year, the committee's jurisdiction pulled it into the consideration of President Reagan's proposed sale of AWACS surveillance planes to Saudi Arabia. Israel was strongly opposed to the sale. And the issue piqued a special degree of interest on the part of the Indiana senator. The ultimate decision would come on a Senate resolution disapproving the sale. And primary jurisdiction over that resolution lay with the Foreign Relations Committee. But the Armed Services Committee took testimony on the impact of the arms sale on our national defense posture and took its own separate vote on the resolution.

The issue was exactly the kind of foreign policy-related issue that had led Quayle to the committee in the first place. As he explained his initial interest in the AWACS controversy, "I've always been interested in foreign policy. I was on the House Foreign Affairs Committee. I'm on the Armed Services Committee and I'm interested in problems of our strategic balance in the world." At year's end, when I asked him what activity had given him the most satisfaction thus far, he replied, "It's hard to say one thing gave me the most satisfaction. But maybe you should judge by the amount of time I spent. And I spent the most time this year on AWACS." A top staffer concurred in this judgment. "I think AWACS was a big step forward for Dan," he said, "because he played a pretty important part in it and because it gave him confidence. He learned that he could do it." His participation in the AWACS issue was certainly an adjustment milestone for him.

He became an active negotiator in the decision-making process, getting a group of freshmen Republican senators together to work out a compromise that affected the work of the party leadership, the action of the administration, and the vote of some colleagues. The desirability of some compromise grew out of sentiment in the Senate that the United States had to keep some strings—or appear to keep some strings—on these highly sophisticated intelligence-gathering airplanes. The necessity for compromise grew out of the feeling that without it the sale would be disapproved. Other than his general interest in foreign policy, Quayle's driving motivation throughout was his desire to help the new Republican president. "When I first read about AWACS, I was lukewarm toward it. . . ," he said in September, "but I like this president and I want him to succeed. This is the president's first foreign policy vote. We don't want to lose it."

In the period before October 1 when the president formally sent his request to the Senate (with a one-month, up-or-down deadline attached) Quayle met twice with the special Saudi representative to discuss compromises that would either give the United States direct control over half the airplanes or provide for joint U.S.-Saudi crews on all the planes. Simultaneously, he served as liaison with the party leadership, canvassing some fellow freshmen to see whether they would look favorably on some such compromise. He had identified a handful of Republican newcomers who were supportive of the president but reluctant to oppose Israel. None of them was a member of the Foreign Relations or Armed Services committees. "That was [Sen.] Mark Andrews on the phone. I've already talked with [Sen. Robert] Kasten and I have calls in to a few more," he said one day late in September. "[Majority Leader Howard] Baker is trying to find out who might be willing to move if we went to some compromise on joint crewing like [Sen. John] Glenn suggests. Then the administration could get on the phone and bring them in." To the end of his involvement, he described his activity modestly as "helping Howard Baker with the freshmen."

The Saudis, as it turned out, refused all compromise. And the president sent forward his proposal for outright sale of fifty airplanes—the largest arms sale in American history. Whereupon, Quayle's maneuvering turned to another device. "When the Saudis said they wouldn't accept any joint crewing idea . . . things looked pretty bad," he recalled afterward. And he recounted the story of his involvement.

We started thinking about an alternative in the Armed Services Committee when [Secretary of Defense Caspar] Weinberger was testifying in closed session about some of the agreements we had with the Saudis. Several of us said that the administration would have to give some guarantees in public or the sale was dead. That's the way I felt—that I could not vote for the sale unless some changes were made. We began searching for a mechanism. Sam Nunn came up with the idea of some legislation tying the president down, and out of that came the Nunn-Warner resolution. The people I had been talking with thought we needed some kind of letter from the president. I said I thought that was what was needed. Well, what will we call it? So we went back and forth and someone suggested we call it a "letter of certification."

I went back and with [his Armed Services staffer] wrote a draft of the kind of letter we would want. I showed it to [Sen.] Slade Gorton and he worked it over very carefully in his own language. The letter went through several drafts. . . . Gorton, [Sen. Frank] Murkowski, [Sen. Mack] Mattingly, and I went to the White House and met with [White House Chief of Staff] Jim Baker. . . . We told him that our letter was what we needed if we were to go along—that otherwise we would vote against the sale. . . . That afternoon Baker and [chief of White House congressional liaison] Max Friedersdorf came to my office. It was the crucial meeting. Present were Kasten, Gorton, Mattingly, Murkowski, and myself. That was the meeting where they told us they accepted 95 percent of our letter. . . . I knew then that Murkowski and Mattingly and Gorton and myself would go. Andrews was still holding out, though we thought he might go. Kasten we weren't sure of, and he's the one we never did get. . . . The only language the administration would not accept was Kasten's. They said it went too far. And he voted against them.

The president signed the "letter of certification." The sale passed the Senate, 52-48.

When we first met after the vote, Quayle enthused, "Well, the letter of certification worked, didn't it?" "The letter became the mechanism for winning over doubting senators," he explained. "Each one would read it, change it a little bit, put his Hancock on it somewhere. A lot of people had their language in it. We have a copy in the office that shows our original draft, and we got 75 percent to 80 percent of what was in it." That was plenty enough for him to be pleased about. "Slade Gorton was interested in the fine print," he said. "I was not interested in the fine print. I was only interested in the concepts. The main idea came down to an institutional one—can the president conduct our foreign policy? . . .

That was the issue here." And the letter had helped a few senators, at least, to vote "yes" on this question. For his part, Quayle had identified those senators, drafted their letter, gathered them in his office, and acted as a liaison from the party leader to them. It was a modest, facilitative accomplishment. It was not a matter of persuading anyone to vote his way. "There was no lobbying of other senators," he said. "It was a matter of talking it through. . . . 'Why do you think this?' 'Why do you think that?' Nobody said, 'Go this way or that way.' When someone told you how he was going, that was that, nothing more was said." His accomplishment lay in the extent of his involvement.

Out of his participation came a heightened understanding of the Senate, too. In March when we first described it, he had observed:

> They take themselves more importantly here. The analogy I use is that when you say "senator" in the House, everybody turns around, wishing it were so. Over here, when you say "president," everybody turns around, wishing it were so.

When he began working on the AWACS issue, in September, he ran into a concrete manifestation of that phenomenon. "The egos are so great around here," he said as he tried to get the senators together. "I thought it was bad in the House; but the Senate is a hundred times worse. Every one of 'em thinks he ought to be the goddamned president." And, when the AWACS fight was over, he returned to this same individualistic theme. But now he saw it in a more benign, even constructive form. Not only did senators take themselves seriously, they took their work seriously. "Every senator took it very seriously and thought it through for himself," said Quayle.

> I know I was on the House Foreign Affairs Committee and I never took anything as seriously as I took this. You feel it's important and you take more time on it. . . . I think senators do put themselves in the president's shoes. House members do not. . . . So many presidents come from the Senate that you can do that. You look around and you say, "It might be him, or him."

It was the comment of an impressionable newcomer. But it suggests the two faces of Senate individualism—one holding the potential for paralysis, the other holding the potential for deliberation.

Since Quayle probably had never been so involved in so serious a matter of governing as this, there were other aspects of the process to be learned. One was the extent to which the politics of governing is intertwined with the politics of credit and blame. And the extent to which the politics of credit and blame is played out in the media. The Paula Parkinson episode aside, Quayle received more national media attention from his AWACS involvement than he did from anything else in his first year. When he began, he expressed the view that "I don't care about the publicity on this one. I just want to get the job done." And he operated on this premise throughout. "He held back and didn't rush into it," said his press secretary. "He may have been a little too conservative from a publicity standpoint. But still he was on television three times—with people like Tom Pettit [NBC] and Phil Jones [CBS]."

As victory drew near, however, Quayle found that he was unable to garner even what little public credit may have been due him for his effort. It was the cause of some chagrin. His press secretary said,

> He didn't get the credit he deserved. He missed it by two days. Instead of staying here [after the meeting with James Baker] he went to Indianapolis to hold a press conference to announce and explain his position. When he got back to Washington, the wave had rolled over him. He hadn't had the confidence to announce that he had had the idea of the letter of certification and that he had called the meeting of freshmen in his office. He had made me deny that there was such a meeting—even as it was going on. When he got back, he found that the president had signed the letter, that another senator had taken credit for being "THE guy," and that he wasn't disposed to share it. When he saw what had happened, Dan tried to get back in, but it was too late. I said to him, "You've been in a poker game. You had a pair of jacks, and you folded because you didn't think a pair of jacks would win. Now you see that a pair of sevens won the pot, and you're saying, 'Look, I had a pair of jacks.' The game is over." He learned a lot from that.

It was a lesson about credit and publicity he had never been in a position to learn before. And, as his press secretary concluded, "What the hell, there's a lot of time left." Time is something senators have more of than House members do.

In his first year, he began to display a recognizable legislative style. And the AWACS experience contained clues. Most basic was his obvious desire to get involved and to get something done. That is what drove him out of the House and propelled him to the Senate in the first place, he had said. At year's end, the hopes expressed on the campaign trail had been fulfilled. "I get the most satisfaction out of getting involved in the issues, taking some initiatives, doing the work, and getting things accomplished," he said. AWACS was a prime example of all these things. He had been an active negotiator and he could see the results of his activity.

Related to this preference for action was his preference for a breadth of focus—revealed in his comment that he was not interested in "the fine print" only the "concepts." The statement was reminiscent of his earliest postelection comment that he was "sloshing around" his committee preferences. He wanted, he said, to be "creative," to "innovate," "to specialize but . . . save myself to go where the action is." In the AWACS case, that is exactly what he had done.

When we first talked about the Armed Services Committee he had evinced this attraction to broad problems and a corresponding distaste for the details of implementation. "I don't like the mechanical, engineering details," he had said. "I don't care whether we have a fixed wing or a mobile wing or what thrust the turbines have or whether the pistons broke or whatever. I like the policy aspects, the MX missile, the tactical bomber, the rapid deployment force." These were the kinds of strategic questions that attracted him to the AWACS issues—and kept him interested. "We took Dan out to see the AWACS plane yesterday," said a staffer in September, "and he was bored by the whole thing. He doesn't like the toys. . . . He likes the policy aspects." What he likes best about "the policy aspects" is not the philosophical or analytical argumentation that may be involved but the close proximity to "the action," the opportunity as he put it with AWACS "to get the job done."

His willingness to search out a variety of compromises in pursuit of his ultimate "concept" of presidential leadership showed a pragmatism in implementation that we might have expected in view of what we have called his instrumental independence. He shopped around for ideas until he settled on the "letter of certification." "I even went so far," he said of AWACS, "as to call my friend George Will and I asked him, 'George, how do we get the president out of this mess?' "

In recounting his first year's activities he exuded enthusiasm for legislative work in general. "I had fun on all of them," he said after canvassing his first-year interests. "There was no one highlight. The highlight was getting involved and accomplishing a whole lot of things." He was, indeed, reluctant to compartmentalize or narrow his efforts in a way that made AWACS seem extraordinary. In talking about his work on the Budget Committee, a staffer commented that "He's so optimistic about everything. The process is a disaster. But he says, 'Let's get in and fix it up, fix it up, fix it up.' " There is a certain restlessness here, too. Once he identifies a problem, he is impatient to get on with solving it. He told an early interviewer, "I really have few low moments. But when I lose at something—whether it be a fight in a committee or I lose on the floor . . . I shift and go on to something else the very next moment." [56] Enthusiasm, optimism, impatience—these are attributes of a kid, a self-confident kid. They, too, were identifiable elements of an emerging legislative style.

When we talked in December, he seemed well along in his adjustment period. "I feel comfortable and I enjoy it," he said. "I'm where I want to be and where I belong." He looked back on a year of legislative immersion unlike any he had spent in the House. "You have to go back and understand the situation I was in in the House," he explained.

My first year I spent getting my family moved to Washington. The second year I ran for reelection. Then as soon as I was elected, I started running for the Senate. I talked with Bowen in December. So this is the first year I've been able to consider issues without worrying about their overt political consequences. It's the first year I've been able to concentrate on Washington. That's what I've done.

As for his future as a senator he emphasized his desire for a reputation as a legislator—one he had never enjoyed in the House. "I want to be known as an effective senator," he said.

It's hard to tell whether I'll be known as someone who initiates legislation or as someone who takes issues that come to him and moves them through the Senate.... My advisers back home ask me the same question. "What kind of a senator do you want to be?" "When people hear the name Dan Quayle [he snaps his fingers] what will they immediately think of?" It's a good question. But it's too early to tell. I haven't developed any themes yet. If they are still asking me that question after four years, then I'm in big trouble.

Time, he seemed confident, would take care of that problem. And he expressed a clear sense of himself in time.

I feel that this is my first year, that next year is an election year, that the third year is the mid point and that the fourth year is the last chance I'll have to make a record since the last two years, I'll be a candidate again. Everything I do in those last two years will be posturing for the election. But right now I don't have to do that.

For the moment, he was savoring the four years available to him to secure legislative accomplishment and a legislative reputation.

After one year, however, he had no reputation. Among his staffers he already deserved one totally different from the one he had enjoyed as a House member. "He's such a good senator and he was such a shitty congressman," said one staffer. "I don't mean he went from being an OK congressman to being an OK senator. I mean it's a huge change." But among the media scorekeepers who put him at ground zero at the beginning of the year there was no perceptible change. "You've seen these year-end summaries on the freshmen," commented one staffer.

Dan isn't even mentioned. Which is pretty lucky considering what they said about some of them. But they say, "Andrews is good; Gorton is good." I think what happened was that the press expected to be able to say, "Look what Indiana did, trading Birch Bayh for someone without a brain in his head." It ain't so; and they are beginning to find that out. So they can't place him yet. . . . And the Paula Parkinson thing was so devastating. That's what the press thought they would get, so they pointed and said, "See there." The fact that we crawled out of that hole and made it back to zero with the press is a miracle.

He had not yet "surprised everyone but myself" in the governing realm to a degree that would match his success in the campaigning realm. But, unbeknownst to anyone beyond his Senate office, the self-confident kid had been equipping himself for just such a performance. And he would not have to wait four years to undertake it.

NOTES

1. John Kingdon, *Agendas, Alternatives, and Public Policies* (Boston: Little, Brown, 1984).
2. Mark Helmke, "Now the Work Begins for Quayle," *Fort Wayne News Sentinel,* December 4, 1976.
3. Robert P. Mooney, "Quayle to Start by Attacking Evaders," *Indianapolis Star,* December 19, 1976.
4. Gary Jacobson and Sam Kernell, *Strategy and Choice in Congressional Elections,* 2d ed. (New Haven: Yale University Press, 1983).
5. Mark Helmke, "Fates Favor Quayle's Mercurial Career," *Fort Wayne News Sentinel,* May 15, 1979.
6. Mark Helmke, "Opponent Role Spurs 'No' Votes," *Fort Wayne News Sentinel,* January 9, 1978.
7. Jerry Graff, *Fort Wayne News Sentinel,* October 17, 1977; Mark Souder, "Hoosier Perspective," *Allen County Times,* April 14, 1977; Helmke, "Now the Work Begins"; Mooney, "Quayle to Start."
8. Mooney, "Quayle to Start."
9. Charlie Green, "Bowen Decision Brightens Democrats' Senate Outlook," *Anderson Bulletin,* May 14, 1979; Edward Ziegner, "Bayh-Quayle Skirmish Set," *Indianapolis Star,* May 20, 1979.
10. Ziegner, "Bayh-Quayle Skirmish Set."
11. Joyce Wadler, "A Senator Faces the Limelight," *Washington Post,* August 8, 1980.
12. Jerry Graff, "Quayle's Victory Margin Nearly 2-1," *Indianapolis Star,* November 8, 1978.
13. *Indianapolis Star,* May 10, 1979. A little-known opponent did, however, contest the primary against Quayle and was crushed.
14. Mike Perkins, "Quayle Makes It Official," *Huntington Herald Press,* May 14, 1979.

15. David Rohde, "Risk Bearing and Progressive Ambition: The Case of Members of the United States House of Representatives," *American Journal of Political Science* (February 1979).
16. Ibid.
17. "Economics," *Fort Wayne Journal Gazette*, January 18, 1978.
18. Mike Perkins, "In the 4th District, A Clear Choice," *Huntington Herald Press*, November 5, 1978.
19. Helmke, "Opponent Role."
20. Mark Helmke, "Quayle's Future Is Bright," *Fort Wayne News Sentinel*, January 6, 1977; Mark Helmke, "Quayle to Spearhead 'Town Meeting Tour'?" *Fort Wayne News Sentinel*, February 16, 1977.
21. Sylvia Smith, *Fort Wayne Journal Gazette*, July 6, 1977.
22. Helmke, "Opponent Role."
23. Mark Helmke, "Quayle's Smalltown-Boy Manner Covers Uncertainties," *Fort Wayne News Sentinel*, January 10, 1978.
24. Souder, "Hoosier Perspectives"; Ziegner, "Bayh-Quayle Skirmish Set."
25. For example, see Marjorie Hunter and David Rosenbaum, "Defeats Split Bitter House Democrats," *New York Times*, July 2, 1975; Charles Tidmarch, "The Second Time Around: Freshman Democratic House Members' 1976 Reelection Experiences" (paper prepared for delivery at American Political Science Association Convention, Washington, D.C., 1977); Diane Granat, "Whatever Happened to the Watergate Babies?" *Congressional Quarterly Weekly Report*, March 3, 1984.
26. Michael Barone, ed., *The Almanac of American Politics* (Washington, D.C.: National Journal, 1974, 1976.)
27. Mooney, "Quayle to Start"; Hortense Meyers, "Quayle Announces Senate Candidacy," *South Bend Tribune*, May 14, 1979; Elizabeth Bumiller, "The Charmed Life of Indiana's Golden Boy," *Washington Post*, January 11, 1981; Steven Hess, *The Ultimate Insiders* (Washington, D.C.: The Brookings Institution, 1987).
28. Helmke, "Quayle's Smalltown-Boy Manner"; Bill Jackson, "Quayle: Not A Household Word-Yet," *Evansville Courier*, May 19, 1979; Green, "Bowen Decision Brightens"; Donald Benn, *La Porte Herald*, October 24, 1977; Dave Kurtz, *Auburn Evening Star*, November 8, 1977.
29. Kurtz, *Auburn Evening Star*, November 8, 1977.
30. Mooney, "Quayle to Start."
31. Helmke, "Now the Work Begins."
32. Mooney, "Quayle to Start."
33. Helmke, "Fates Favor Quayle's Mercurial Career"; Mooney, "Quayle to Start"; Helmke, "Now the Work Begins."
34. Helmke, "Now the Work Begins"; Perkins, "In the 4th District, A Clear Choice."
35. Sylvia Smith, "Quayle Says It'll Cost Us More if He Turns Down Raise," *Fort Wayne Journal Gazette*, January 8, 1977.
36. Stu Engle, "Quayle Launches New Mobile Office," *Fort Wayne News Sentinel*, May 31, 1977.
37. Helmke, "Quayle to Spearhead"; Gary Marx, " 'Worst' Is Over for Quayle," *Wabash Plain Dealer*, January 6, 1978.
38. "Congressman Quayle Has Open Line Policy," *Berne News*, March 11, 1977; "Quayle Taking Own Calls," *Wabash Plain Dealer*, March 14, 1977.

39. Smith, "Quayle Says It'll Cost Us"; "Constituents," *Fort Wayne Journal Gazette,* January 18, 1978.
40. Helmke, "Quayle's Smalltown-Boy Manner."
41. Smith, "Quayle Says It'll Cost Us."
42. Dave Kurtz, *Auburn Evening Star,* February 15, 1977.
43. Mark Helmke, *Fort Wayne News Sentinel,* March 19, 1977.
44. *Fort Wayne News Sentinel,* August 16, 1977.
45. Marx, " 'Worst' Is Over"; Smith, "Quayle Says It'll Cost Us."
46. *Steuben Republican,* February 22, 1978.
47. Gary Graham, "Quayle Helps to Defeat No-Vote Pay Hike Measure," *Wabash Plain Dealer,* November 5, 1977; Helmke, "Quayle's Smalltown-Boy Manner."
48. Kurtz, *Auburn Evening Star,* February 15, 1977.
49. Richard Fenno, *Home Style: House Members in Their Districts* (Boston: Little, Brown, 1978).
50. Jack Anderson and Tony Capaccio, "Jack Anderson Rates the Congress," *The Washingtonian,* October 1980.
51. Anderson and Capaccio, "Jack Anderson Rates." On Quayle, see also Bumiller, "The Charmed Life of Indiana's Golden Boy."
52. Fenno, *Home Style.*
53. For the Quayle-Bayh race, see Xandra Kayden, "Campaign Under Siege: Reflections on One Senator's Defeat," *New York University Review of Law and Social Change* 10, 1 (1980-1981); more generally, see Marjorie Hershey, *Running for Office: The Political Education of Campaigners* (Chatham, N.J.: Chatham House, 1984).
54. *Indianapolis Star,* July 31, 1981.
55. Bumiller, "The Charmed Life of Indiana's Golden Boy."
56. Ibid.

A Season of Governing I

THE SUBCOMMITTEE CHAIRMAN:
PROBLEM AND PREPARATION

The year 1982 became a time of major legislative accomplishment for the junior senator from Indiana. It came about not because of some long-pursued policy interest nor because of some carefully plotted course of career development. It came about because an opportunity—predetermined by Congress four years earlier and magnified by the politics of the intervening years—presented itself to whatever senator happened to be the chairman in 1982 of the Labor and Human Resources Subcommittee on Employment and Productivity. And that chairman happened to be Dan Quayle.

In the beginning, he had not wanted that subcommittee chairmanship, much less, as we have seen, the parent committee itself. Once on the committee, his first desire was to chair the Subcommittee on Health.[1] But Labor and Human Resources Chairman Orrin Hatch, R-Utah, decided to reserve that area for himself by keeping it under the control of the full committee. The next ranking Republican, Robert Stafford, Vt., chose to pursue a lifetime interest by chairing the other prominent subcommittee—Education. From among the remaining alternatives, Quayle chose to chair the Employment Subcommittee—probably because it covered a subject that bulked large in his campaign and in his electoral interpretation. Within the jurisdiction of that subcommittee lay the $8 billion, highly controversial Comprehensive Employment and Training Act (CETA). And the act was set to expire on September 30, 1982. The question—what to do about it—awaited him on the subcommittee's agenda. Timing and position thus conspired to create a legislative opportunity that could not be

avoided. What he would make of that opportunity, however, remained to be seen.

Chairman Quayle came to his subcommittee position as a committed
supporter of all of Ronald Reagan's political principles and, hence, of the
putative "Reagan Revolution." He was devoted to the idea of reducing
the size and the impact of the federal government. His public record and
his public pronouncements proclaimed his economic and social conservatism. During the first two years, the "revolutionary" years, of the
Reagan administration, he was as loyal a supporter of the president as
there was in the Senate—with scores for supporting the president's
position on legislation of 87 percent and 84 percent, respectively. The
1981 score was 7 points higher and the 1982 score was 10 points higher
than the average score of all Republican senators. In 1981 only five
Republican senators scored higher than he, and in 1982, only four.

His support scores on conservative coalition votes (where a majority
of Republicans and southern Democrats opposes a majority of northern
Democrats) were 88 percent and 86 percent, according to *Congressional
Quarterly*; and he ranked twenty-second, 8 points higher than the
Republican average, and twentieth, 10 points higher than the Republican average, in 1981 and 1982, respectively.[2] On *National Journal*'s 1981
voting scorecard, his conservatism score was 27 points higher than that
of the average Republican senator on economic policy issues, 86 points
higher on social policy issues, and 22 points higher on foreign policy
issues. Only two Republican senators were more conservative than he
on social matters; seventeen were more conservative on economic issues;
and twenty-six were more so on foreign policy issues. All of his general
political predispositions were loyally Republican, strongly conservative,
and wholeheartedly supportive of the exciting antigovernmental
Reaganite thrust. Those were the lenses with which he would see every
important domestic public policy problem in the Ninety-seventh Congress. With national unemployment at 8 percent and moving upward to
post-Depression highs, employment and training policy certainly qualified as one such crucial problem.

But central tendencies, however strongly they may be held and
expressed, do not tell us all we need to know about individual instances.
In Quayle's case we have already noted his "instrumental independence"—a willingness to entertain a somewhat independent policy position when confronted by an identifiable problem. Once he recognized a
problem, that is, he would want to do something about it. And at that
point his conservatism might be attenuated by his desire to "get something done," to "fix it up, fix it up." His dislike for government might be
tempered by a felt necessity to use government. "The distrust of government is deeply ingrained within me," he explained later in his term.

So I start with that basic principle. . . . But I like to accomplish things. It doesn't do any good to take a pure position against government when there are national problems that have to be solved. It may make you feel good, but it ain't the way the world is. The government has to have a role in some things, and always will. So I always ask myself, "Is there a role for government here? What should the government's role be? How can it be kept to a minimum?" I think that's a valuable intellectual exercise no matter how you come out in the end.

He brought to his subcommittee chairmanship both his conservatism and his open-mindedness.

His first task as chairman was to learn something about "the way the world is" in the tangle of issues encompassing manpower, employment, and training. He was totally unfamiliar with the policy area and with the issue networks that had formed over time to shape policy making in that area. But he knew there was a problem—at least an Indiana problem. During his campaign, he had hit hard, he said, on "one theme—that 300,000 people were without jobs and that Birch Bayh was to blame." And Bayh himself had attributed his defeat largely to "18 percent unemployment among Indiana autoworkers." [3] In our first interview following his subcommittee selection, Quayle volunteered that

the problems I talked about in the campaign are the problems I'm still interested in—the auto industry. But I'm interested in them on a larger scale than I was before. Now, I'm worried about the auto industry throughout the whole state. Problems that we had in my district are much worse in other parts of the state. The scale of problems Gary has is so much greater than in Fort Wayne.

His statewide campaign, followed by his statewide responsibilities, had widened his horizons. He was clearly in the midst of a transition in his thinking from House member to senator.

As subcommittee chairman, he was positioned to make a still further transition—to a national perspective. At the very end of that first, March interview of him as senator, my notes read that he spoke "with some passion" about one part of the CETA program. "The administration is going to cut out the youth employment programs," he said.

OK, I agree, we've got to cut these programs. But what are they going to put in their place? That's what they've got to decide. They are so preoccupied with the budget, they aren't thinking about it. I hope this doesn't put me at odds with the administration. But there's an employment problem out there and the question is: what are they going to do about it? It's a Gary problem. I get more people coming in here from that part of the state than from any other part. They want to tell me about their problems. And they've got 'em.

He was seeing the unemployment problem through the eyes of a conservative Indiana senator, but the problem he was seeing was "the Gary problem." And that problem was a national problem—a problem of a 40 percent unemployment rate among low income black teenagers as well as the displacement of skilled auto workers. In incremental steps—from campaigner, to senator, to subcommittee chairman—Dan Quayle was coming to recognize the problem sitting on his subcommittee's agenda.

The CETA program, as established in 1973, contained both employment and training components. The employment segment provided public service jobs for people who were unemployed either by virtue of long-term (structural) economic change—mostly the poor and unskilled—or short-term (countercyclical) economic downturn—mostly the skilled. At its peak CETA was funded at $10 billion and provided 750,000 jobs. By 1980 the number was down to about 300,000, and its beneficiaries were primarily the poor and the unskilled. Their wages were provided by grants to state and local governments, and their jobs were provided and/or organized by those—mostly local—governments.

It was a program besieged by criticism. Conservatives claimed that it was awash in "fraud, abuse, and waste," that it was a prime example of a paternalistic governmental bureaucracy at its worst.[4] Neo-liberal Democrats used it as exhibit A in the futility of a liberalism that reflexively threw money at problems without careful calculation of long-term benefits.[5] The program had its defenders; but in the wake of Republican victories for White House and Senate, they had been weakened and put on the defensive. To the incoming administration, the $4 billion price tag the proposed Carter budget placed on this public service employment program represented the biggest and the most vulnerable domestic spending request available to them. Predictably, the massive budget-cutting 1981 reconciliation bill eliminated all funding for public service employment and killed it.[6] Dan Quayle welcomed the execution. "No one campaigned any harder against CETA than Dan," said one of his campaigners. And though I had never heard him mention the program, everything I did hear was consistent with that statement. So, too, was his voting record in the House.[7]

The second component of the CETA program involved job training for long-term and short-term unemployed persons. In 1980, $5 billion was spent training 2.5 million of the unemployed for what were hoped to be permanent jobs. These were both on-the-job and off-the-job training programs. These programs, too, were run by 476 state and local—mostly local—governmental units called "prime sponsors." The success of these training programs—how well they trained the poorest and the least skilled—was a matter of some dispute.[8] But their desirability was not. The Reagan administration proposed to keep the job training elements of CETA. But they budgeted them at $1 million below the Carter budget and proposed to consolidate a number of separate CETA job training programs into one single "block grant"—that is, a lump sum for training to be used at the discretion of the state and local government.[9] Block grants, however, threaten (as they are designed to do) discrete "categorical" programs. And the administration's training proposal ran into some difficulty on this score.

Defenders of CETA's special youth employment and training programs feared their demise if they were folded into a larger block grant.[10] So they sought to keep youth programs as separate entities. Their pleas went to the subcommittee of jurisdiction, chaired by the senator from Indiana. Quayle was a major defender of the block-grant concept. And, as a member of the House, he had joined a minority of his own party in opposing several youth training programs.[11] Now, however, as his March comments about Gary indicate, he was well aware of the youth employment problem. And he was receptive to arguments asking his subcommittee to keep youth programs intact—at least until his subcommittee could consider the entire employment problem.

On March 18 the subcommittee held its first, brief hearing—on the Youth Employment Demonstration Amendments of 1981. During the hearing, Quayle indicated strong support for the extension.

> If we don't do something with this authorization, if we don't do something with the young people, then we are simply turning our back. And that, to me is not an option. It is not an option that we can pursue. I don't think it's an option this administration wants to pursue. What I am concerned about is that we don't just zero out these youth programs in a course of two months and not have any kind of replacement. That would be a course of action that is unacceptable, as far as I am concerned.[12]

On April 7 he wrote to Office of Management and Budget (OMB) Director David Stockman and Presidential Assistant Martin Anderson urging that CETA's youth training programs be exempted from the block grant and extended for one year. "As you know, CETA expires in 1982," he wrote. "By extending the youth [sic] for one year, we will be able to deal with youth and adults together in 1982." In the memo, he also argued substantively that "Letting the youth program expire would mean a drastic reduction in service to youth which is difficult to

justify in light of the severity and persistence of the youth unemployment problem." [13]

The next day, his subcommittee voted out the one-year extension.
The full committee, the Senate, and the House quickly followed suit.
The bill passed in June. The major portion of the CETA training
component was given reduced authorization but in conventional form.
And the reconciliation bill provided that if Congress did not complete
action on reauthorization or replacement of CETA by September 30,
1982, the 1982 authorization levels would hold for 1983. In effect, then,
job training under CETA would continue for another year if Congress
failed to act in 1982.[14]

The Reagan administration was not happy. But, "preoccupied
with its budget cutting efforts, the administration did not oppose the
simple extension." [15] As Quayle had worried, however, his action did
put him "at odds with the administration." The administration
refused to send anyone to testify at the subcommittee hearing.
"Secretary [of Labor Raymond] Donovan fought us every inch of the
way on it," said Quayle later. And Donovan got some support from
among the conservative members of Quayle's subcommittee and the
full committee. To the degree that Quayle had begun to contemplate
the much larger task of formulating new training legislation, the
youth extension bill might suggest future difficulties. By itself,
however, the postponement proved to be a simple legislative matter.
It took far less of his time than his preoccupation with AWACS. "We
thought we would try a small bill, to get one under our belt," said a
subcommittee staffer. And that seems a fair assessment of Dan
Quayle's earliest effort at governing. It was a simple trial run, not a
strenuous test.

It would make for a tidy story line if we could say that Quayle's experience with the youth training bill left him with a clear understanding of the importance—or even the potential importance—that job
training policy making had for his legislative and his political career,
that he moved thereafter in a straight line and with single-minded
determination to capitalize on the good fortune that had brought him to
his subcommittee position. But such is not the case. He came to that
recognition slowly and at later stages in the process. Looking ahead, at
the end of his first year, he said,

> It's not clear yet just what I'll be working on [in the long
> run].... Next year I'll probably be active on the Budget
> Committee. And on Armed Services, I had just begun to get
> active on the MX basing amendment at the end of the session.
> Labor and Human Resources has been a pretty quiet committee.
> But I'll be the leader on youth training again.

He conveyed no developed sense that the training legislation presented a special priority or a special opportunity for him.

Some Quayle staffers, too, predicted a full range of activity across his various committees. One staffer opined that his boss would be "most interested" in budget matters, that he would "have to do something about CETA," and that his activity on Armed Services would be "problematical." Another predicted simply, "He's got the jobs bill, the budget bill, and defense legislation." "He goes in fits and starts, and he's got a short attention span," said one staffer in describing Quayle's work habits at year's end. "He'll get interested in something and the whole staff will get in motion. But he may forget it and not ask about it for a long time afterward." Looking toward 1982, it seems, the young senator contemplated a broad range of interests—more action than focus.

For his subcommittee staff, however, there was both action and focus. From the beginning of 1981 they pointed toward the larger task of replacing CETA. For them, it was the only task; and the youth training bill was the curtain raiser for "a long hard look at the employment problem." Steadily, and with increasing degrees of specificity, they built a public record to support their ultimate legislative objective. One week after the youth extension plan passed the Senate, they produced an outline of eight "major issues of particular concern to the Subcommittee" in reformulating employment and training policy. On May 19, Quayle announced a schedule of summertime subcommittee hearings and inserted the outline in the *Congressional Record* as a guide for witnesses.[16]

In June and August the subcommittee held hearings on employment problems in general—four days in Washington, two days in Indiana. "I can't have the people in Indiana shooting at my back," said Quayle. The subcommittee took testimony from business groups, labor groups, community groups, education groups, minority groups, mayors, governors, administrators, and clients of the local training enterprises.[17] The fact of the hearings and "more than 100 witnesses" was used at all subsequent decision points in the process to legitimate the subcommittee's policy leadership.[18] The staff used the hearings "to find out what was important to the various interest groups and what was not . . . [in order to] make some first cuts at what they would buy." By September the staff had identified fourteen "major issues" for private circulation among interested parties.[19] In November, Quayle set forth in the *Congressional Record* both "some broad principles" and an annotated "outline of a new approach to employment problems."[20] And by the end of December the subcommittee staff had produced forty-one pages of "very preliminary specifications for a job training bill."[21]

For the success of this incremental, bill-building process, Dan Quayle's very first decision as subcommittee chairman was crucial. Recognizing that he lacked expertise, and confident of his political instincts, he had deliberately put himself in the hands of a substantive expert. For staff director of the subcommittee he selected Robert Guttman, a seasoned manpower policy consultant from the Congressional Research Service (CRS). Guttman understood the employment policy area as well as anyone in the business, and he had operated easily and knowledgeably within that issue network. In the words of a full committee staff member, "He had been involved in the training field since day one. He knew all the pitfalls that lay ahead." A lawyer by training, he was equally at home in argumentation, bargaining, and bill writing. He supervised a staff of two other professionals and a secretary. He became the intellectual keystone of the legislative effort. He and the chairman were total strangers when Guttman—anxious to leave CRS and learning of the opening—solicited an interview. They were something of an odd couple—veteran and kid, liberal and conservative, intellectual and plunger—but they "hit it off" immediately. And they established and maintained an easy working partnership of respect and trust.

The chairman's attention to the work of his subcommittee staff was discontinuous. But for him, too, there was incremental movement toward the legislative goal. The summertime hearings gave him a further education in the nature and scope of the problem and forced him to conduct his "intellectual exercise" concerning "the role of the government here." When they were over, he expressed his threshold conclusion "that the federal government should play a significant role in providing training opportunities to those who cannot succeed in the labor market without help." That solid conviction underlay all subsequent ideas about how to do it. He also concluded from the hearings that "the major groups in trouble" were "disadvantaged youth," "female family heads," and, "experienced workers ... suffering dislocation." And finally, the hearings had revealed that "the shape of the delivery system" would be "the most contentious issue" in the area of implementation.[22] This issue—how and by whom the training programs would be designed and run—pitted the groups that dominated in the CETA program—that is, mayors and labor groups—against groups that wanted a larger voice—governors and business groups.

In his November *Congressional Record* statement, the subcommittee chairman set forth the four guiding principles of his approach to job training. They exemplified his central concern for broad "concepts" of legislation rather than the "fine print" expressed during his AWACS activity. They were, also, conservative principles. They were to: (1)

"strengthen the involvement of the private sector," (2) "give to the states a preponderant voice in designing programs," (3) "design programs that prepared people for jobs ... [and avoided] income maintenance," and (4) design "a system that is result-oriented ... [and] measures outcomes." [23] As he predicted, sharp differences came over the first two items—the delivery system. Equally, however, they arose over the third item, payments to trainees. But he never lost sight of these four fundamental "concepts" with which he began. From subcommittee to conference committee, they governed his substantive decisions.

STRATEGIC DECISIONS: BIPARTISANSHIP AND THE POLICY INITIATIVE

The most basic strategic decisions facing the subcommittee chairman also got identified in the course of the preliminary record-building, bill-building processes of 1981. They were of two sorts: support and timing. How to win the support of a committee majority and the administration? When to begin and how fast to move in the subcommittee relative to the administration? These, of course, were decisions only the chairman could make.

Quayle's fundamental decision about support was his decision to build a bipartisan majority inside the Labor and Human Resources Committee. It was shaped by arithmetic and confirmed by instinct. From the moment the makeup of the committee was settled, it was clear to all observers that the nominal 9-7 Republican majority was not, in fact, a working majority. Lowell Weicker, Conn., was one of the two most liberal and least dependable of Senate Republicans. And his maverick tendencies were particularly pronounced on matters before this committee.[24] His defection to the solid phalanx of Democrats would create an 8-8 tie, thus frustrating action by the majority party. A second member, Robert Stafford, was also among the more liberal Senate Republicans; and he, too, often brought his moderate Republican views to bear on matters coming before this committee.[25] His defection could create a committee majority. Indeed, it had done just that in 1981, forcing Chairman Orrin Hatch to backtrack and compromise on the administration's block-grant proposals and weakening his leadership potential.[26]

"Hatch is completely disorganized," said Quayle in December. "There are a whole lot of issues before the committee that he doesn't want to handle. He wishes they would go away. The committee is badly split along party lines. ... The situation ... is totally unpredictable." Quayle understood the arithmetic of the situation, not the least of the reasons being that the committee had passed his youth training exten-

sion bill with the support of seven Democrats and four Republicans
(Weicker, Stafford, Hatch, and himself) and over the opposition of the
five other Republicans.[27] Lacking strong Republican leadership and a
dependable Republican majority, the prospect for building a Republican
majority and holding one throughout the legislative process was exceed-
ingly dim.

Besides, it was not Dan Quayle's preferred method of proceeding.
His personal goal was to gain a reputation as "an effective senator,"
and for that he needed a bill. And the surest way to get a bill, as he
saw it, was to forge the broadest possible committee consensus in
support of that bill. That meant a bipartisan strategy. "It's been a
bipartisan bill from the beginning," he explained shortly after he
introduced it in 1982.

> I never thought of it in any other way. It's my first piece of leg-
> islation and it should be bipartisan. That's the way I think.
> That's what my instincts are. After all, it is a national prob-
> lem. . . . Besides, there's no way you can get it out of committee
> unless it's bipartisan—with Weicker going his own way. I want
> to pass this bill.

As he explained later, the instinct that governed this view concerned the Senate as well as the committee. When I asked if his
preference for bipartisanship grew out of his experience in the House,
he laughed. "Hell, no. The House is completely partisan. The Democrats
run it and won't let the Republicans do anything. The House is the
worst training ground in the world for bipartisanship. If anything, you
come out of the House filled with hate—with venom." "But," he
continued, "when you get to the Senate you realize immediately that
things are different, that the only way anything gets done here, with
few exceptions, is through bipartisanship. If you want to get results, you
have to be bipartisan. And I'm a results-oriented person." It was one
more piece of evidence of his strong desire for accomplishment. But it
was the first sign of the legislative instincts that would underwrite his
committee accomplishments.

The decision about bipartisanship carried some serious risks. Prime
among them was the risk that the pursuit of Democratic support might
put him, again, "at odds" with the Reagan administration. And in the final analysis he could not pass a job training bill without the support of
the administration. Substantively, the Democrats were more favorable to
a CETA-style program, while the administration was vehemently opposed to anything that would bring back public service jobs through the
side door—an approach they labelled "CETA revisited." Less substantively, the key to a bipartisan strategy was the ranking Democratic
member of the committee, Edward Kennedy, Mass. And administration

sentiment was at least as antipathetic to political arch-rival Kennedy as it was to "CETA revisited."

Quayle faced these risks with the same self-confidence that governed his decisions to run for office. "I don't worry about things. My problem is that sometimes I act too quickly and I'll make a mistake," he admitted later.

> But if I do, my attitude is, "I'll fix that up when I get to it." It's that old saying that if you see ten troubles coming down the road, nine will go away before they get to you. Some people spend a lot of time thinking, "Should I do this or that?" I don't. I just decide what I want to do and do it. I don't go over and over decisions. My wife does, but I don't. It's a matter of self-confidence.

The decision to travel the bipartisan route and to solicit the help of Edward Kennedy was his earliest strategic decision. It caused him a lot of trouble; but he never looked back.

The decision about support had the effect of shaping the decision about timing. On the matter of timing, his choice was whether to wait for the administration to act. Once he decided to go down the path of bipartisanship, there was no reason not to proceed as quickly as possible to use that support to move the bill through the committee. His instincts too—his impatience, his desire to get in and "fix it up, fix it up"—inclined him to action. He saw no reason to wait for the administration, lest its actions disrupt bipartisan agreements and force recalculations about support. Above all else, the "results-oriented" subcommittee chairman wanted a bill. He was not sure the administration wanted one. So he decided to assume active, positive leadership.

On September 15, Quayle wrote to committee Chairman Hatch outlining his subcommittee's activities and future plans. He ended with the following prospectus:

> Bob Guttman of my staff has started informal discussions with interested groups with a view to developing a consensus bill. . . . I would look forward to developing a bill that could be cosponsored by the Chairman and Ranking Minority member of the Committee. We are, of course, also working as closely as we can with the Administration which is engaging in a similar endeavor. I would hope that we could have a bill ready for introduction at the beginning of the next session. . . .

This was the first indication of his decision to seek bipartisan support. The letter also indicated that he was undertaking a bill-writing effort that was—for the time being at least—separate from that of the administration. And it further indicated that, one way or another, he intended to introduce a bill in January. It was a clear signal of his readiness to move and his intention to move quickly. A copy of the letter was sent to Senator Kennedy. On October 4, in a speech to the National Alliance of Business, he repeated, publicly, his bipartisan hopes and his January timetable.[28] He had not yet talked privately to either Hatch or Kennedy; and he awaited their reactions to his initiative.

It was five or six weeks before the Quayle people received a response from Kennedy that "could be interpreted" as expressing an interest in bipartisanship. And a follow-up meeting between the two senators was arranged by Guttman and his counterpart on the Kennedy staff, Kitty Higgins. "We got them together, but the main thing was that they wanted to get together." The two staffers were long-time acquaintances within the issue network; and they retained, throughout, an ease in their relationship that smoothed bipartisan negotiation.

At the same time, however, their friendship hindered relations with the administration, whose Labor Department operatives were distrustful of Guttman because of it. Throughout the fall, "I only knew what I read in the *Washington Post* about what the administration was thinking," said Guttman. One of Senate Leader Howard Baker's staffers explained, "Bob Guttman knows more about the program than anyone else. But the administration does not trust him. They felt he would not listen to them, that he had some kind of liaison with the Kennedy staff so they tried to go around him." But he added that "the decisions weren't Guttman's, they were Quayle's."

Quayle and Kennedy agreed to work together in shaping a bill. One year later, Quayle recalled: "Way back at the beginning, when we had the meeting to work out a conceptual agreement with Kennedy, I remember we came out and Bob [Guttman] said, 'We've got a bill.' I said, 'Don't be so sure.'" Kennedy had yielded to Quayle on a basic "concept" regarding the issue of the service delivery system. "For Kennedy," said Guttman,

> it meant deciding that he was willing to compromise on that which we absolutely could not give up. We could not agree to a direct line from the federal government—the Labor Department—to the localities. We were committed to working through the governors. Kennedy agreed to our basic position; and we agreed to put in procedural protections for the mayors. His willingness to give in on such an important provision showed that he had a real interest in solving the problem.

On the basis of their mutual interest in solving a national problem, a veteran liberal leader of the Democratic party and an unknown conservative freshman Republican launched their unlikely partnership.

Committee Chairman Hatch's response to Quayle's letter was tentative. Unlike Kennedy, Hatch did not have to weigh any serious substantive disagreements with Quayle. He had none. But, unlike Kennedy, he faced problems of procedure and of credit. For Kennedy, there was only one train leaving the station. For Hatch, there might be two—Quayle's and the administration's. He believed that his role as chairman required that he be especially solicitous of administration wishes, whatever those might be. Furthermore, Hatch's staff chief, George Pritts, had a long-standing political association with the Labor Department's chief congressional liaison, Assistant Secretary Don Shasteen. It was an important back-channel for Hatch/administration cooperation—the equivalent of the Guttman/Higgins tie—but exacerbating rather than smoothing Quayle's course. If Hatch waited to sponsor an administration proposal, he would get a larger share of the credit. The administration, and his staff, wanted him to wait. So he wavered.

On November 24 the three senators placed their respective public positions in the *Congressional Record*. Quayle set forth the basic "principles" of his approach (see pp. 42-43) and expressed "my firm intention to proceed on a bipartisan basis." Kennedy called "bipartisan cooperation" a "hallmark" of past employment and training policy, welcomed "the opportunity to work ... to achieve a bipartisan approach," and concluded that "the principles I have outlined are compatible with many of the objectives Senator Quayle has proposed." Hatch, on the other hand, emphasized the administration's role, by saying that "after the administration's views and recommendations are taken into careful account" his committee would work out "a new bill." He added tepidly, "I look forward to cosponsoring a bill along with Senator Quayle which ... should have broad bipartisan support." [29]

A week later, the Quayle staff seized upon the positive aspects of these comments in a memo to the Kennedy and Hatch staffers. "Now that our principals have agreed to work on a bipartisan bill, it is important that we lose no time in turning the generalities of the statements in the *Record* into the specifics of a bill," wrote Guttman. And he added, "As you know, it is Senator Quayle's firm intention to have a bill ready to introduce on the first day of the next session." [30] Quayle's fundamental decision about timing seemed clear. He would keep the initiative, move as early as possible, and set the pace—certainly with Kennedy, maybe with Hatch, and with or without the Reagan administration.

In the weeks that followed, it became increasingly clear that Quayle would be moving without the administration and without his full committee chairman, who had decided to wait for the administration. Both Hatch and the administration requested that Quayle not introduce his own bill, that he, too, wait for the administration to work up its own training legislation. But Quayle did not wish to give up either the substance of his own bill or the policy momentum it would give him. As he said later, "The only way I could deal with those guys downtown was to force them to pay attention to me by moving the bill along." He declined the request.

For one thing, Quayle reacted to both requests with skepticism born of Senate experience. In 1981, when he had wanted to introduce a bill to cut back the Department of Education, the administration had asked him to wait for their bill on the subject, and he had done so. But they had never produced a relevant bill, and his legislation subsequently "fell into the bottom of the legislative swamp." Besides, there was no administration training bill in sight; and he did not believe that the administration was capable of producing draft legislation in a timely fashion. Nor was he sure the administration was deeply committed to new legislation—a view strengthened by news in early December that OMB had proposed a reduction in the training program budget from the existing $3.9 billion to $1.5 billion. Quayle fired off an immediate protest to OMB Director Stockman stating that "It seems to me that the Administration should be looking for ways to make training programs a higher priority. . . ." [31]

As for his chairman's request, Quayle had, from the beginning, found Orrin Hatch hard to understand. They had begun their careers in 1979 as twin poster stars of the Conservative Conference; and they had shared billing as two of the six "rising stars" of Congress as selected by the *Chicago Tribune.*[32] Their differences were less philosophical than personal, political, and practical. "He's a funny guy. I can't figure him out," Quayle had commented during our first interview in March. Later, he believed he had seen Hatch take another program, and credit for it, out of the hands of another subcommittee chairman. "He doesn't like the idea of giving a freshman credit for such a major bill as ours," said a Quayle staffer. Furthermore, the Quayle staff had found the Hatch staff difficult to work with. So the subcommittee chairman had not developed a sufficiently smooth or trusting personal relationship with the full committee chairman to be responsive to his request on those grounds.

More than his experience, however, it was Quayle's own desire to lead, his eagerness to "get something done" that governed his decision to proceed with his own piece of legislation. "The thing that inspires me," he said in December,

> is when I can take an issue, make certain it is consistent with my philosophy, massage it, articulate it, and go to committee or

to the floor and see it through. I like the excitement of the battle—the debate on the floor, the lobbying in committee.

The job training bill was his best chance yet to do exactly that. And he did not want to miss it.

As the new year began, his staff noted his growing state of readiness. "He's much more confident than he was last year about jumping in and mixing it up," said one, speaking generally. "He still has the same attitude, 'Let's get in and fix it up, fix it up.'" As for the jobs bill, another said,

> In terms of the development of a senator, he has pursued a steady course. He has not been rash or brash. He has told everyone what he was going to do and has stayed with it— even when some big logs were thrown in his path. He said in September that he was going to introduce a bill in January.... Last August he would not have had the confidence to do this. He had the status of subcommittee chairman but he wasn't willing to use it. Now he's willing to say to the chairman of the committee that he's going ahead with the bill even if the chairman won't come along with him.

Quayle's bill, this staffer offered, "is the biggest thing he's done thus far. It may be the biggest piece of legislation in his whole first term." A subcommittee staffer added that "This bill will be the big bill coming out of the Labor Committee this year." I never heard Quayle talk at all in that vein. But the self-confident, "results-oriented" kid did see it as an opportunity to legislate. "For the past five years, I've done nothing but run for election," he said in late January. "For the next three years I want to establish a solid legislative record." He could not wait to get started.

OBSERVATIONS AND REFLECTIONS: PRESS CONFERENCE

On February 2, I watched Senators Quayle and Kennedy hold a joint press conference to introduce their "Quayle-Kennedy Training for Jobs Bill." My notes and reflections follow.

A dozen reporters and three TV camera crews—one covering Indianapolis, one covering both Indianapolis and Fort Wayne plus the Independent News Network—are here. But none of the major national television networks have come. As an issue, says a subcommittee staffer, job training "is not a life-and-death matter. People want to have a program, but few lose sleep over it. Interest is always there, but it's not deep." About ninety people are in the audience—attracted, say the

Quayle people, more by the presence of Ted Kennedy than by the issue, and, certainly, not by Dan Quayle.

Altogether, it is an event that attracts modest interest. But the dynamics of the relationship between the two senators is fascinating. Watching them, I recall how Dan Quayle had used Ted Kennedy as a whipping boy during his election campaign. [My notes show that to the dentists of Warrick County he had prophesied, "Let me tell you one thing. Your friend Ted Kennedy will not be chairman of the Judiciary. (applause) And there won't be any Kennedy national health insurance bill." (applause)] Yet here they are two years later sharing the podium, as legislative partners.

Quayle speaks first, then Kennedy. They thank and praise each other—Kennedy's references to "Chairman Quayle," his "diligence, effort, and energies" being particularly generous. Each describes what Quayle calls "the pain and misery of unemployment" and Kennedy calls "the pleas of the unemployed." Quayle sees the figures at "12 percent in Indiana"; Kennedy sees them about to reach "the highest level since the Great Depression" nationally.[33] Quayle's concluding comment is: "It replaces CETA and we hope it will have broad bipartisan support."

Scorekeeper questions indicate their exclusive interest in the politics of the cosponsorship. The first one asks Kennedy what the key compromises were. Kennedy defers to Quayle, who mentions, first, the funding level and, second, protection for local officials in the face of the increased role for governors and for "the Private Industry Councils." "These two main differences took a lot of negotiation." Next, Quayle is asked: "Why shouldn't the private sector do the job?" He answers that "there is a certain segment of our society that private industry will not touch.... Therein lies the responsibility of government." Kennedy agrees—at greater length and in stronger language. Quayle is then asked, "Do you have a White House commitment?" "No, we've told them what we're doing.... There is no commitment.... I'm convinced at some point they will come forth." "What will convince them, 10 percent unemployment?" "I imagine that would be an incentive." (laughter)

A fourth scorekeeper asks, "Senator Quayle, isn't this a rather unusual alliance? How will it play back home?" Kennedy butts in, "You mean in Massachusetts?" (laughter) Says Quayle, "They don't know who Dan Quayle is in Massachusetts. But they do know who Ted Kennedy is in Indiana. (laughter) I don't think there will be any recall. Actually, the fact that the two of us would get together underscores the seriousness of the problem of unemployment and it emphasizes our commitment.... A high rate of unemployment is unacceptable." There is a repeat question about the administration, and the thirty-minute conference ends.

Shortly after noon, the two principals go over to the Senate floor to exchange more flattery and make their speeches introducing the bill.[34] It is given the number S 2036.

ADMINISTRATION RESPONSE

At this point the subcommittee chairman wanted to hold hearings as soon as possible and then swing directly into subcommittee markup. He believed that he had worked out a good bill, a bill that—with the usual intra-Senate negotiation—could command "broad bipartisan support" in his subcommittee, in the full committee, and in the Senate. Before the press conference, he had proposed to the counterpart subcommittee in the Democratic House of Representatives that they hold joint hearings on all job training proposals. Chairman Augustus Hawkins, D-Calif., of the House Education and Labor Subcommittee on Employment Opportunities had agreed; and a February 22 date for hearings already had been set.

This small gesture reflected Quayle's instinctive desire to establish working relationships with the broadest range of congressional groups. It held the possibility, too, of easing the inevitable negotiations that would take place when a more CETA-like bill from the Democratic House would have to be reconciled with the product of the Republican Senate. On the day of the press conference, Quayle and Hawkins cosigned a letter inviting Secretary of Labor Raymond Donovan to be their leadoff witness on February 22.[35]

On the day S 2036 was introduced, it did not have the support of the administration. The Quayle people knew that their bill could not succeed without it. "The administration is the big unknown factor...," said a subcommittee aide that day.

> We would like to move from hearings right into markup, but we will have to engage the administration. We can't move a piece of legislation without administration support or benevolent silence. We could get it out of subcommittee, but then Hatch wouldn't schedule it [for a full committee vote].

They were hopeful, however, that the administration and the committee chairman would recognize the merits of their bill, grant them the policy initiative, and adopt S 2036 as their negotiating vehicle, too. As a second staffer put it,

> Maybe the administration will look at it as it goes along and see that it's a good bill, ask to change a section or two, and join us. I hope so. As for Hatch, he may join too. If he does, we'll give

him seventy-five columns of print on what a great committee chairman he is.

They were encouraged in this hope by their view that any administration bill—as it got worked out—would inevitably look very much like S 2036. "The administration bill is coming closer to ours all the time," continued the first aide,

> because they are responding to the same people and the same concerns we are. Legislation doesn't develop out of thin air. It develops out of a concrete set of concerns on the part of certain people. And the administration listens to the same people we do.

He recognized, however, that some of the obstacles were not substantive but political. "The administration has two problems with our bill. One is the size of the budget [$3.9 billion] and the other is the cosponsorship of Kennedy. And I'm not so sure but what the second one isn't worse than the first." Still, he ended his February 2 assessment on an optimistic note. "We've tried to convince them to take the bipartisan bill, and I think we've got a shot. There are mostly ruffled feathers at this point." "Maybe," he laughed, "Dan could go out and play golf with Donovan and that would do it."

Informal negotiation of any sort, however, was not in the cards. Nor was administration acceptance of S 2036. Budget Director Stockman's cool reply on February 10 to Quayle's December protest indicated that the administration would proceed with their own bill.[36] Donovan's response to the Quayle-Hawkins invitation to testify was to request a one-month postponement of the hearings to give the administration time to produce a bill of its own. Quayle was impatient. "There's no way I'll postpone them a month. If you wait for the Labor Department to come up with a bill, you'll wait forever." But in the face of a "no-postponement, no-testimony" threat from the secretary, a three-week postponement—to March 15—was eventually agreed upon. The very idea that the Senate Republicans would share their hearing with House Democrats "ticked off the administration," said an aide to Chairman Hatch.

In view of the scheduled demise of CETA and the centrality of job training policy to their mission, Labor Department tardiness in preparing new legislation is, by any standards, remarkable. We cannot be sure what executive branch thinking was at this time, because our view comes from the perspective of the Quayle enterprise. But the Quayle people attributed the delay largely to a lack of administration enthusiasm for any large, new job training program.

"I think there are a lot of people in the administration who hope Congress can't come up with a bill," said Quayle. "They may just continue CETA ... till it expires on September 30." There was, after all, the fall-back position of an automatic one-year extension. And the Quayle enterprise believed that the administration probably preferred this status quo position to a new bill they could not control. The Quayle group believed that only the constant pressure of their legislative buildup had caused the administration to move at all. "At one point," said Quayle, "they weren't even going to introduce a bill."

Another reason for the delay, they believed, was disorganization inside the Labor Department. "We've had so little communication with them," complained a subcommittee staff member, "we can't find anyone to bargain with." Quayle requested a meeting with Donovan, who declined. The staff asked to meet with Assistant Secretary for Employment and Training Albert Angrisani, who declined. Donovan, they believed, was embattled and weakened by political troubles; and Angrisani would not move without Donovan. Overall administration confusion, they believed too, was further aggravated by the Quayle-Kennedy alliance. "They were caught by surprise," said a staffer. "They didn't think we could ever get Kennedy. It threw their timetable off. They haven't recovered."

While the Kennedy connection probably did cause them to sputter, it probably doubled their determination to write their own bill. "We keep telling them," said a subcommittee aide, "that if we get a consensus bill out of the Senate, we'll be in a much stronger position in conference with the House. If we keep Kennedy on board, he will be worth his weight in gold. ... But they are torn between not wanting to help Kennedy and wanting the legislation." In terms of emotion, the first pull was undoubtedly stronger. "They hate 2036," said a Hatch confidant, "because Kennedy's name is on it."

No matter what the explanation of the administration's tardiness, the response of the subcommittee chairman was to continue to push his bipartisan bill. But a week after the press conference, hope in the face of adversity was turning to determination in the face of opposition. "The administration doesn't like the bill. And they like it less because of Kennedy," he exclaimed.

> I've lost the Labor Department; and the Cabinet Council is not supporting it because of Labor. I've got a call in to [Treasury Secretary Donald] Regan now. He's the chairman of the council. I want to tell him I have the best bill, and that Kennedy is the ranking member of the committee. They probably can't get anything through that committee unless they work with him. I've got to, damn it, have administration support.

He was at a similar impasse with his committee chairman. "I can't deal with him. I had to go around him," he said of Hatch.

I asked him to join me, but that's not his conception—joining. He wants to be the leader. He thinks it should be his bill. Well, it's my bill. I did all the work on it. I told him, "Maybe you can get away with this with somebody else, but not me." . . . Hatch doesn't accomplish anything. What has he ever done?

All of this was said less in anger than as straightforward commentary—and certainly not in despair. Dan Quayle does not know the meaning of the word. "I'm sure I've stepped on some toes and made some enemies—forever," he concluded. "But that's the way it is. No one said it would be easy."

As their separate bill took final form, both Hatch and the administration asked Quayle to be its chief sponsor. Hatch wrote a formal note to Quayle regretting any "misunderstanding" about who should be the main sponsor and admitting that "we have differed on the appropriate timing of all this." He said,

I would be pleased if you would be the prime sponsor of the administration's proposal. . . . I will go on as the second name. You are our Committee expert on training issues and it is fitting that you should guide this legislation with your own. . . .

Hatch also requested that he be made a cosponsor of the Quayle-Kennedy bill.[37] The administration also invited Quayle and Hatch to be present at Donovan's press conference unveiling the administration bill.

Apparently they had come to believe that they could not succeed without Quayle. "The fundamental reason [for the request] was that we had the support," said an aide.

The administration had to go around to the same people we went to. We have the same constituencies—businessmen and governors. When they went around to these groups they heard that we had not sold out to Kennedy. They heard, "This is a good bill." So the administration learned they couldn't ram an alternative down Quayle's throat. People are a lot more cooperative when you have the horses.

Quayle agreed to sponsor the administration bill. "We said, 'Sure.' We had always been willing to do that. It was a given," said an aide. "But they treated it like we had been forced to make a big concession. It's hard to figure out."

There is reason to believe that the administration thought that once they got their act together, they could pressure Quayle to sponsor their bill, that they would then be in control of the agenda, and that they and their bill would dominate the proceedings from thereon. If that is what the administration thought—and they often acted that way—then they failed to understand the degree to which their slowness to act had already surrendered the policy initiative. And they failed to reckon with the determination of the young subcommittee chairman who had seized the initiative.

Quayle told the press that his sponsorship of the administration's bill was only a courtesy to the administration and that he was "not about to abandon the Quayle-Kennedy bill." [38] Privately he said, "They wanted me to go down to the White House to endorse their bill. They told everyone I was going to go down there. There was no way I was going down there to endorse it." He did not. He was now the main sponsor of two bills. But, as a top staffer put it at the time, "Dan will push the first bill, not the second."

NEGOTIATION: FROM HEARINGS TO MARKUP

On March 15 the chairman of the Employment and Productivity Subcommittee opened four days of joint hearings (with its House counterpart) by reading a statement stressing the necessity and the urgency of job training legislation. He called it "perhaps the most important piece of legislation, domestic legislation, that will pass this Congress." The tone was typically upbeat. "In my opinion, CETA is broken and needs to be fixed.... I say, let's fix it!" The tone also conveyed a familiar impatience. "There are some rough spots to be ironed out, and I am hoping that this can be accommodated quickly and to the satisfaction of most." [39]

Throughout the hearings, Quayle leaned on friendly and neutral witnesses alike to acknowledge their agreement with him; and to the recalcitrants he portrayed a bleak alternative—that is, nothing. He exerted the same pressure on some of the ninety-odd witnesses that he had been exerting on the administration. And, more important even, he kept the pressure on the administration, too. If they ever presumed that he was now in their pocket or, at least, that his pressure would be off, they were disabused of that belief within the first hour.

As leadoff witness, Secretary Donovan spoke in favor of "the administration proposal introduced last week by Senator Quayle and Senator Hatch...." When he finished, Quayle concluded that "we now have a commitment from ... the administration that we do have to do something about our training program [and that] ... we are in fact moving toward getting a ... program." And Quayle then made clear his continued support for "the bipartisan bill that is presently before the Senate, S 2036." He said to Donovan, "You and the administration have come up with a fine proposal, introduced by Senator Hatch.... I know you are not prepared to endorse our proposal today. If you would be, we

would certainly find that very profound and interesting." To which the
secretary replied mildly that "a bipartisan approach is most welcome
and we want to be a part of it." [40] Moments later, however, a major
obstacle to any such agreement to "our proposal" appeared in the form
of a sharp, hostile, and confrontational set of exchanges between
Secretary Donovan and Senator Kennedy. The tension in the hearing
room was thick. And it presaged a problem for the subcommittee
chairman when and if he ever found himself caught between these two
combatants.

For the time being, however, the young senator plunged ahead,
pressing witnesses to support his Quayle-Kennedy bill in preference to
the administration bill. Consider this exchange between himself and
three big-city mayors—representatives of the group least in favor of
changes in the CETA-style legislation.

> SENATOR QUAYLE: Having talked about the bipartisan bill in the
> Senate, let me just get to the political reality, at least in the Senate.
> There are two bills pending over there. One is a bipartisan
> proposal submitted by myself, Senator Kennedy . . . and others;
> and the other is the administration proposal. Which one would
> you prefer?
>
> MAYOR SLOANE (Louisville): Well, sir, yours. (laughter)
>
> QUAYLE: Mayor Fraser, you have been around this place before.
> You know how things operate. We've got a couple of bills over
> there, so which one would you like to see?
>
> MAYOR FRASER (Minneapolis): Well, of the two you mentioned, there
> is no choice. Yours is far superior to the Administration's bill.
>
> SLOANE: I agree.
>
> QUAYLE: Mayor Sloane, you agree?
>
> SLOANE: I certainly do.
>
> QUAYLE: Mayor Schaefer, I assume you agree. Are you going to
> support the Administration bill?
>
> MAYOR SCHAEFER (Baltimore): No, no. Wait a minute. (laughter)
> You're a fine Senator, but let me . . .
>
> QUAYLE: You only have an either/or.
>
> SCHAEFER: No, I think that is wrong. You're saying to us, "Take it or
> leave it."
>
> QUAYLE: No, I'm just saying that the political reality over there is
> you've got two pieces of legislation that we're going to be
> discussing, and I would just like to have some input from the
> prominent mayors around the country as we get into markup on
> which bills they prefer, the Administration bill or the Quayle-
> Kennedy bill.
>
> SCHAEFER: Senator, if it were just that simple, that would be fine.
>
> QUAYLE: And if it was that simple, which would you choose?

SCHAEFER: You know you can keep pinning me like this, because you're a Senator and I'm only a mayor. . . .

QUAYLE: All right. Then let me ask this question, since you don't want to answer that one.

SCHAEFER: I'll answer it. Neither one.

QUAYLE: Either one?

SCHAEFER: Neither one.

QUAYLE: No, that's not the choice.

SCHAEFER: Let me write your bill for you.

QUAYLE: In other words, you would rather not have legislation.

SCHAEFER: No, no.

QUAYLE: No legislation. All right, if you want to go on record on no training legislation, that's fine. I don't think you will find too much support here. We all want training legislation.

REPRESENTATIVE HAWKINS: How about an amendment?

QUAYLE: Actually, Congressman Hawkins, I wish you would consider coming over to the other body. . . . We would like to have you over there.

HAWKINS: Either bill has to pass both houses.[41]

When I saw Quayle the next morning, he was still chuckling over his exchange with the mayor of Baltimore. And, more pointedly, he enthused, "We've got the administration going, haven't we?"

Representative Hawkins had, of course, gently intruded to remind his feisty counterpart of a reality beyond the administration. Hawkins's own bill was certain to dominate in the House. It retained the local, "prime-sponsor" arrangement of CETA and provided for the payment of wages to trainees. Quayle-Kennedy provided for some participation by local government and was silent on wage payments. The administration bill was least solicitous of local authorities and prohibited all wage payments. (See Table 2-1.)

For the mayors, then, their order of preference among the bills was Hawkins, Quayle-Kennedy, administration. And they probably preferred the one-year extension of CETA—that is, no action—to the administration bill.

For another beneficiary of the CETA program, however—organized labor—the most preferred alternative was the one-year CETA extension. To labor, and indirectly to Hawkins, Quayle's standard riposte was to pose the threat of no program at all. On the third day of the hearings, he argued to the AFL-CIO that

it would really be very much to our disadvantage if in fact we don't get a training bill this year, because I am not sure we could get through Congress a simple one-year extension. I think it would be very very difficult, from a political sense to

TABLE 2-1 Comparison of the Reagan Administration's CETA Reauthorization Proposal with the Quayle and Hawkins Proposals

	Senator Quayle proposal, S 2036	Representative Hawkins proposal, HR 5320	Administration proposal, S 2184
Authorized levels for appropriations	$3.8 billion for training .1 billion for displaced workers	$4.5 billion for training .5 billion for displaced workers	$2.4 billion for training
Who has primary government responsibility?	State government, but with transitional provisions and procedural safeguards for local governments	Local government (prime sponsors)	State government
Who plans services?	Local Private Industry Council (PIC)	The prime sponsor and the PIC would jointly plan services.	The governor plans, subject to approval by the local PIC. The governor appoints PIC membership.
Who administers and provides the services?	If the existing prime sponsor agrees to the PIC's plan, it would administer. If it does not agree, then the PIC can administer.	Local prime sponsor	The State Job Training Council (appointed by the governor) chooses the administrator. Money is passed through to the local level.
Types of services allowed	50 percent of money must be spent on youth. Broad range of activities; local PIC must certify that level of training is acceptable to employers. No stipends.	50 percent of money must be spent on youth. All existing CETA activities and temporary public service employment. Stipends and subsidized wages allowed.	Training, on-the-job training, apprenticeships, etc. No stipends or subsidized wages.

Source: Subcommittee on Employment and Productivity.

get through.... Believe me, there are plenty of opponents in Congress.... And that's why I believe it is imperative that we all get in this boat together and row toward a new structure.[42]

He did not expect the AFL-CIO to listen. "They aren't interested in our approach because there's nothing in it for them. They want public service."

But he did expect Hawkins to listen. And to Hawkins he argued that if the two houses could not agree "you would find a mounting political pressure to further reduce training ... [to] say, 'Well, if the Congress can't get together on a training program, maybe we don't need one.' I can hear the arguments right now. And they will be forthcoming." [43] He was using the perception of an unfriendly administration plus some congressional opposition to keep his House counterpart in a cooperative, compromising mood. This was all he could expect and all he wanted from "the other body" while he attended to the fate of S 2036.

The hearings made it amply clear that Quayle had no intention of substituting the administration bill for the bipartisan bill. Throughout, he had pitted "our bill" against "their bill." More openly than ever, he was defining the situation as a competitive one. Thus, "We've got the administration going, haven't we?" Looking back, afterward, at the hearings, a top aide said, "He wasn't neutral, was he? Our first plan was to be neutral at the hearings, but he abandoned that." (Fenno: "You mean, once he got into them?")

> Yes. This administration made a big mistake in the way they treated Dan Quayle. They thought the way to deal with him was to hit him over the head. It's not. They thought, "Here's this young, junior senator. We'll just tell him what to do." They didn't call and say, "We need your help." They can't quite figure him out.

For starters, they might have studied the upset electoral victories that got him where he was. In each case, his self-confidence had sustained him against long odds, and he had "surprised everyone but myself."

The situation was similar to the one in 1980. "Birch Bayh underestimated Quayle," said a staffer. "He took a poll, found he was 18 to 20 points ahead, went on television and assumed Dan would fold and he would blow him away. He had no idea how competitive Dan is." "He's the most competitive person I've ever met...," said a staffer who had campaigned with him and governed with him. "And he's very smart. He won't argue about angels on the head of a pin. But if there's some problem he can get his arms around, he'll go right to the center of it. He'll know just what it takes to win. And what he wants is to win." Job training legislation was the problem he now had encircled; bipartisan support plus the legislative initiative were what he thought it would take to win. And, as always, he wanted to win.

Three days before the hearings began, the administration apparently decided at last that the subcommittee chairman deserved their personal attention. "Donovan came to my office," said Quayle. "We went through the bill, and there are five things we disagreed on. I asked him to put them down on paper. They don't want to do that. They say there are five things, but they're like an eel when you try to pin them down." The two problems Quayle mentioned during our conversation, however, were the delivery system and payments to trainees.

> One of the big issues will be over the role of the PICs [Private Industry Councils]. We want to give more responsibility to the PICs. . . . [And] there's going to be a problem with wages. They don't want any wage subsidies. I don't care about them. We didn't prohibit them—as a concession to Kennedy. Maybe he will yield on them. I don't know.

The next day, a subcommittee aide elaborated on the emerging three-sided relationship.

> [The Labor Department] says they have a comparison between the two bills, but they won't put it in writing. . . . We need it in writing so we can deal with Kennedy. We can't deal with him off the administration bill. We have to deal with him off our bill. Our biggest problem now may be having Kennedy on the bill. As the businessmen said yesterday [in hearings], "You can get the right people in a room for an hour and iron out the technical differences, but the political differences have to be dealt with elsewhere." I think the administration doesn't want Kennedy's name on a major domestic initiative. But you'd have to talk to [White House aides Edwin] Meese or [James] Baker to find that out.

A move to the administration would risk losing Kennedy; continued devotion to Kennedy would risk further conflict with the administration. Quayle was gradually being drawn into the middle—between Kennedy and Donovan. And the dilemma sharpened almost daily over the next couple of weeks.

Quayle's first response was to stay on course, stick with Kennedy, and push for the subcommittee markup of S 2036. "We're going to markup on Thursday [March 25]," he said after discussing his meeting with Donovan.

> I want to get moving. I want to report out a bill by Easter. I hope Kennedy will agree. I'll have to talk to Kennedy about it. I think his staff knows. I want to move fast, before everything

gets backed up. I also want to put the administration's feet to the fire to see what they will come up with.

A subcommittee staffer echoed, "We're going to markup on Thursday. That's our go-get-'em senator."

From the beginning of his effort, in late January, the chairman had thought about legislative prospects in his seven-member subcommittee. And he had said early on that "I know I can get it out of subcommittee." Once he had secured Kennedy as the chief cosponsor, he had quickly signed on two other members of his subcommittee as the other "original cosponsors," Republican Paula Hawkins, Fla., and Democrat Claiborne Pell, R.I.

So he had a majority from the outset. He "didn't deal at all" with the labor-oriented ranking Democrat of his subcommittee, Howard Metzenbaum, Ohio. "I'll have trouble with Metzenbaum," he predicted; and as markup approached a staffer said, "Metzenbaum will be off in left field somewhere." For some time, Quayle's staff had been trying to work out an amendment tying training to education, to be offered by the third subcommittee Republican, Don Nickles, Okla. "If we get him, we're golden," said an aide. "You can't get more conservative than he is." But as the markup approached, Nickles was "being pressured by the administration to go with their bill."

Finally, there was the enigma of the fourth Republican—Chairman Orrin Hatch. Ever since his original refusal to cosponsor, the Quayle people had worried about what Hatch would do when S 2036 passed the subcommittee. Quayle had "worked around him" and the two leaders had "almost no direct communication." Discussing the impending markup, an aide worried the question.

> He's the committee chairman. If he wants to move our bill, there's not much the administration can say. If he doesn't, we can get the bill out of subcommittee and it won't go anywhere. He's so hard to figure. I think he's softening. He's up for reelection and he needs something to show. His committee has not been very productive. This is the most important bill to come out of the committee this year. He ought to want it.

But Hatch remained extremely solicitous of the administration's wishes. Quayle mused, "We may run into the Hatch thing again in markup."

The subcommittee chairman used his prerogative to schedule a markup session. And this act created a deadline. The administration reacted to it by inviting the subcommittee chairman to the White House the day before the markup. They asked for a postponement and an effort by both sides to reach "a consensus bill." They wanted time to submit, to Quayle, "five or six amendments" to S 2036. Quayle agreed to a five-day postponement. He also agreed that if the administration's amendments were found acceptable to him, and incorporated into S 2036, the product would constitute "the consensus bill." As such, it would be given a *new* bill number. And the new, consensus bill would be marked up on the following Tuesday. If, however, no consensus could be reached S 2036, "the bipartisan bill," would be marked up as planned.

The meeting was attended by Quayle, Donovan, Counsel to the President Edwin Meese, OMB Director Stockman, and White House congressional liaison staffer Pam Turner.[44] It marked the first visible intervention of Meese, whose close relationship with the president was well known. The substantive and political sides of the administration position were clear. They wanted new provisions. And they wanted—by way of a new bill number—to wipe out Ted Kennedy's association with the legislation. The White House negotiation was carried on "as if there were no Kennedy involved," because the White House refused to have any negotiating connection with Kennedy. But Quayle intended, nonetheless, to use any "consensus bill" as a basis for further negotiation with Kennedy.

Dan Quayle, Raymond Donovan, Bob Guttman, and Albert Angrisani (mostly the latter two) spent the next few days bargaining over the provisions of the consensus bill. When it was over, there remained ambiguity about how they would treat the matter of payments to trainees. Have all income-support payments been explicitly and totally prohibited? What proportion of the money would be available for "support services" for trainees, such as transportation, meals, and day care? Despite what the Quayle people believed was "a very ambiguous consensus bill," the Labor Department issued a press release claiming that a compromise had been reached with Quayle *and Kennedy*, and stating that income-support payments had been prohibited.

Quayle had argued against any public statement, but, an aide said, "The administration kept bugging him and bugging him. At the end of a long weekend of negotiation, he finally said OK." It was a mistake; and it was compounded when his staff failed to catch the implications of the press release when it was sent to them. Before Quayle could talk with Kennedy, the senator from Massachusetts read the public statement. He interpreted it as the administration's declaration of victory over him— which it was—after a negotiation to which he was not a party. And he then felt totally cut out of the process he helped initiate.

The other Democrats also interpreted the announced prohibition against wage subsidies as taking off the table the one issue of greatest importance to them. The Democrats reacted by refusing to attend the markup. Without at least one minority member, there could be no quorum. So the subcommittee markup was postponed for the second time. "This time we got the same thing from the left that we got last time from the right," said a subcommittee staffer.

To members of the Quayle enterprise, the Democratic refusal indicated that "the passage of time had changed the situation and complicated things for us." "The Democrats have gradually come together," said one staffer.

> As they have come together, Kennedy has become less independent. He's not the ranking member of the subcommittee; Metzenbaum is. Kennedy [as ranking member of the full committee] won't do anything that would make Metzenbaum unhappy. They have circled the wagons. Whereas we originally could deal with Kennedy alone and rely on him to keep in touch with the others, now he feels he can't do anything the others would object to.

At least that was the position Kennedy and the Democrats were taking for purposes of bargaining with Quayle. "The Democrats want 2036," said a staffer. "But that's not their bottom line. The bottom line is who gets credit for the bill. In a sense, that's been the central issue from the beginning." The Democrats who joined the bipartisan bill expected bipartisan credit. But, on the other side, that is much of what the administration had been negotiating over, too. A subcommittee staffer noted that "The administration has accommodated us far more than I thought they would. They've made major accommodations on substance. The question is whether there's any give on procedure. . . . We've settled the substantive wars and we're into the ego wars—who gets credit for the thing." Even Chairman Hatch had begun nudging his way back into the credit picture.

> He wants to be number two in the list of sponsors. In the beginning he had said, "I don't care if my name is third on the list; let's get the bill out." But that was when he didn't think Quayle's bill would go anywhere.

As between the Democrats and the administration, the staffer continued, "The suspicion between them is made more difficult because of the personal enmity between Kennedy and Donovan. You heard Kennedy question him in the hearings. That wasn't tough. That was vicious." Since that exchange, the subcommittee chairman had, indeed, gotten squarely in the middle. There were three sides to the conflict. But it was impossible to have a three-way negotiation. Only Dan Quayle could deal with all parties concerned.

Quayle picked up the thread of negotiation that had been cut by the Democrats' action and returned to bipartisan negotiations, at the staff level, inside the subcommittee. At the same time, he sought to shore up his *bona fides* with the administration by asking to see the president and, having failed that, writing the president a letter setting forth the concepts on which his subcommittee bill would be based—"the principles which you and I share." The letter emphasized "the use of our limited resources for training and not for income maintenance" and "no provisions for public service employment." [45] "What I'm afraid of," said Quayle, "is that the president will get the idea in his head that he doesn't like stipends and doesn't like training and that he'll veto our bill." The veto was, of course, the ultimate administration stick, and the threat of it began to hang over all sides of the negotiations.

The administration asked Senate Leader Howard Baker to "help" their negotiations with Quayle; and a top Baker staffer explained their strategic thinking. "There are a lot of people in the administration who don't like the idea of any training bill," he said. "The administration has three or four philosophical points they are sticking in. If they aren't satisfied, there will be a veto. And Reagan will veto the hell out of that bill." Baker knew, of course, that Quayle wanted a bill; and he wanted to persuade Quayle to work with the administration. He also tried to persuade Quayle not to negotiate further with Kennedy. "[Kennedy] says they pulled a swifty on him. . . . He wants two bites of the apple. He negotiated with Quayle once. Then the administration negotiated with Quayle. Now Kennedy wants another crack at the bill." It is, of course, Quayle not Baker who made the original bipartisan agreement with Kennedy. But it was the majority leader's natural pitch for Republican harmony.

Quayle was being pressured on two fronts to abandon his strategic premise of bipartisanship. And for a time his strategy hung in the balance. In the end, Quayle did not take Baker's advice nor did he succumb to the veto threat. Instead, he used the veto threat to soften up subcommittee Democrats and negotiated out his differences with them. "My negotiating position," said a top Quayle aide,

> is that the president will use the veto. I think he will. The administration really doesn't care about this program. If we don't pass a bill, the program will be funded under the continuing [appropriations] resolution [for fiscal 1983], and it will be cut way back because it is the CETA program.

Out of the internal subcommittee negotiations, "three major changes were made" in the consensus bill and "a new markup document" was prepared and sent to the administration for approval.

The Quayle people knew that the three changes—all concessions to the Democrats—courted administration disapproval. "On the critical provision involving wage subsidies," said a staffer,

We have left that part of the bill sufficiently vague. That may be the final philosophical controversy. . . . The administration has to come up with a bill that is perceived as a major change from the CETA system. That was such an unpopular program. They cannot accept anything that can be portrayed as "the same old CETA system." That is the bottom line for the administration. . . . I'm trying to get them to declare victory. Whether they will or not, I don't know. They have taken so many positions in the last six months, from zero to 180 degrees, that I don't know what to expect.

The "new markup document" retained, despite administration apoplexy, the original label, S 2036. By number as well as content, therefore, it represented a decision to preserve bipartisanship in the face of concerted pressure. Having made the decision, the subcommittee chairman scheduled the markup for April 22.

Two days before the scheduled markup date, Secretary Donovan issued the administration's reply to the latest subcommittee draft. He issued it first by press release and then by letters to Quayle and Hatch. The Quayle office got press inquiries before they got the letter. It was the second time the administration had put Quayle on the spot using press releases. It was altogether a heavy-handed, hostile tactic. And so was the substance. Donovan wrote, "The Bill you plan to mark up is unacceptable to the administration." He accused Quayle of reneging on the agreement on "the consensus bill." He stressed, as the three remaining areas of difference, "the area of wages, allowances and stipends and to some extent . . . the Delivery System," plus the matter of cost.[46]

Two days later, on the day of the subcommittee meeting, Assistant Secretary Angrisani wrote to Quayle detailing more specifically the outstanding differences between "the consensus bill" and the markup bill. "Unfortunately," he concluded, "the changes made to the 'Consensus Bill' have made it impossible for the Administration to support the Bill being marked up in Subcommittee today."[47] Three weeks of postponements and negotiations had failed to produce agreement. Quayle had tried to reach an accommodation with the administration without breaching his bipartisan subcommittee agreement. It had not been possible.

Much later, two participants looked back on Quayle's decisions. Howard Baker's negotiator recalled,

When I got into it, there were all these power games going on at all levels. Negotiations between Quayle and the administration had broken down. Kennedy felt left out. The administration wanted Quayle to go out and beat Kennedy. Quayle, for whatever reason, opted to work out a deal with Kennedy. Whether he did that because he thought he needed Democratic support or whether he did it because that was his own preference, I don't know—probably a little of each.

The guess seems a good one—Quayle's preference for bipartisanship came from a combination of instinct and strategic calculation. Quayle recalled his premarkup decision as a crucial one.

> When he [Kennedy] felt that our negotiations with the administration went against the original compromise, we gave him back three out of the four disagreements. When the administration wanted to use the consensus bill as the markup document in subcommittee, we might have had serious trouble [with Kennedy]. . . . The consensus bill was the one where Hatch wanted to be second on the list ahead of Kennedy. And the administration had already announced that we were going to take up the consensus bill. They couldn't stand the thought of having Kennedy's name on the bill. I finally said, "We're not going to get into this nonsense." And we went back to Quayle-Kennedy as the markup document. That is the only point at which we could have lost the bipartisanship.

At the time, however, the subcommittee chairman went to subcommittee markup with the assurance that his bill would pass its first formal test. But he was very seriously "at odds" with the Labor Department, and presumably, with the White House as well.

NOTES

1. Elizabeth Bumiller, "The Charmed Life of Indiana's Golden Boy," *Washington Post,* January 11, 1981.
2. For presidential support and conservative coalition scores, see *Congressional Quarterly Almanac,* vols. 37, 38 (Washington, D.C.: Congressional Quarterly, 1982, 1983). For *National Journal* scores, see Richard Cohen, "Rating Congress—A Guide to Separating the Liberals from the Conservatives," *National Journal,* May 8, 1982.
3. *Indianapolis Star,* July 31, 1981.
4. Harrison Donnelly, "New, Smaller Job Training Program Emerging to Help the Hard Core Unemployed," *Congressional Quarterly Weekly Report,* March 6, 1982; William J. Lanouette, "Life After Death—CETA's Demise Won't Mean the End of Manpower Training," *National Journal,* February 6, 1982.
5. For example, Paul Tsongas, *The Road from Here: Liberalism and Realities in the 1980s* (New York: Knopf, 1981).
6. Harrison Donnelly and Dale Tate, "Reagan Seeks Halt in CETA Public Service Employment," *Congressional Quarterly Weekly Report,* March 14, 1981; Harrison Donnelly, "CETA Public Service Jobs Programs Reach End of Line;

Training Efforts Trimmed," *Congressional Quarterly Weekly Report*, August 15, 1981; "The $350 Billion in Cuts OK'd by Congress," *Boston Globe*, August 3, 1981.

7. "Economics," *Fort Wayne Journal Gazette*, January 18, 1978.
8. Lanouette, "Life After Death."
9. "For the Jobless: Jobs," *Washington Post*, March 6, 1981; Donnelly and Tate, "Reagan Seeks Halt in CETA."
10. Donnelly and Tate, "Reagan Seeks Halt in CETA"; Major Cuts in Programs for the Poor," *Congressional Quarterly Weekly Report*, April 18, 1981.
11. Harrison Donnelly, "Scaled-Down Block Grants Near Enactment," *Congressional Quarterly Weekly Report*, July 4, 1981; "Economics," *Fort Wayne Journal Gazette*, January 18, 1978. Quayle's attitude toward block grants can be found in *Congressional Record*, June 24, 1981, S13536-S13537.
12. U.S. Senate, Subcommittee on Employment and Productivity, Committee on Labor and Human Resources, *Hearings on Youth Employment Demonstration Amendments of 1981*, 97th Cong., 1st sess., March 18, 1981, 13. Quayle's introduction and explanation of the bill can be found in *Congressional Record*, March 6, 1981, S1911-S1193.
13. Memorandum to David Stockman and Martin Anderson, April 7, 1981.
14. Donnelly, "CETA Public Service Jobs Programs Reach End of Line." Quayle's defense of the relevent provisions of the reconciliation bill will be found in *Congressional Record*, April 1, 1981, S6014-S6015. The occasion was an amendment by ranking subcommittee member Howard Metzenbaum, D-Ohio, to add $300 million to the Youth Employment Program. It failed 24-74. See *Congressional Record*, April 1, 1981, S6011-S6018.
15. Harrison Donnelly, "Federal Youth Jobs Programs Extended Through Fiscal '82," *Congressional Quarterly Weekly Report*, June 6, 1981.
16. *Congressional Record*, May 19, 1981, S10199-S10200.
17. U.S. Senate, Subcommittee on Employment and Productivity, Committee on Labor and Human Resources, *Hearings on Employment and Training Programs in the United States*, 97th Cong., 1st sess., Washington, D.C., June 11, 15, 18, 19, 1981, and Indianapolis, Indiana, August 25, 26, 1981. On the Indiana hearings, see "City, State, Private Sector Call CETA a Mess; Vie for Control," *Indianapolis Star*, August 26, 1981.
18. For example, see *Congressional Record*, July 1, 1982, S7820-S7823; *Congressional Record*, September 30, 1982, S12711-S12715.
19. Memorandum, Committee on Labor and Human Resources, "Developing an Employment and Training Bill," September 22, 1981.
20. Dan Quayle, "A New Approach to Employment Training," *Congressional Record*, November 24, 1981, S28990-S28991.
21. Bob Guttman to Kitty Higgins and Kris Iverson, "Developing an Employment and Training Bill: Suggested Procedure," December 2, 1981.
22. Letter from Dan Quayle to Orrin Hatch, September 15, 1981.
23. Quayle, "A New Approach to Employment Training."
24. See, for example, Richard Madden, "Ties to Party Are Contrasted in Weicker-Moffett Debate, *New York Times*, October 5, 1982; Howard Kurtz, "How Lowell Weicker Gets Even—He Raises Reagan's Budgets," *Washington Post Weekly*, May 6, 1985; Lawrence Evans, "Influence in Senate Committees" (Ph.D. dissertation, University of Rochester, 1987).
25. See, for example, Benjamin Taylor, "Stafford's Bottom Line," *Boston Globe*, June 14, 1981; Francis X. Clines, "A Vermont Republican Gently Resists

Reagan," *New York Times,* July 6, 1981; "Solid Senator Stafford," *Washington Post,* December 4, 1987; Evans, "Influence in Senate Committees."

26. Donnelly, "Scaled-Down Block Grants."
27. Donnelly, "Federal Youth Jobs Program." See also Alan Murray, "Senate Panel Recommends $9 Billion Cuts," *Congressional Quarterly Weekly Report,* March 14, 1981.
28. Press release, "Quayle Tells NAB New Training Program to Demand Results," October 5, 1981.
29. *Congressional Record,* November 24, 1981, S28990-S28993.
30. Guttman, "Developing an Employment and Training Bill."
31. Letter from Dan Quayle to David Stockman, December 7, 1981; See also Spencer Rich, "OMB Seeks New Cuts at Labor Department," *Washington Post,* December 6, 1981.
32. Mark Helmke, "Quayle's Future Is Bright," *Fort Wayne News Sentinel,* January 6, 1977; Mark Helmke, "Opponent Role Spurs 'No' Votes," *Fort Wayne News Sentinel,* January 9, 1978.
33. Press release, "Statement of Edward M. Kennedy on the Training for Jobs Act," February 2, 1982; Quayle press release, "Quayle-Kennedy Introduce 'Training for Jobs Bill,'" February 2, 1982. See also Quayle press release, "Quayle-Kennedy to Introduce Training for Jobs Bill," January 28, 1982.
34. *Congressional Record,* February 2, 1982, S242-S260.
35. Letter from Dan Quayle and Augustus Hawkins to Raymond Donovan, February 2, 1982.
36. Letter from David Stockman to Dan Quayle, February 10, 1982.
37. Letter from Orrin Hatch to Dan Quayle, February 25, 1982.
38. Paul Taylor, "Job-Training Plan Leaves GOP Tepid," *Washington Post,* March 11, 1982.
39. U.S. Congress, Senate Subcommittee on Employment and Productivity, House Subcommittee on Employment Opportunities, *Joint Hearings on Employment Training Policy,* 97th Cong., 2d sess., part 1, March 15, 1982, 1-6.
40. Ibid., 22-23
41. Ibid., 591-592.
42. Ibid., Part 2, March 17, 18, 1982, 117.
43. Ibid., 118.
44. Memorandum from Dan Quayle to Raymond Donovan, March 25, 1982.
45. Letter from Dan Quayle to Ronald Reagan, April 1, 1982.
46. Letter from Raymond Donovan to Orrin Hatch and Dan Quayle, April 20, 1982.
47. Letter from Albert Angrisani to Orrin Hatch, April 22, 1982.

3

A Season of Governing II

OBSERVATIONS AND REFLECTIONS: SUBCOMMITTEE MARKUP

The April 22 meeting of the Subcommittee on Employment and Productivity was the third in its sixteen-month existence; but it was the first meeting at which all members were present and the first at which there was any substantive discussion.[1] It was a group without any established patterns of behavior, formal or informal. Chairman Dan Quayle had no doubt about the outcome. "I guess you thought we never would get to this day," he said as we walked into the meeting. "We're going to get a bill." He knew he had the votes; but he did not know how the proceedings might unfold. And he was untested under such conditions. The following account comes from my notes taken during the meeting and from the printed record.

Both Quayle and Edward Kennedy read from their press releases to open the meeting. Quayle describes the bill to be marked up, S 2036, as a "bipartisan document," a combination of the "tentative consensus bill" worked out with the Labor Department and "additional input from both majority and minority members of the subcommittee." He does not mention Reagan administration objections. His intention is to pass the bill in subcommittee and deal later with "the ten troubles coming down the road" (from the administration).

Kennedy congratulates Quayle as "the guiding force in the development of this legislation. . . . You have worked very hard to develop a common consensus . . . and still remained consistent with your own principles." Quayle urges that "I . . . want to see this moved with the greatest dispatch, hopefully maybe in early May." Both men say there are matters that will have to be negotiated and settled before markup in the full committee. Each takes special pains to point out that one such matter is an amendment relating training to education more generally— the amendment subcommittee member Don Nickles wants as the price of his agreement.[2] Clearly, their alliance remains intact.

But that cannot be said about Quayle's untended relationship with his ranking minority member, Democrat Howard Metzenbaum. He has little idea what Metzenbaum will do. The senator from Ohio launches into an excoriation of Ronald Reagan and a commentary on the bill's inadequacies. "It does not provide one job for the over 10 million unemployed people in the country. It does not provide wages to be paid during the training period ... to people suffering from the Reagan recession." [3] Quayle replies that "it is necessary to deal with the situation where we find ourselves today and that is to come forth with a training program that will be signed by the president of the United States. That is my objective." Metzenbaum demurs that "My remarks were to a fellow who is not in the room." "In that case," says the chairman, brightly, "we can proceed. I just want the record to show I was listening very carefully." There is general laughter.

The exchange and the laughter seem to indicate that the committee's most obstreperous Democrat[4] is prepared to work under the leadership of the subcommittee chairman, that members of both parties appreciate the uncomfortable position Quayle is in, and that he has their support in his dealings with the administration. Republican Paula Hawkins expresses this sense immediately thereafter. Praising Quayle for his "patience and stamina," she says that "the opposition [to this bill] has not been the normal opposition ... [but] we will produce a bill that will make the administration proud." There is more laughter. Says Quayle, "I could not have said it better myself." Hawkins has her own animus—administration opposition to her own special contribution to the bill, a loan fund to provide for "allowances" for disadvantaged trainees. Democrat Claiborne Pell and Republican Nickles join in praise for the "patience and care," the "energy and diligence" of their chairman.

As he manages the business part of the meeting, Quayle displays a recognizably upbeat style. When the first amendment comes from Metzenbaum, proposing that the important local Private Industry Council be chaired by a business person, Quayle reaches over to pat the Ohioan on the back and says exuberantly, "That is progress. I like these amendments. How many more do you have? I hope everybody notices that Senator Metzenbaum wants to give it all to the business community. I would like to be a cosponsor of that amendment." The byplay also produces much laughter.

Metzenbaum's next amendment comes with the support of Orrin Hatch—to mandate Job Corps funding at existing levels. Quayle argues that writing protection for specific programs is unwise and that he does not want "to go down this road." He says he likes the program and will work for it. He asks Metzenbaum how strongly he feels about it; Metzenbaum replies that the full committee chairman, Hatch, is strongly for it. Hatch has not yet joined the group. A lengthy discussion ensues about where the money will come from, during which Hawkins expresses her support. "I know when I'm going to get rolled," says Quayle genially. "I am prepared to accept defeat." The amendment passes by voice vote. Metzenbaum jokes, "I hope we can continue in this pattern." Quayle jokes back, "I am going to check my proxies here." It is a good-humored beginning.

Metzenbaum's third amendment is a substantively important one. It provides for a Summer Youth Employment Program with wages to be paid to participants. He invokes the memory of a "long hot summer" with cities burning, and he describes black teenage unemployment at 42 percent and the alarm of business people. The "wages" provision, says Quayle, is one he cannot support. His bill, he explains, is deliberately "silent on the issue" of wages, leaving it to the judgment of the local PICs. "When we get into wages and stipends, I think you know as well as I do the red flag and the problems we are going to have with that . . . now and into the conference committee." He pledges, "I will work with you and others that are concerned about the summer program to see what in fact we can do to accommodate the concerns."

Committee Chairman Hatch, who has just joined the group, enters the discussion to remind participants of the administration's clout.

> What I don't want this bill to be is CETA revisited. . . . We've had a heck of a time here on this committee because we have a bunch of forces that have to be accommodated. . . . I personally appreciate Senator Quayle's leadership on this bill and Senator Kennedy's willingness to make this a bipartisan effort, but I also want the administration—they have a tremendous imprimatur on this bill. . . . It's a composite bill. . . .

Metzenbaum makes a pitch for Senator Hawkins's support. "I would also guess that in Miami, Florida, it must be one hell of a problem and will be even greater this summer." Hawkins agrees. Quayle says he will work something out. Metzenbaum asks for a roll-call vote. Hawkins votes no "with the understanding that we work it out." The vote is 4-3, a straight party vote. Quayle says, "The record shows that Senator Hawkins pointed her pencil at me and said, 'with the understanding that we work it out.' I get the message, senator." "We are going to try to work it out between now and full committee," he says, and, "I will consult with [all of you]." With that, the one formal expression of subcommittee division had passed.

It is, of course, a characteristic of the subcommittee stage that divisive or unsettled issues can be postponed for later consideration at a committee meeting, and for further negotiation between the two stages. Furthermore, no one has an incentive to kill the bill at this early stage. The administration makes no fight at this point. The desirability of postponement—given administration opposition to the bill the subcommittee was passing—seemed tacitly understood by the subcommittee members. It is an understanding that Quayle employs to move the proceedings. He suggests, and Metzenbaum agrees, to postpone the Ohioan's last two amendments. "I will withhold my amendment with the understanding that we will work out some language on it," he says on one. And, "Based on your desire to move things along," he tells Quayle on the second one, "I am not going to offer it. I will do so in full committee." A couple of Hatch amendments are similarly postponed.

One Hatch amendment, however, displays the continuing breach between the subcommittee chairman and the full committee chairman. Hatch proposes an affirmative action amendment, which Quayle turns into a matter of prerogative and procedure because he does not wish to deal with it. "I had not anticipated this amendment being offered," he tells Hatch. "I did not know it would be offered. I am not even prepared at this point to judge the merits of it." Hatch persists. "I would like to see it put in the bill at this time.... I would hope the chairman would support me on this today." To which Quayle replies,

> I have not looked at it and I have not talked with you about it and you have not mentioned it to me either.... As I have deliberated this bill, it has been my style and my desire ... [not] to take substantive amendments without having a thorough discussion on both sides of the aisle.... I have established a precedent. I would like to keep that precedent. I do not want to get in a position to be in any kind of opposition to my chairman for whom I have the greatest respect and affection.

Hatch avoids a further face-down by withdrawing the amendment. Quayle says he has every reason to believe it will be worked out before the full committee meets and that he will support it. Quayle's behavior seemed partly a rebuke, partly a reassertion of his independence. It was testimony to the cool and distant relationship between the two Republicans. And, as it turned out, it was a prelude to a more serious confrontation minutes later.

With Quayle pushing for a final vote, Hatch intervenes to anticipate what will happen farther down the line and to express the administration's viewpoint. "I want to chat a bit about what the administration would like to see between now and full committee," he says, to see if we can have some room to work on it, because we need everybody to go down the same pathway here and frankly it is very difficult to get everybody together.... There are some problems with this bill as we will pass it today that may cause us severe problems in the future.

Quayle says that he "would like to vote the bill." Hatch replies that "It will not take long.... I would like to have a discussion before we vote the bill out." Quayle responds somewhat saucily, "Well, you are the chairman of the full committee and who would I be to say no? I prefer to vote it out and then have a discussion because Senator Pell and others have to leave.... [But] if you want to talk...." Hatch begins, "This is a very important bill, but it is a long way from home." He starts reading from Secretary Donovan's letter of two days earlier. But when Metzenbaum gets up to leave, Hatch gives in. "Let's vote," he says. And S 2036 is voted out of subcommittee unanimously, 7-0. It is a moment of triumph for the subcommittee chairman.

But it is a brief moment. Chairman Hatch resumes his warnings about the trouble ahead. "We have to face whatever the president does," he warns. "... I think it is safe for me to say that he is going to do everything he can to stop it.... [So] we should work hard to make sure that this is satisfactory to the administration." He reads the letter from the assistant secretary of labor, Albert Angrisani, again stressing the administration's desire for a prohibition against all wages. And he says, "I am asking the chairman to work with me and with Senator Kennedy" to "bring together" a bill that will meet administration objections.

Quayle picks up on the issue of wages by repeating his statement that this matter has been left to the discretion of the local PICs, that the PICs are business-dominated, and that they will never permit wages to be paid. "So I believe that issue has been answered," he says flatly. And Hatch replies, "The administration wanted to make sure of it." Whereupon Quayle gives the back of his hand to the administration. "They can read the record, or perhaps somebody can be in the room that can report back. I do not know. Or, they can read the papers tomorrow and I assume the news accounts will be accurate, perhaps more than the commitments we have around here." The taunt draws laughter. But Hatch does not think it is funny. "Let us make it clear," he snaps. "It is going to be difficult to have a bill without the administration."

At this point, Senator Hawkins weighs in with help for the subcommittee chairman. "We read daily in the headlines," she says, "that several prominent players, actors in the play need to compromise and negotiate and I think we are demonstrating today our great willingness to compromise and negotiate.... We have a document today and I think they ought to commend us for a job well done." From start to finish in the life of S 2036, Hawkins has been and will be the most unstinting and the most generous ally of the subcommittee chairman, a rock of support on whom he can depend amid all the other uncertainties. Her role is invaluable for any legislative leader—particularly a new one. And Quayle recognizes it often.[5] Hatch says that he will help to keep her loan fund idea in the bill.

Rather than let it go at that, Quayle takes another swipe at the administration. He ostentatiously picks up the Angrisani letter with its five objections and answers each one with a sentence. He slaps at the letter with each sentence and then throws it, with a dramatic sweep of his arm, onto the table. "I would think," he says with finality, "that each one of the questions that the administration raised has been fully answered. And I look forward to further discussions with them and with you; and I hope we can proceed with great dispatch at this full committee level." With this impatient suggestion, however, the subcommittee chairman has touched the prerogatives of the full committee chairman. It is dangerous territory, but the self-confident kid wades in, nonetheless, alternately teasing and pushing the full committee chairman. As Quayle grows increasingly expansive in mood, Hatch grows increasingly irritated. Their exchange escalates until the stern chairman of the full committee puts the feisty subcommittee chairman in his place.

> SENATOR HATCH: I do not think they [the administration's questions] have been fully answered. I think you think they have been fully answered and I appreciate that. I tend to agree with this [sub]committee chairman on some of those areas.
>
> SENATOR QUAYLE: Good. Let the record show, in capital letters.
>
> HATCH: I always tend to agree.
>
> QUAYLE: Tend to agree?
>
> HATCH: Let us understand something. There are a lot of egos involved here, not just yours or mine or Senator Kennedy's. . . . It is a tough problem here and it is a very important bill. I want the bill to pass in the worst possible way. . . . Maybe it won't. . . . I think I have made it clear to you that I have worked my tail off to try to get this problem resolved.
>
> QUAYLE: You have.
>
> HATCH: I have tried to get everybody together. I am trying to do that now. So I do not think you bring them together by, you know, ridiculing some of the feelings that the White House may have or the Labor Department may have. Now they advanced these in good faith. . . . I tend to agree with you that you have made some good strides in resolving these problems and I voted for this bill today and I will probably vote for the bill in full committee because I think it is a darn good bill. That doesn't

mean I think it is perfect. The administration doesn't think it's perfect. I don't think Senator Kennedy thinks it's perfect and I do not think you do and I know the House does not. When we get to the House, we will get this done and I will help you.

QUAYLE: I wonder if we could shoot at a target so that everybody will have an understanding that the full committee will be meeting on May 5 or 6, and agree to take it up in full committee.

HATCH: That will not be the day. But we will give it full consideration. I have the fourth, the fifth, and the sixth [of May] taken already.

QUAYLE: In the full committee?

HATCH: [getting up out of his chair and walking away] In the Judiciary. Let's us, you and I, discuss it in private and we will resolve that issue.

QUAYLE: [still sitting at the table] I will work with you and get a date as soon as possible.

HATCH: [over his shoulder as he leaves the room] I hope so.

The subcommittee chairman and the full committee chairman have never had a good working relationship. Now the gulf between them has been widened—by differences in legislative prerogative, bargaining stance, and personality. Orrin Hatch now has the power to dictate the pace of the bill; Dan Quayle does not. Quayle's bill has now become subject to mercies that he has worried about from the very beginning. His instinct is, "Let's keep going"; Hatch's instinct is, "Let's stop and talk." Further, Quayle has gotten locked into combat with the administration and Hatch has become the protector—though not the advocate—of the administration's position.

Finally, their markup clash reveals two very different personal styles. It is a difference I observed travelling with each of them in their home states. And it is a large enough difference so that misunderstanding lies just below the surface of their relationship. Dan Quayle is an exuberant, expansive young man. He is a "kidder," with a spontaneous, hyperbolic, golf course, locker room brand of humor. He has a backslapping style of camaraderie to match. Orrin Hatch is a very serious, self-contained person. He is not naturally gregarious, and he has to work at a sense of humor. He is at home pursuing an ideological mission; he is not at home bargaining with his fellow man. On my experience they are both very kind human beings. But they are different. Dan Quayle skates along the edge of brashness; Orrin Hatch skates along the edge of solemnity. The coltish Quayle does not appreciate a tight rein; the intense Hatch does not appreciate a teasing. By the close of the markup, each had given the other a taste of his unwanted medicine. The exchange was no aid to problem solving.

The Quayle-Hatch contretemps dominated post-mortems within the subcommittee chairman's enterprise. "Weren't you surprised when Hatch walked out like that?" began one staffer. "He got up while Dan was still talking. Dan had no idea Hatch was mad until Hatch's aide came over and told Dan his boss was mad and he'd better apologize." The comment confirmed my own feeling that the action-oriented kid had been unaware of, and certainly unperturbed by, the rising tension in the room. His staffers, however, were very aware. "Everything went about as I expected," said another aide afterward, "all but the exchange between Quayle and Hatch. I didn't expect that. I didn't expect the open hostility. I guess I should have. Dan's a very feisty guy."

Quayle's aides weighed the consequences. "Everything went fine except the last ten minutes," said a third. "That was not productive. It was not productive for Dan Quayle to get into a public dispute with Orrin Hatch." To a fourth Quayle staffer, it was proof of the difficulty of working with Hatch.

> He's stone-cold. . . . He's indecisive. He always says, "I tend to agree." "I will probably support Senator Quayle. . . ." He's scared to death about his reelection. . . . He does what the administration tells him to do. Didn't you notice how he would say something to Dan, then look over to [Don] Shasteen [assistant secretary of labor for congressional relations] and then say something else to Dan?

A fifth staffer worried that Quayle's bipartisan bill might be "flawed," that it might be so "liberal" that the eventual compromise with an even more liberal House bill would inevitably produce a presidential veto. From the Kennedy staff came praise for Quayle's "absolute faithfulness to the bipartisan agreement." "Right now," replied a Quayle staffer, "we don't need that kind of praise." Later in the day Quayle called Hatch and they exchanged apologies—"according to Dan's optimistic interpretation of the telephone conversation." The two men would have to work together if there was to be a job training bill.

MORE NEGOTIATION: BETWEEN MARKUPS

Subcommittee passage of S 2036 changed the negotiating context for Dan Quayle. He had gained policy momentum; but he had lost procedural control. Formal leverage had passed to the full committee chairman. And the chairman proposed to use it to bring administration views into play. One of Hatch's aides described the situation.

Now the ball was in Hatch's court. The administration still opposed the bill. Hatch told Quayle, "If you don't get together with the administration, I'll sit on the bill forever." The administration was pleased to hear him talk this way. But at the same time, he was on the phone to Ed Meese telling him the administration was going to have to give a little. He was basically sympathetic to Quayle's position, but there was no way he was going to hold that markup until they worked out an agreement. He kept a low profile. He was trying to get the warring factions together, to get them around the table . . . [to get] a "Treaty of Jobs."

Just as Quayle had manipulated Hatch in the subcommittee setting, Hatch was manipulating Quayle in the full committee setting.

"I don't know where we are on the jobs bill," said Quayle nearly three weeks after markup. "I don't know whether Hatch will call a [full committee] markup. . . . I talked with him last night. He said, 'We've got to have the administration.' I said, 'You'll never get the administration until you actually have a bill.'" He was typically optimistic about his ability to get a bill.

> Oh, there's no problem at all in committee. I may lose [John] East [R-N.C.] and [Gordon] Humphrey [R-N.H.]. But all the others are for it. . . . I had no idea it would take so long and be so tedious and petty when I started. But we'll get a jobs bill.

While his committee chairman temporized, however, the impatient subcommittee chairman remained, as one observer put it, "in orbit."

Hatch's desire for some kind of "treaty" was certainly on target. When the markup ended, the subcommittee chairman and the Labor Department were, indeed, at war. The secretary and the assistant secretary had flatly and formally opposed S 2036. But the subcommittee had ridden roughshod over their objections in passing the bill. The losers immediately began talking veto. Quayle's view was that,

> The Labor Department ruined things with their press release just before markup saying what they would and would not accept. That was stupid. They took everything off the table. The people down there are not very smart about dealing with the Hill. . . . I've given up dealing with the Department of Labor. The Department of Labor is impossible to deal with.

The Hatch staffers saw two sides to the situation. "The administration thought Quayle was impetuous and presumptuous," said one. "Quayle felt the administration had had its chance to get aboard and had refused." In any case it was a standoff. As a subcommittee staffer put it the day after markup, "Now each side will make the other sweat and we'll see who blinks."

In view of the administration's hostility to S 2036, the Quayle-Kennedy bill, I asked the Indiana senator if he had any regrets about his alliance with the senator from Massachusetts. There were none. "If I had gone it alone," he said,

> my bill would have been treated by Hatch and by the adminis-tration as just another bill. They would have considered their own bills and some time or other, maybe, they would have considered my bill. In order to elevate it the way I wanted to, I needed a bipartisan bill. In order to avoid bitterness and rancor and name calling in getting the bill out of committee, I needed a bipartisan bill. In order to be able to deal with the House effectively, I had to be bipartisan. So I think it was the right thing to do. But I've gotten into a lot of trouble over it. It's a jungle out there.

He conceded that a different Democrat might have made for a smoother path.

> The Reagan administration, of course, doesn't like Kennedy. . . . Well, he's been around here a long time and he occupies some very important positions. In my case, he is the ranking member of the committee. If someone else was in that position, things might have been easier. After all, Donovan thinks Kennedy wants to put him in jail. Hypothetically, if Eagleton [Tom Eagleton, D-Mo.,] had been the ranking member, I would have the benefits of bipartisanship without the drawbacks. Kennedy has made it more difficult. There's no doubt about that. But I've enjoyed working with him. He's a lot better than his image. And he's given up a lot. You heard him say in markup that the bill isn't what he would want. It isn't. It's a real compromise.

For the time being, he would have to attend to his relations with the ad-ministration. But he did not intend to abandon his bipartisan strategy in the process.

The political standoff with the administration lasted three weeks. During that period neither Quayle nor his staff heard from or dealt with the Labor Department. Bob Guttman and his counterpart on the Hatch staff, Kris Iverson, cooperated to keep track of the substantive disagree-ments between S 2036 and the administration and to present options to their principals.

Here, too, the subcommittee markup had changed the context. The Metzenbaum amendment had added a new complication to what was already a major area of disagreement—payments during training. Wage subsidies were the kind of payment most adamantly opposed by the administration. Metzenbaum had proposed wage subsidies for a sum-mer youth program. Moreover, subcommittee support for a summer program had been made manifest. In a memo prepared for Quayle and Hatch, Guttman and Iverson wrote that the

> Metzenbaum amendment . . . was defeated in Subcommittee by a party line 4-3 vote, with a majority of Senators making clear that they thought the issue of a summer program must be dealt with in Full Committee. It appears likely that the Metzenbaum amendment would pass if offered in Full Committee. We could try to defer the issue, but the likelihood of success is low.[6]

If, that is, the administration continued to insist on a flat prohibition against wage subsidies, they would be defeated on the summer program. Thus, another layer of substantive disagreement had been added to those that separated subcommittee from administration.

In the period after the markup, the focus of the subcommittee chairman's strategy shifted from the Labor Department to the higher echelons of the administration. "If there is no bill, there will be an extension of CETA," said an aide the day after markup. "The president knows he'll never get as good a bill as this one two years from now. So our bill is the only game in town for him. We're hoping he sees it that way." To that point, however, there was no evidence of any presidential involvement in the matter. Nor was there any evidence that anyone in the White House had yet grasped the situation from the president's perspective. But the Quayle people believed that, from the presidential perspective, subcommittee passage of S 2036 had raised public expectations sufficiently to rule out the status quo as a viable option. The president, they believed, would want—perhaps need—a bill.

"I can't imagine they'd veto," said Quayle. "[S 2036] would give people something to run on," he explained, thinking ahead to Republican chances in the fall elections.

> It would help with the rich/poor thing; the bill helps do something about the poor. It would help with unemployment; the bill helps people without jobs. It will help with the whole compassion argument. It's a natural. You'd think the people down there would see it. But they don't—the bastards.

The problem, Quayle thought, was that the top-level White House people had not yet focused on the situation. "I've stopped dealing with the Department of Labor. I haven't had any communication with them since the markup. I will only deal with the White House. . . . But I can't tell where I am with the White House. It's not a high priority with them. . . . They aren't paying attention."

On May 11, two and a half weeks after the markup, something happened to change that situation. President Reagan called Senator Quayle personally about another bill, to ask him to withdraw a proposed amendment regarding the MX missile. Quayle agreed. And he seized the opportunity to do what he had been unable to do several weeks earlier—talk to the president about his job training bill. "I told him that I thought we were spending too much money on things like MX, but that I wouldn't do anything to harm his negotiations," Quayle recounted a day later.

> Then I said, "While I've got you here, there's something coming up I want to alert you to"—and I told him about the jobs bill. I told him it had passed the committee 7-0. I told him all the money went to the PICs, with 51 percent [membership of] business. I told him the governors would have more say than before. I told him that we had an absolute prohibition against public service jobs. I told him that 90 percent of the money went for training. He said, "If what you say is true, that sounds like something we should support." I told him that if we didn't get a jobs bill, we'd get CETA. He said he didn't want that and that he'd speak to some people about it. I didn't push him. I just wanted to tell him about it. We'll see what happens.

When it was all over Quayle looked back on that chance conversation and said,

> I don't know what would have happened if Reagan hadn't called me about the MX missile that day. That's when I asked him, "What about the job training program? We've got a good program." He said, "I'm for that, and I'll look into it." Right after that, things started to move. The administration started to change.

Two days after the call, Quayle was invited to the White House by the president's top political person, Chief of Staff James Baker, for a high-level negotiation on the jobs bill.

White House intervention changed the context of negotiation again. It moved the entire negotiation to a new level within the administration and brought new players into the picture. Quayle gained important new allies. The political people, Chief of Staff Baker and Congressional Liaison Chief Kenneth Duberstein, also wanted a bill and they began exerting pressure in that direction. But new opponents emerged as well. Resistance came, now, from Budget Director Stockman and Counsel to the President Edwin Meese. "The administration is of two minds," said a Hatch staffer. "The budget people want to pick up money wherever they can; and they would be very happy to save $3.5 billion. But the political people want a program to show that the president isn't against the disadvantaged."

The Labor Department had ceased to be an independent force— both because of White House intervention and because Labor Secretary

Donovan had become embroiled in an increasingly damaging dispute with the Judiciary Committee over his conduct as a private contractor. Shortly before the White House meeting, in fact, Orrin Hatch had called for Donovan's resignation because of it.[7] Their relationship had become enveloped in bitterness. Hatch no longer could do business with Donovan. He could do business with Assistant Secretary Angrisani. But Angrisani, who had insisted on dealing only with Hatch and not Quayle, had become dependent for his instructions on the White House. He remained a dogged but crippled combatant.

The White House meeting on the morning of May 13 was attended by Quayle, Hatch, Baker, Stockman, Duberstein, Donovan, Angrisani, and Pam Turner, a Duberstein assistant. "It turned out that the principals were Stockman and myself," said Quayle later,

> I had the most trouble with Stockman—my friend! He was adamantly opposed to a summer youth program, and he did not like the idea of spending money on supportive services. Jim Baker wanted a bill. He's very different from Meese. When I talked to Meese, he wanted to know just what was in the bill. He was interested in its purity and didn't want any bill that wasn't pure. Baker wanted to get together to work out an agreement. That's the way you run the government. You don't run it on ideology. You don't get anywhere if you are hung up on purity.

A Quayle staffer added that the meeting had produced "some movement."

> The legislative people in the White House made it clear they wanted a new jobs bill. . . . Baker told the Labor Department to "move toward" a bill. Donovan and Angrisani had to be given some support. After all, they have been running around saying the bill ought to be vetoed.

It was agreed that the two senators and their staffs would meet that same afternoon with Angrisani and Turner to reach agreement on such amendments to S 2036 as would be necessary to produce administration support.

After this follow-up meeting, the Quayle and Hatch people believed they had an agreement with Angrisani on the payments issue. "Supportive services" to trainees and program administration would be increased and capped at 30 percent of the available funds. The list of likely supportive services would be changed from "health care, transportation, temporary shelter, child care, financial counseling, and necessary cash assistance payments to individuals to enable them to participate in training" to "in-kind provision, cash assistance or loans for transportation, child care, meals, financial counseling or other *reasonable* expenses required for participation in the training program." [8] [Emphasis added.] "Wages, allowances, and stipends" would be prohibited, but with an explicit exception made for a summer youth program.

Accordingly, that evening, the Quayle enterprise began preparing for full committee markup. "Stockman was the one who was tough on this," said Quayle. "I'm going to call him and tell him not to throw a monkey wrench into it." He added, "And I've got to get Stafford's proxy. I've talked to him about it once already." "I think we've got an agreement," echoed Guttman. "We'll have to see how it goes down with the Democrats. I think if Dan gets in touch with Kennedy right now, that will help." He was anticipating only two votes in markup—one on the summer youth program, one on the 70/30 agreement.

But Assistant Secretary of Labor Angrisani had a different interpretation of the agreement. He drafted a set of amendments that included an absolute prohibition on wages and contained no mention of a summer youth program. He prepared a letter for Secretary Donovan stating that the administration would support S 2036 if all its amendments were approved, and that the administration would "withhold its support" if its amendments were not passed. In the letter, Donovan also said that the summer youth proposal was being "reviewed . . . outside the provisions of this letter."

The letter—with "withhold" changed to "reconsider"—went to each of the executive branch participants in the White House meeting and to Meese.[9] Angrisani added his comment: "These documents fulfill the offer made by the Administration to Senators Hatch and Quayle. To date they have not officially communicated their acceptance or rejection of these Amendments." [10] As a courtesy to Hatch, Angrisani sent Iverson a copy of these communications. As a snub to Quayle, he made Guttman go down to the Labor Department to get copies. When he read the documents, Guttman concluded that "Angrisani has reneged. . . . He won't budge until he has unambiguous instructions from the White House. Until he does, he will just keep going back to the department's original position. That's what he's done. Why he made a deal on Thursday, I don't know."

The Labor Department's continuing inability to bargain confirmed the wisdom of Quayle's decision not to deal with it. So he produced his version of the agreement and sent the relevant amendments to Chief of Staff Baker at the White House, with copies to the other participants. Its cover letter set forth the political realities as the subcommittee chairman saw them.

> I believe these amendments can pass in the Committee, but *only if* there is public assurance that the Administration will support the bill with these amendments included.

The amendments include a prohibition of wages, allowances and stipends but with an exception for a tightly drawn summer youth program. Support for a summer youth program in the Committee is sufficiently strong that we cannot report a bill that does not authorize such a program. The key question therefore is whether you can support a wage prohibition with the summer youth exception.[11]

With the conflicting Angrisani interpretation-plus-amendments and the Quayle interpretation-plus-amendments sitting on his desk, Baker did nothing.

Several days after Quayle's letter to Baker, a top subcommittee staffer expressed concern about the effect of delay on the chances for committee approval. He was particularly worried about swing voter Lowell Weicker. "At the time we offered our amendments, we thought we could sell them to the committee," he said.

I had talked to people close to Weicker and had gotten the idea that he would go for our package. He wants a summer program to campaign on this summer. But we needed quick and enthusiastic support for it by the administration. Baker hasn't answered the letter. The Kennedy people have lobbied Weicker. . . . Timing is everything. The time for taking him aside, explaining it, and asking for his vote may have passed.

Chairman Hatch apparently shared these concerns about timing. He had scheduled a full committee markup for May 26. On May 24 Stockman asked for a postponement of "just one more day while we work things out."

At this point the impatient subcommittee chairman once again became a prime force for action. As he described it, "We weren't getting anywhere with Angrisani. They wanted us to delay the markup again. Hatch wanted to delay it. I said to him, 'No, we can't do that again. We've got to go ahead.'" Hatch agreed. He refused Stockman's request. By this time, the Quayle people believed that, because of his bitter feud with Secretary Donovan, Orrin Hatch's relationship with the Labor Department had soured and that his actions had to be interpreted in that light. He too, they believed, had become impatient with the department. "The Donovan blowup is a lot more important than all the amendments," said a Quayle staffer.

The markup deadline put pressure on all parties. Quayle applied added pressure to ensure a successful markup. He may not have realized how important the outcome would be to his career. But more than any participant he wanted a bill. He also knew that more than anyone else's the bill he got would be his. He knew he needed administration support for that bill. He believed that such a bill was very much in the president's interest, too. He pressed this line of argument with the White House on May 25.

> I said to myself, "I don't have to deal with Angrisani." So I called Jim Baker. And I said to him, "You've got to do something if you want a bill. The Labor Department is killing it. It's your president who will be hurt. We are going to hold a markup tomorrow. Can't we do something?" Baker said that the Labor Department was their administrator, that they couldn't go around them. But he said the decision would be made in the White House. He said they would pretend to deal with the Labor Department, while really making the decision themselves. I called him in the morning. At 2:30 we had a meeting.

"Hatch was not happy when Dan called and said they were going [to the White House] to meet with Donovan," laughed a staffer. "But Dan said, 'I'll protect you.'" More as allies, now, than as competitors, they went to negotiate for a jobs bill—Hatch to draw the lines, Quayle to fight the battle.

The participants in the second White House meeting were Baker, Quayle, Hatch, Donovan, Stockman, Duberstein, Turner, and Assistant Secretary of Labor for Congressional Relations Don Shasteen. Once again, in Quayle's words, "The principals were Stockman and myself." He recalled,

> Donovan and Shasteen were there, but they sort of sat off to one side. That was fine with me. Donovan is very hard to bargain with. He's used to dealing with those guys up in New Jersey. Stockman and I were the principals. Stockman agreed to a separate summer program and I agreed to try to get the wage prohibition. I said, "I don't know if I can sell it, but I'll try. If we lose that in committee, we may stop the markup, regroup, and see what we can do." Then I left for Atlanta.

On the way to the airport from the White House, he called to report the deal to staff chief Guttman.

The essence of the deal was that the summer youth program was added to the bill "as a separate title, creating a separate and free standing program to be authorized at a level of 'such sums as may be necessary,'" that no prohibition against wages would be placed in that title, but that an absolute prohibition against wages would be applied to all other titles of the bill.[12] The administration won its central position regarding the wage prohibition and thus maintained its stand against a job training bill that looked like "CETA revisited." The price it paid was a summer program it did not want, with wages it did not want. But it was able to separate that program from the main body of the bill. Quayle, on the other hand, got the summer program, "the sweetener" he needed, but at the expense of a programmatic separation from his training bill that he had never contemplated and never wanted. He also paid the price of a total wage ban that he had heretofore resisted as the one provision that could cost him his majority in the full committee.

A "Memo of Understanding" from Duberstein to Quayle also contained a reaffirmation "of our previous agreement that 70 percent of program funding should be dedicated to training and that 30 percent of program funding shall be dedicated to administrative and support services." It also included an agreement that if the amendments incorporating these several provisions "shall tie or fail" in committee, "Hatch will recess the committee to allow further discussions." [13]

Guttman's reaction to Quayle's phone call was one of agony and dismay—philosophically and politically. "It's the worst of both worlds," he expostulated to Quayle at the other end of the line.

> When you separate the summer program from the training and from all the quality control—no performance standards, no flexibility, no local initiative—you get a crummy program. You give up the notion of a block grant with which we started and create another categorical program. You lose the argument on the merits. A separate summer program is not meritorious. Maybe it will appeal to people for that reason. It's politically attractive and it will just get pumped up and pumped up with money. That's where your costs will go. It's an income-maintenance program, not a training program. You will lose the programmatic people ... because programmatically it's not good. But you may attract people ... who don't care about the program. We'll be going back on all the things we talked about.

It was the quintessential plea from the staff expert to the politician, a plea for programmatic coherence in the face of coalition-building pressures. It was, of course, the politician who most wanted the bill and who, therefore, needed to bargain for support. And as Quayle himself had put it, "You can't get anywhere if you are hung up on purity." Privately, no doubt, he and Guttman had drawn the line against the administration many times. But in the more complex world the line had proven impossible to hold. And Guttman's outburst provided a measure of how much Quayle had forsaken their blueprint in the end.

Guttman expressed political reservations as well. "You'll have a hard time selling the wage prohibition," he continued. "The Democrats have been holding their staff meetings all day telling each other to hang together on that one. You'll have trouble with Weicker and probably Stafford on it, too.... It's impossible to predict how it will go. You just can't tell." But, he concluded, "I'll start peddling it in the morning to each of the Democrats and we'll see if it sells to any of them." Quayle said he would call Weicker when he got to Atlanta. The conversation ended.

Guttman was visibly upset. But within a catch of his breath he turned from disappointed architect to loyal builder. "It stinks," he said. "It will take us back to the same bad old programs. They'll pump it up with money without any controls. But the real problem is: Can we get nine votes for it?" Another subcommittee staffer reacted similarly. "Talk about CETA revisited! That's just what we tried to get away from." But a few minutes later she was heard saying, "Whatever Senator Quayle is for, we are for. Whatever he wants to get through, that's what we'll try to get through." The griping was over; the enterprise turned to its new task, preparing for markup.

To conclude Quayle's own account of his activities, he made two phone calls as soon as he reached Atlanta—one to Kennedy, one to Weicker.

> I called Kennedy and had a brief conversation. He was at dinner. I told him what had happened. I said, "I hope you won't give me too much trouble tomorrow. I need this one. I hope you won't get too rambunctious. I know you are opposed [to the wage prohibition], but I need some room." He said, "You'll do all right," or something like that. I called Weicker, filled him in briefly and asked if I could come around and talk with him when I got back the next day. He said, "Sure."

With the conservatives now on board, with the administration and with moderate Senator Stafford's proxy in his pocket, Quayle's remaining Republican uncertainty lay in the attitude of Lowell Weicker—"the key, the swing vote in the committee," as Quayle put it.

The next morning, he went to Weicker's office.

> I explained the situation to him. He said, "If that's the best you can do, I'll be with you." I thought I had him, but I did not know for sure that I had him. He's not the kind of person who says, "I will support you whatever bill you come up with." So I felt comfortable going into the markup.

His success in the markup would depend less on what he did in the meeting than what he had done before that. But the markup was his biggest governing test yet. And unpredictability remained.

OBSERVATIONS AND REFLECTIONS: FULL COMMITTEE MARKUP

In midafternoon on May 26, the members of the Labor and Human Resources Committee and their staffs crowded into a small (fifteen by twenty-five feet) room just off the Senate floor on the West Front of the Capitol. The senators sat nose to nose around a long table; the staffers stood against the wall behind their principals. Three committee members did not come at all; three others stayed very briefly; nine remained throughout most of the one hour and twenty-five minute session.[14] Among the nine were all seven members of the subcommittee, and they monopolized the proceedings. Thirty amendments were offered; most of them were dispatched without debate, three were debated at some length, and four drew recorded votes.

As the meeting begins, Chairman Hatch sits at the head of the table with the gavel—Quayle on one side of him, Kennedy on the other. "We have come a long way," he says. Then, "I turn to Senator Quayle who has worked so long and hard on this. I hope we can help Senator Quayle today and get this matter resolved." Quayle repeats that it has been "a rather long process," and moves to the heart of the matter.

> Although there has been a consensus developed in the Congress, we have not had agreement from the Administration. We have worked in the past to get an agreement and have been unsuccessful. I am glad to report we do have an accommodation on the summer program with the administration which has had a change of position and of heart. . . . It has been suggested and I agree that we would put in a prohibition on the payment of wages in the training program, which will be in every title except the new title, Summer Employment. I believe this is a good compromise. . . . I hope when the time comes for debate on these amendments everyone will keep their powder dry and listen to the arguments and support them.[15]

Kennedy, Metzenbaum, and Pell then praise Quayle for his leadership of the legislative effort. As he has in every public forum so far, Kennedy is especially generous in his praise.

> Senator Quayle has spent hours on this issue. He has taken his subcommittee to different parts of this country. He has solicited ideas from a number of us on this side of the aisle. He has been willing to accommodate many of the points we have made. He has worked in good faith all the way through these negotiations.

Metzenbaum "commends" the Indiana senator "for his effort to move forward" and calls him "sensitive to the problem." Pell "congratulates" him because "he has combined the Democratic views and the Republican views." They take cognizance of Quayle's battles with the administration, which have been, to a degree, their battles too. After all, S 2036 is not an administration bill spoonfed to the Congress. It is a homegrown bill, a congressional initiative—and a bipartisan one at that.

Kennedy notes that "the toughest negotiators ... appeared to be members of the administration." Metzenbaum observes that Quayle "is acting under some restraints, which are obvious, from the administration." The atmosphere is informal and cordial, and the stakes seem well understood.

After the easy passage of a dozen amendments—including Nickles's vocational education provision and Hawkins's loan fund—Kennedy argues for greater flexibility under the 70/30 division in the definition of "supportive services." He argues that different areas have different needs for financial aid. Quayle says he thinks the phrase "reasonable expenses" will ensure flexibility, but he says he will make a "good-faith effort to try and work out, with the people whom I have to deal with, an exception." Saying that "we've gone around quite a bit on this particular one," Kennedy accepts Quayle's assurances.[16]

"The next two [amendments] go together," says Quayle as he offers the amendments establishing a summer youth program and prohibiting the payment of wages in the rest of the bill. "This is the basic compromise," he begins.

> A compromise is a compromise. It is not what I prefer. It is not everything the administration prefers, but here is what it does. For the first time, if we are able to pass these amendments, we will have the support of the administration, which I think is critical to the passage of this bill and having the president sign it. There is no doubt that if he would veto a bill, in all probability it would be sustained. Everybody at this table in good-faith effort has worked exceedingly hard to get a training and unemployment bill through. These amendments are a compromise that have been worked out with the administration because they have been, up until yesterday, in opposition to a summer employment training program and ... in opposition to paying wages through a summer employment training program.

Again, he stresses that "reasonable expenses," to be determined by the local Private Industry Councils, provide flexibility in aiding people who need help in getting training. And he ends his brief discussion: "Friends, this is the best I could do. I hope you will support me." He is all business. There is none of the anti-administration or Hatch-teasing friskiness that marked his debut in the subcommittee.

Metzenbaum praises Quayle, ("It has not been an easy task for him."), speaks at length about the necessity of a summer program and says that, except for the wage prohibition, he will support the bill. Kennedy praises Quayle for the summer program but argues at length that the wage prohibition and "the stringent formula" for supportive services plus the 30 percent cap, puts the program "in a straightjacket" as far as the poor are concerned. The best training program, he argues, is a long-term program, and without financial support the poor will be unable to take advantage of the best training programs. It is a strong speech. Quayle refers again to the flexibility of the "reasonable expenses" provision. Kennedy says, "We've been talking to each other over a long period of time and have been unable to convince each other." At that moment there are nine senators present—seven subcommittee members, Weicker, and Jennings Randolph, D-W.Va. The summer program is approved by voice vote, but Kennedy asks for a roll-call vote on the wage prohibition.

For Quayle, it is the most important vote to be taken in the Senate on S 2036. It begins:

SENATOR STAFFORD: Aye by proxy.
SENATOR QUAYLE: Aye.
SENATOR WEICKER: Aye. . . .

It is very matter of fact. There are no signals of recognition that the pivotal vote has been cast. The roll-call flows swiftly on; the wage prohibition amendment passes by a party-line 9-7 vote. On the next two 8-8 roll calls, Weicker votes with the Democrats in losing causes. But on the showdown vote he has stood with Quayle. Shortly thereafter, S 2036 is voted out of full committee by a unanimous 16-0 vote. It caps Quayle's most strenuous effort and his most significant accomplishment thus far as a United States senator.

Most striking to the observer about the meeting is the good humor that accompanies the seriousness of the matter—particularly on the part of the ranking minority member. When a vote is called for, on reducing the size of service delivery areas, Kennedy says, "We've been over this so many times . . . let's just put 8-8 on this one." Hatch agrees. Quayle says, "He's not serious." And, amid laughter, Kennedy quips, "You never can tell about these things." So they have a roll call, 8-8. Before the next roll call, on his amendment to change a distribution formula, Kennedy smiles, "It's nickles and dimes. But it's the principle that counts." Amid laughter he says, "Let the record show laughter." Again the vote is 8-8. My own notes read: "Kennedy dominates the meeting—in victory, in defeat, in keeping a light atmosphere. I think he has come to trust Quayle over the months." If so, the absence of bitterness in the meeting and the unanimity of the vote were dividends from Quayle's bipartisan strategy and the skill with which he fostered it.

Quayle's own post-mortems centered on Ted Kennedy, too, and his relation to the pivotal vote. "The important thing," he said, was that Kennedy did not work actively against me on the wage prohibition. His people were opposed to it, but they did not lobby Weicker—or Stafford—against it. They could have made a decision that they were going all out to defeat the wage prohibition. They did not make that decision. What would have happened if the AFL-CIO had turned their people loose? They could have said to Weicker, "What do you owe the administration?" He can't get any credit at home for his votes for the bill, only inside the committee. But if his labor people at home say he voted against them, then he would be hurt at home. I have no idea whether we could have gotten a bill under those circumstances.

As is so often the case in a close political situation, it is intensity of preference that seems to matter more than the mere preference itself.

The question remains, of course, as to why the lack of intensity. "I'm not sure," said Quayle. But he speculated on a number of possibilities as far as the unions were concerned. For one thing, "There is something in the bill for the unions—retraining for displaced workers. That's what I kept telling them, 'There's money for displaced workers. They are your guys.' " For another thing, the deal with the administration may have caught them unprepared. "The thing happened so quickly, the opponents may not have had time to react. If they had had a couple of days to think about it, they might have decided differently." Besides, there was plenty of time left to act at other stages. "Both Kennedy and the unions may hope to strengthen their position in the House and in conference and they knew it was this bill or nothing in the Senate." There were, in short, sufficient strategic reasons for the opponents of wage prohibition to pull their punches in the Senate committee.

But Quayle, not surprisingly, placed greatest emphasis on his original bipartisan strategy and Kennedy's loyalty to that concept. "It's a bipartisan bill," he said.

We could not have done it any other way. If Kennedy had not supported the bill, we would have had a whole lot of other bills . . . and none of them would have been seen as having a chance of getting out of committee. Once Kennedy supported it, everyone knew the bill could get out of committee.

And Kennedy's support remained steadfast. "Kennedy has always wanted a bill. And his decision not to oppose the prohibition strongly was a good-faith effort on his part," said Quayle.

There never was a time that Kennedy threatened to close the door and withdraw his support for the bill. He wanted a bill. He got a lot of things he wanted in his original compromise. At

one point when he felt that our negotiations with the administration went against the original compromise we gave him back
three out of the four disagreements. . . . It's a bipartisan bill. It
will be known as the Quayle-Kennedy bill.

In the final analysis, it was the unlikely alliance—the one that the
administration so disliked—that had brought the bill through the
difficult Labor Committee.

If, as seems evident, the alliance had survived because of the mutual
trust established between Quayle and Kennedy during their lengthy
"good-faith effort," credit accrues as much to the unexpected and
untested political acumen of the newcomer as to the established
senatorial skill of the veteran. Seizing the bipartisan initiative and
holding it is, perhaps, the main piece of evidence. But Quayle's
interpersonal skills in carrying out his strategy obviously counted, too.
While he behaved often like an overexuberant kid, he also seemed very
much at ease in dealing with fellow senators.

Some of the explanation of Lowell Weicker's support, for example,
can be attributed to Quayle's personal appeal on the morning of the
markup. I asked Weicker's top legislative aide about the decision of his
boss. "I was not sure how Weicker was going to vote," said the aide.

I told the Kennedy people that. After his meeting with Quayle,
I got the feeling that he would go with Quayle. He did not say
how he was going to vote, but he did say he thought Quayle
had done a good job in the context of getting a bill out.
Especially, Quayle convinced him that there was enough
looseness in the language concerning expenses so that help
could be given in cases where training was otherwise impossible. I don't know how hard the Kennedy people were pushing
the other view. I was at the markup and I didn't think Kennedy
acted as if it meant all that much to him. There is no doubt that
the meeting with Quayle was important. It got Weicker to focus
on the issue, and it convinced him that Quayle had done as
good a job as could be done with the bill.

The maneuvering for S 2036, as for AWACS, produced further evidence
of Quayle's coalition-building skills.

I asked Quayle to reflect on his personal accomplishment—first by
asking what would have happened if he had not put the bill on such a
fast track, but had waited instead. "I'm not sure what would have
happened," he answered, as he slowly puzzled it out.

[Rep. Augustus] Hawkins wanted to extend CETA and wait for
a change of administration in 1984. But that would not have
carried in the Senate. The administration might never have put
in a bill. I'd like to think there would have been some

responsible people here in the Senate. But I'm not sure who would have really pushed hard for it. Nobody else did. So I guess I'd have to say, "No, if I had not pushed it, we probably wouldn't have had a bill." Institutionally, it was a congressional initiative. There's no doubt about that part of it. The administration fought us every step of the way.

It was a conclusion reached with more reluctance than eagerness. It was a characteristic of Quayle's attitude toward the bill that he was always slower to claim credit for the bill than I thought he would be—or, indeed, should be.

I asked him how he felt after the committee passage and suggested that it might have been a confidence-building experience. He saw it differently. "I've learned how difficult it is to get things done," he answered.

It hasn't affected my confidence. I've always had that. But I think it increases the confidence of the staff in me. They will say, "Here is someone who said a year and a half ago that he was going to get a bill and he's done it." They will look upon me as someone who can get things done. As far as my peers are concerned, the reaction will be favorable, I'm sure. After the markup, several people came up and congratulated me— Kennedy, Nickles, Hawkins, she's been a strong supporter all the way through, Metzenbaum, Riegle [Donald W. Riegle, Jr., D-Mich.].

He was, of course, describing progress in the achievement of his personal goal—to be known as an effective senator. He was getting, he believed, both the legislation and the legislative reputation he most wanted.

DECISION: THE SENATE FLOOR

Both achievements would be in jeopardy, however, if the bill could not surmount its next hurdle—passage on the Senate floor. The subcommittee chairman turned to that prospect immediately. And, as always, his objective was to keep the steam in the boiler. Because the majority leader controlled access to the floor, Quayle wasted no time in pressing his case with Howard Baker. On June 10 he sent a letter to Baker. "I am anxious to move this bill to the Senate floor as expeditiously as possible," he wrote, pledging "to do whatever else I can to facilitate quick consideration and passage of this important legislation." [17]

That same day, he expressed his sense of urgency privately and displayed the uncertainties of a neophyte about what awaited him on the Senate floor. "I want to get it passed in the Senate during June," he stated,

> If I can get a time agreement [a unanimous agreement among all senators to limit the length of debate on a bill] with the Democrats, Baker will schedule it. If we can't get a time agreement, I'm not sure what he will do. There are so many other bills coming up.... I've got to talk to Kennedy. Unless there are controversial amendments, our side could do it in two hours. Hopefully, Kennedy will agree to two hours—or four hours. I don't know what they'll try on the floor. If they try to take out the wage prohibition, I'll beat them....

On June 22 I watched Quayle jump up and down and wave his arms under Baker's nose during one of the majority leader's regular colloquys with Minority Leader Robert Byrd over the schedule—after which Baker added "a jobs training bill which is on the calendar" to his list of possible items to be taken up the following week.[18]

It was, however, neither Baker nor the Democrats that Quayle should have worried about, but—no surprise—the Reagan administration. For while they supported the bill during markup, they did not do so wholeheartedly or enthusiastically. During a break in those proceedings one of Hatch's assistants had said, "We are pushing the administration to endorse the bill more openly. But they are still very skittish." And when the bill had passed, members of Quayle's staff spoke of the administration not as their ally but their opponent.

They vented their disapproval on the emissary of the administration to the markup, Assistant Secretary Shasteen. "To have a bill reported out of that committee by 16-0 is really something," exclaimed one staffer afterwards. "That ought to be quite a blow to Donovan. I wonder how Shasteen must have felt when he saw the degree of cooperation between the two sides." "Shasteen couldn't get in the room at first," another staffer laughed. "He told a guard, 'I'm a representative of the Labor Department,' and the guard just told him, 'Stand back.' It was great. I guess he got in after a while." And a third staffer chipped in,

> Shasteen was clawing and scratching right to the end. He went up to Bob [Guttman] during the markup and said, "I don't know whether we can support this." Bob told him not to worry, that it was good language.

These tales of victory over the enemy were not exactly grounds for optimism about future relations. Quayle himself was characteristically optimistic—but not about the Labor Department. "I think we'll get a bill," he said after the markup.

The administration has decided to support us. The White House
wants the bill. If we can only get Angrisani out of the country
or give him something else to do. The Labor Department is in a
shambles. Donovan is under a cloud. You can't get anything
out of them.

But his troubles with the department were not over yet.

On June 18 Stockman wrote to the subcommittee chairman stating
that "the Administration supports speedy enactment of job training
legislation along the lines of S 2036," but adding in the next sentence
that "several changes made during the markup of the bill constrain the
potential effectiveness of the program." He then listed three suggested
sorts of amendments the administration would support on the Senate
floor "to remove those constraints." He tendered administration cooperation in drafting these "necessary" amendments.[19] His suggestions had
to be Labor Department-inspired. Howard Baker's aides reported that
Meese, too, was supporting the Labor Department efforts.

Stockman's letter was interpreted by the Quayle people as "obstruc-
tionist." And Quayle fired back an "I-cannot-agree" and "I-trust-you-
will-reconsider" letter to the budget director. In the letter, he attacked
Stockman's three amendment suggestions. The first, he said, "Is doomed
to failure and . . . will only undermine the administration's credibility."
The second, he said, would reverse a previous administration endorsement and "it is too late to go back on that agreement now." The third
suggestion, he said, simply "is incomprehensible to me."[20] He did not
know how intensely or how persistently the Labor Department would
pursue Stockman's letter. But the possibility now appeared that the
simmering war would heat up again.

Which it did. One week after Majority Leader Baker had put S 2036
on his tentative floor schedule, it was nowhere to be found on the list.[21]
The administration—that is, the Labor Department—had lodged objections with Baker and had arranged for a number of senators to put
"holds" on the bill. A "hold" is a personal request to the leader not to
move a bill forward on the floor; and it is normally honored for a period
of time by the leader. One of Baker's top aides told the story from their
perspective.

Baker asked me to see if I couldn't get a time agreement for the
bill. I called in the majority and minority staff people on the
committee and the staff of the other interested senators to see
what could be done and to see if we picked up any burrs under
the saddle. As soon as I did that, we began to get these calls to
put a hold on the bill. It was the administration asking senators
to do this—senators who had no interest in the bill. They were
doing it because they knew the bill would pass if it ever got to

the floor. We scheduled the bill for the floor two or three times
and each time we had to pull it back.

He continued, "Quayle was one upset senator. He had to go around and
talk to each senator and persuade him to take off the hold. At that point,
the fate of the bill depended on Quayle's steadfastness in going around
to each senator."

Dan Quayle is nothing if not steadfast, and he proceeded to do just
that. As he described it,

[The Labor Department] put holds all over the Senate. I've
spent the last day and a half running around talking guys out
of it—East, Simpson [Alan K. Simpson, R-Wyo.], Helms [Jesse
Helms, R-N.C.], Humphrey, you name it. Someone told me
Donovan was going to call Howard Baker and tell him to stop
the bill. I went to Baker and said, "If you stop this bill now. . . ."
He said, "Don't worry, I'll call the White House if I have to."

At this point, Chairman Hatch, too, was counseling Baker to move.
"Baker called Hatch," reported one of the chairman's staffers, "and said,
'A lot of people are asking me to put a hold on this. What should I do?'
Hatch said, 'They've had enough time.' Hatch knew they had been
stalling since the beginning. They were still stalling."

When, on June 30, Quayle successfully completed his round of
person-to-person pleading, Baker scheduled S 2036 for floor action the
next day. When I arrived at the Quayle office on the morning of July 1, I
learned that the Labor Department had not yet fired its last shot at the
subcommittee chairman. Two staffers described what had happened the
day before. "Last night, Shasteen called," reported one,

and he said he had sixteen "merely technical amendments"
that the Labor Department wanted before they would support
the bill. . . . I don't know who is going to introduce them. Dan
has made it clear that he is not going to introduce any
substantive amendments. . . . Duberstein says the administration is in full support of the bill. But the Labor Department is
still fighting us. I don't think the administration knows how
important this bill is—for us and for them. It's still not a high-
priority item for them.

A second staffer recounted a similar experience. "All day yesterday," he
said,

I got calls from other [Senate] offices asking if the administration had withdrawn its support for the bill. They said they had
rumors that the administration had withdrawn support. We
spent the day pouring water on that fire. We told them that
Stockman was strongly in favor of it. Last night Dan called

Duberstein to make certain the administration was on board. He said they were completely on board. . . . There's a conflict between the bureaucrats in the Labor Department and the White House.

"It's still a struggle," concluded the first staffer. "It's been like false labor. You go to the hospital and come back, go and come back. . . . This morning Dan came in and asked, 'Well, what did they do to us while we were asleep?' "

The query was not an idle one. Overnight, the Labor Department had prepared an eleven-page packet containing fourteen amendments, with explanations of each, that it wanted to have passed on the floor. On the front page of the packet—stretching from top to bottom of the page—was the title: "S 2036 *AMENDMENTS* which the Administration deems *ESSENTIAL TO*, a Manageable, Workable, Effective *JOB TRAIN-ING LAW* to replace the Comprehensive Employment and Training Act (CETA)." In the morning, along with a cover letter from Don Shasteen dated July 1 and stamped URGENT, the Labor Department representatives distributed the packet of amendments to Senate offices.[22] It was their final effort to throw roadblocks in the way of the bill. And it failed—for lack of support from any of the other participants.

At about 11:00 A.M. the subcommittee chairman opened debate on the bill. Shortly thereafter the Labor Department gave up the fight and officially withdrew its opposition. "They even called around to the offices to tell people—as if it made any difference," said a staffer. Surely, it did not—not at that stage. At 2:45 P.M. S 2036, with a few minor changes, passed the Senate, 95-0. It was called the Training for Jobs Act.

The bitter-end quality of the Labor Department's performance overwhelmed all commentary afterward. "It was a real pissing match," exclaimed Howard Baker's negotiator.

> The bunch of bumblers down in the Labor Department couldn't have screwed up worse than they did. They really thought they were going to beat Quayle! You can't treat a United States senator like they did today—sneaking around here with a big stack of amendments and saying, "We're going to get these introduced." You knew not one of them was going to go through unless it was approved by Quayle and Kennedy, or unless they got some great mass of senators to support them.

The gist of this comment had been made at earlier stages of the process, too—that the administration underestimated Dan Quayle's competitiveness and that their treatment of him was damagingly heavyhanded. Quayle was angry. "The Labor Department withdrew their opposition and we won," he said after a champagne celebration in his office.

It was one horror story after another. They ought to be hung—
the bastards. That's enough of a reason right there to fire
Donovan. . . . I called Ken Duberstein and told him that if they
didn't call off the dogs I would go out on the floor and tell the
whole story. They didn't want that. Pam Turner called me to
say that "heads will roll if they don't stop it." And they shut
down the Labor Department.

"Shasteen fought it right down to the last moment," added a celebrating
staff member. "They withdrew their opposition when the vote reached
90-0."

As the margin of victory indicates, Dan Quayle's difficulties on July
1 occurred off the Senate floor, not on it. Almost nothing transpired
there that could be called a debate. Quayle's initial presentation featured
lavish praise from the newcomer to the veteran, Kennedy, who he said
was "well known for the energy he has expended in the training area, in
helping the less fortunate, the downtrodden in our society. [His]
thoughts and idealism, which have been with him in all the days of his
public life, are indelibly impressed upon this piece of legislation."

Quayle called S 2036 "a compromise, a bipartisan measure." He
stressed "the comprehensive support we have for this legislation [which
has] traversed the legislative route for a long time." And he described
the bill as "one of the most, and perhaps, the most, important pieces of
domestic legislation that will be dealt with by this Congress." [23] It was
an expansive presentation, delivered from a yellow pad of notes as he
remained in constant motion, standing behind his chair, then walking
back and forth into the aisle, putting his hands in his pocket and then
thrusting his arms forward.

Kennedy reciprocated, as he had so often before, in generous
commendation of the subcommittee chairman who "as a new member
on the Committee . . . showed great interest in this issue and worked
effectively with the members of his party as well as with the Democrats"
and who "was extremely forthcoming in working with those of us who
have been interested in this issue for a number of years in considering
our various proposals while at the same time balancing the administration interests." He too described S 2036 as "an extremely important bill"
and "the first real initiative that recognizes and responds to the human
dimensions of the serious economic problems facing our country" and
"a bill we can all be proud of." [24] It was an unexpressive presentation,
read from behind a lectern in a droning monotone. It seemed, from the
gallery, to be Quayle's day of triumph not Kennedy's.

Quayle approved thirteen minor amendments and the handful of
senators on the floor—between three and six—adopted them by voice
vote. No amendment opposed by Quayle passed. No serious amend-

ments were pressed to a vote. Both Kennedy and Metzenbaum introduced amendments of the sort that had lost in full committee, providing far more flexibility in both the 70/30 split of funds and in supportive services and/or administrative costs. In both cases, Quayle expressed sympathy, said that he was constrained to oppose them at this stage, and assured their sponsors that the subject would come up again in conference. Both amendments were strategically withdrawn. As he withdrew his amendment, Metzenbaum said, "I want to congratulate the senator from Indiana and express my appreciation to him for his efforts in handling this legislation and, I think, making good progress under very difficult circumstances vis-à-vis the administration."[25]

Twice, Quayle used a quorum call to negotiate privately on amendments he did not expect. On one, he arranged for Sen. Arlen Specter, R-Pa., to get a hearing before the Finance Committee for a tax proposal affecting training. On the other, he yielded to Sen. Pete V. Domenici, R-N.M., on an amendment he had first opposed. "That one came out of the blue. We were getting ready to vote. I told him I'd consider it. He kept pushing. I leaned over to him and kidded him, 'You take care of your committee and let me take care of mine.' But we put in some innocuous language." He announced the solution, "in all humility"; he praised Domenici for "his usual intestinal fortitude in getting his way" and "for pointing out to me my shortcomings";[26] and he added, stretching both arms toward Domenici across the aisle, "Who am I to disagree with my distinguished [Budget Committee] chairman?" Privately, he said that only one amendment "got me mad"—one by Jeremiah Denton, R-Ala., that violated a prior agreement. "I talked to him and he took it back." His entire public performance, however, exhibited the expansive good humor of a self-confident kid.

Back in his office afterward, he was on the phone with White House Congressional Liaison Chief Duberstein, making the quick transition to the next stage in the process.[27] "Thank you, my friend, thank you for calling off the dogs," he was saying.

> We took a few amendments we had to. But we preserved the 70/30 and they didn't attack the wage provision. Both of them will come up in conference, I guarantee you. . . . I'll be with you [in conference]. That's part of the deal. We'll have to sit down when it gets through the House and I know what I'm dealing with there. We'll have to sit down and have you tell us what you want us to do in conference, tell us what is acceptable to you.

There would have to be a pause in the push for the bill. But he was eager to keep right on going.

Over in the subcommittee offices, the success of another agreement—equally essential to the bill's passage—was being acknowledged. Quayle staffer Guttman and Kennedy staffer Higgins were preparing to walk down the block to the Monocle restaurant for a celebratory drink. There, they toasted one another. Guttman: "Here's to a bipartisan bill." Higgins: "Today was an anticlimax compared to the two markups. It was easy." No sooner had they lowered their glasses when the Labor Department's Don Shasteen walked by. "Congratulations on getting the bill through," he said. "You deserve a lot of credit." No one smiled. "Thank you," each one said to him curtly. And he moved on.

For Shasteen, the scene must have been more painful proof of the relationship that produced so much consternation and confusion in the executive ranks. For the staffers, Shasteen's appearance then and there must have seemed like one last drop of rain on their parade. "They have no idea how to lobby Congress," said Higgins. "The only people worse than Carter's Labor Department lobbyists are Reagan's Labor Department lobbyists." Guttman agreed. "I think the Carter people must have told them exactly whom to hire so they would look good by comparison." [28] Then the conversation turned to pleasant topics.

DECISION: CONFERENCE COMMITTEE

As they nurtured and battled for their own bill, the subcommittee chairman and his staff paid scant attention—once the joint hearings ended—to the parallel progress of job training legislation in the House. Nor did the administration, pinned down as they were, also, by the fight over the Quayle-Kennedy bill. Nor did this observer—whose interest was tied completely to the legislative activity of the senator from Indiana. It was well understood by all participants that the Democratic House would produce legislation that represented much less of a departure from the CETA program than anything that would come out of the Senate alone or out of a Senate-administration compromise. And it was, therefore, well understood that a fairly wide gulf would have to be bridged by the conference committee. As we have just noted, some senators withheld amendments on the Senate floor lest a defeat there jeopardize their case in the more favorable conference forum. But for most of the time that S 2036 was being shaped in the Senate, the conference was a distant and little-discussed eventuality.

Random expressions of interest did occasionally appear. The clearest of these prior to subcommittee markup was a lengthy mid-April rumination by a top subcommittee aide. "The interesting political situation," he offered,

> is that the administration has concentrated all its attention on the Senate. They have spent their time on the differences between Quayle-Kennedy and their bill. Meanwhile, the House is proceeding to mark up its bill—the Hawkins bill. If they pass that bill and we go to conference with them on that bill, I'm afraid the result will surely be a bill that is "vetoable." Try as you may, the Hawkins bill is just the same old CETA system. The administration has got to have an alternative presented over there—in committee or, at least, on the floor. But there is still no administration bill in the House. I keep kicking them in that direction. But all they can see is our bill. That's because Kennedy's name is on it. There is no Kennedy in the House, so they don't pay attention. So much of that problem results from Donovan's personality.... I think our real problem with the administration is the personality clash between Donovan and Kennedy.

The notion expressed here, that the administration should be more active in the House to nudge legislation closer to the Senate's ideas, had been the Quayle enterprise's strategic preference from the outset.

My conversations with the subcommittee chairman included no mention of the House until his bill had cleared the subcommittee in May. Complaining about administration behavior of that time, he said, "They are smart about some things but not Congress. Why, they could get this bill of ours passed in the House if they would introduce it and push it over there. But they haven't." I asked him if he had been in touch with the House. "I'm going to have to sit down with [Minority Leader Robert] Michel and [Minority Whip Trent] Lott," he said. "But I decided that I ought to get the bill out of the Senate committee before I do that." In June, with S 2036 safely through committee, he returned to the strategic situation confronting him. But he was still only a spectator.

"It will be interesting to see what the strategy will be in the House," he began.

> I hope we can pass our bill soon. Then we'll have a better chance of getting a substitute passed over there. Maybe the House will wait for us. But they aren't dummies. So I would expect them to move as quickly as they can to pass their own bill. That way, they get more leverage in conference. I've got to talk to Michel. But he's been so tied down with the budget that

I haven't even tried.... I have no idea what the Republicans are thinking over there.

At that point the Hawkins bill, now the Hawkins-Jeffords bill (HR 5320), had passed in subcommittee and full committee and it, too, was waiting floor consideration. As it turned out, HR 5320 passed the House (356-52) on August 1, one month after the passage of the Senate bill. It was called the Job Training Partnership Act.

The job training bill passed by the House did move substantially away from the CETA program in one respect: it abandoned the creation of public service employment. Its supporters did so reluctantly, not at the subcommittee stage, but during full committee markup—as a concession to political reality, to the public perception of CETA's problems, and to the adamant position of the administration. For Quayle's House counterpart, Augustus Hawkins, it was a necessary but rending defeat. When ranking committee Republican James Jeffords, Vt., offered an amendment to strike public service employment, "for philosophical and practical reasons," Hawkins responded that

> We shouldn't even be considering such an amendment. But the public perception of CETA is there. If the amendment is defeated here, others will offer it on the floor, and we do not have the votes to defeat it on the floor. So I will not oppose the amendment at this time.

He had, he said, introduced a separate job creation bill; and he asked Jeffords if he would "indicate at least some support for presenting this issue on another bill . . . to test the waters at least to see what acceptance there is to the idea." Jeffords agreed. Hawkins salvaged a tiny strategic consolation. And he guaranteed easy passage on the House floor. Except for public service jobs, the Hawkins-Jeffords bill bore a strong resemblance to the CETA system. But when he went to conference, the House subcommittee chairman believed that he had already given away half the store. That belief, in turn, guaranteed a difficult negotiation with the Senate.

The House-Senate conferees met eight times between their opening session on August 16 and their agreement on September 22. My own first-hand observation of the Quayle enterprise ended in early August. So no effort will be made to detail the performance of the Senate subcommittee chairman in surmounting the final legislative hurdle. In later conversations, however, he and his staffers emphasized the difficulty of the negotiation.

The House bill retained the influential relationship between federal government (that is, the secretary of labor) and local elected officials in programmatic matters, kept Private Industry Councils and state government (governors) in weak subordinate roles, provided for allowances and wages for trainees, and inserted flexibility into the 70/30 arrangement.

The Senate bill, on the other hand, drastically reduced the influence of the federal government, inserted the governors in its place, strengthened the Private Industry Councils at the expense of local elected officials, prohibited wages and allowances, and provided for a rigid 70/30 split between training and supportive services/administrative costs. The Senate bill called for a $3.8 billion funding level; the House bill called for $5.4 billion.[29] The two bills grew out of very different philosophies about desirable political and programmatic relations between levels of government, about the contribution of the private sector, and about the uses of federal money. Given the scope of these differences, the conference was set up to be a prototypical Great Society vs. less government clash— except that the politics of the matter made it less of a clash of philosophies than a clash of wills.

In the clash of wills, the House had been put at a disadvantage by the election of 1980, which had determined that two of the three players at this final stage of the legislative process would be of the same party and of the same general persuasion. This advantage was sufficient to give the final bill its Senate number S 2036, so that it would forever bear the original Quayle-Kennedy imprint. If the Senate and the administration could agree, the House would be pressured to give in on substantive grounds as well. Depending, that is, on how badly the House wanted a bill. And depending, of course, on whether the Senate and the administration could agree. For Quayle, according to the reports from his perspective, the twin dangers were that the House might not want a bill badly enough and that the Senate and the administration might not agree.

In the eyes of the subcommittee staff, S 2036 and HR 5320 "were worlds apart." From the beginning, therefore, "the two sets of conferees could not understand each other," reported a subcommittee staffer.

> They operated from such different sets of assumptions that they could not even talk to each other. Each side felt it had already given up all it could give. Hawkins felt he had given up public service employment, so how could he be expected to give up any more. For Quayle, public service employment had always been absolutely out of the question. The bills were so far apart, we couldn't work from the bills. The staff had to work up proposals for the conferees to work on. That was the only way

they could talk to each other. Both sides kept asking us for proposals. . . . The main issues between them became the composition of the Private Industry Council and the role of the governor.

These two matters emerged as "the main issues" because they framed the rock-bottom political question: who will control the job training program? Control by local elected officials, the traditional pattern, was preserved in the House bill and eclipsed by both business interests and governors in the Senate bill. The issue was explosive enough to have driven Kennedy from the conference. "He did not participate," said Quayle,

> because his constituency was kicking the hell out of him. The Conference of Mayors was really mad at him. He told me, "I can't do any more; I'm in hot water with my constituents." But still he kept saying, "We've got to have a bill." That was helpful because so many other people didn't want a bill.

In Quayle's later summary, "The composition of the Private Industry Council was the big substantive issue. The Conference of Mayors hated to give it up. But if the mayors controlled the PICs, we would have had the same old ballgame. That was the issue as far as I was concerned. The 70/30 issue was Mickey Mouse by comparison. You can always fiddle with that."

The 70/30 issue—the other decisive matter of the conference— was less one between the two chambers than between both of them and the administration. It involved the administration's continued, fundamental abhorrence of income payments ("wages, allowances, and stipends") to trainees and the desire of House (and Senate) Democrats to modify the constraints of the Senate bill. In conference, the dispute came to center (as it had in the Senate committee and on the Senate floor) on the 70/30 formula—on the definition of supportive services and flexibility in the 30 percent part of the allowance.

Now, of course, the administration was backing the Senate bill. "The irony of the situation," said a staffer, "is that the administration, after having fought our bill all the way, has now adopted it as its bill and is telling everyone how wonderful it is." With the administration, backed by a veto threat, standing fast for the Senate bill's payment provisions and with the House, backed by a walk-out threat, standing fast for its bill's program control by mayors, the potential for conference deadlock was considerable. And the task of finding a way out fell largely to the Senate's Republican conferees—the only people who could negotiate with all parties and the people who most wanted a bill.

No one, of course, wanted a bill more than the subcommittee chairman. He did not want it to fail. But, as he recalled the situation, "Hawkins and I came at it from completely opposite poles. I would go over to his office whenever we had a problem. He would sit behind his desk and I would sit in the chair in front of him. I think he appreciated that. He would say how nice it was to deal with me. But we were asking him to change something he had been doing for forty years." "There was a period of four or five days when I thought it was lost," Quayle said afterward.

> The House really dug in when they saw all the compromising they were going to have to do, bringing the governors in and so forth. They began to say, "Why should we have any bill? We don't need a bill. We'll just go along with CETA for one more year." They started thinking that way, and their attitude hardened along those lines. The Conference of Mayors was telling them to do it. Boy, are they tough. The Democratic party must be beholden to them. Then the administration—mostly Ed Meese—kept saying, "Don't worry, things won't be so bad if we don't get any bill." And he said, "We'll veto any bill that isn't just what we want." Bob and I said, "Well, we may not get a bill after all."
>
> I was caught in the middle and was being hit by both sides. They were together in not wanting a bill. I used that against them by playing them off against each other. I'd go to Hawkins and tell him, "You're with Donovan; he doesn't want a bill." Then I'd go to the White House and say, "You're with those big city mayors; they don't want a bill." And I told the House guys, "OK, if you go with CETA, I'll guarantee you that it will be cut in half." And I sent that message to the House Appropriations Committee people, too, that CETA was very unpopular. Their thinking began to change. . . . But there was a time when I thought we might not get a bill out of conference.

Quayle's efforts aimed at softening up both sides to the point where a negotiated alternative would be preferable to the status quo. But the negotiation still had to be completed. The final pieces in that puzzle were put in place by the full committee chairman Orrin Hatch. In a formal sense, the leaders of their respective conferees were House Education and Labor Committee Chairman Carl Perkins, D-Ky., and Senate Labor and Human Resources Committee Chairman Hatch. The final bargain was struck between them. According to a top Quayle staffer,

> Perkins was sitting there saying, "The conference is over," when Hatch worked out a special exemption for him. As soon

as Hatch offered it to him and explained it, then he and Perkins started making agreements right and left. Hawkins didn't even know what was happening because Perkins doesn't believe in voting. . . . Without that special exemption for Perkins, there would have been no bill.

The "exemption" provided first for the "grandfathering in" of the service delivery area established under CETA for the area that included Perkins's district and for three or four other rural areas and, second, for an exemption from the 30 percent limit and other restrictions on supportive services for those particular areas. The effect was that long-standing "work experience" programs so cherished in Perkins's impoverished Kentucky district would continue untouched by JTPA.[30]

The pivotal power of Carl Perkins in the decisions of the House Education and Labor Committee was traditional and legendary. In the words of a committee veteran, "In writing education legislation, we always begin with the question: How does this affect the Seventh District in Kentucky?"[31] In conference, Perkins's concerns were equally determinative. Another committee veteran called him "the most persistent, the most dogged, and the most determined" of conferees.[32] And a senator agreed, "When you get into a conference with Carl Perkins, you may end up not having any furniture in your office. He is awesome."[33] The JTPA conference did nothing to dim his reputation.

As the Quayle enterprise saw it, Hatch was the key person in swaying the administration, too. "He also resolved the 70/30 issue, which was the administration's major problem," said a staffer. "We wanted Hatch to come in with that proposal because we knew the administration could not repudiate Hatch. He was up for reelection; and he was Reagan's man." Quayle elaborated the same conclusion. "Hatch's staff person worked out a compromise and we grabbed it so as to bring Hatch into the picture. Up to then, it had always been, 'Make a speech and drag Hatch.' But he became involved and became very helpful in putting it together." The compromise was a carefully circumscribed waiver of the 30 percent supportive services allocation and more generous "needs payments" to trainees under the rubric of supportive services.[34]

More than negotiating the bargain, Hatch was important in selling the conference product to the administration, whose acquiescence could never be assumed. Quayle recalled a conversation with Meese after the conference negotiations were concluded.

I had taken the kids to a soccer game. We stopped at McDonald's and I used a public phone. I called Ed Meese; and he said he was thinking of vetoing the bill. I said, "Over my dead body." He said, we won't sign it unless you change this and this and this. I said, "You're crazy. This is the most important piece of social legislation passed by your administration."

"Right up until the last minute," said Quayle, Meese was threatening to veto the bill. . . . Finally, "We had to pull a Donovan and get him out of town."

With the conference report signed and with Meese "out of town," the committee Republicans, with Hatch as their point man, "went to the White House to argue for the bill." Hatch possessed in this arena something Quayle did not—credibility and credits with the administration. "Hatch told them they had to have a bill. They did not want to offend him. They had to take him seriously," said Quayle. "He was running for reelection and he wanted a bill." Another participant described the denouement at the White House.

It was not a negotiating session. It was an explanation session. Hatch carried the argument that "This is it. It is this bill or no bill." Angrisani argued against it to the end. Meese was in New York, thank goodness. Duberstein and Baker were for it. The final act was Stockman saying, "OK, it's the best we can get."

And the weight of the White House was finally and formally put behind S 2036. On September 21 President Reagan announced his support for the Job Training Partnership Act. Nine days later the CETA program expired. That same day the conference report was accepted by the Senate, 97-0; and the next day it passed the House, 339-12.[35]

THE POLITICS OF CREDIT

All that remained was the signing. But the signing did not proceed any more smoothly for the subcommittee chairman than the rest of the sequence. Success, the proverb tells us, has a thousand fathers. No sooner had the bill passed than the scramble for credit began. In this part of the process the administration seized the lead. A presidential bill-signing ceremony is, or can be made to be, one of the great credit-claiming occasions in our political life. The president—in a setting determined by him, with words written by him, with a supporting cast of politicians chosen by him, and with a magnitude of national publicity guaranteed only by him—reaps a huge amount of credit-by-association for the legislative accomplishment he celebrates.

With unemployment at 9.8 percent and soon to reach 10.1 percent, and with unemployment the number-one public concern in the polls,

President Reagan gave every indication that he would exploit the signing of S 2036 to claim credit for a major effort to address the problem.

On September 28, speaking to a group of corporate leaders in the White House, he said, "The best thing Congress could do would be to pass the job training bill this week." And the statement was featured on the CBS and NBC nightly news.[36] In the opening statement of his press conference later that day, he made it sound, again, as though he was pushing Congress to pass the job training bill. "Before they leave Washington for a campaign recess," he said,

> I urge members of the Congress to devote their energies to essential economic legislation . . . a private sector jobs training bill that can help more than a million unemployed Americans per year, also awaits action this week.[37]

In answer to at least three subsequent questions on the economy he invoked the job training bill as superior to the previous jobs program and touted S 2036 as an exemplary positive, constructive, timely, approach to unemployment problems.[38]

These praises, too, reached a national audience. Ronald Reagan was embracing the job training bill, as the Quayle enterprise had long believed he could, as a flagship accomplishment of his administration. His two performances that day—one week after he had announced his support for the bill—were an augury of much more to come at the signing ceremony, scheduled for October 6.

With this prospect in view, and with the knowledge that JTPA was a bipartisan congressional initiative that the administration had opposed, House Democrats moved to claim their share of the credit by preempting the president's signing ceremony. House Speaker Tip O'Neill staged a ceremony of his own. As he routinely forwarded the bill to the White House with his signature, on October 5, he turned the occasion into a press conference. O'Neill praised S 2036, said that the Democrats deserved much credit for it, and handed out laurels to Quayle, Kennedy, and Gus Hawkins. Even more, he sought to establish the reigning interpretation of the bill's accomplishments before anyone else had a chance, by emphasizing that the task of passing a jobs creation bill still lay ahead. Once more in the history of JTPA, the administration had been upstaged—and surprised.

Under the headline, "Job Training Bill Gives the Democrats Political Mileage," the *Wall Street Journal* story began:

> Score one for the Democrats. Engaged in a tug-of-war with the White House over political credit for a job training measure, congressional Democrats stole a march on President Reagan by

staging their own "bill signing" ceremony at a news conference yesterday. The ploy left White House aides sputtering
with indignation; they had hoped to reap the full political
benefit when Mr. Reagan signs the bill into law today.

The story went on to say that an upset "senior aide" to the
president asserted "that the final version of the bill most closely
resembled one pushed by Senator Dan Quayle and thus the Republicans and President Reagan deserved the credit." [39] It was the first
public acknowledgment, by anyone in the administration, of the
leadership of Dan Quayle in the passage of S 2036. In keeping with administration practice throughout, however, it was a begrudging back-
handed recognition, extracted from them under extreme provocation
by the Democratic party. There was, of course, no mention of Edward
Kennedy. Under certain conditions, credit taking can provoke the
fiercest forms of political warfare.

On the evening of October 5 the Quayle office called to say they
had reserved a place for me at the bill-signing ceremony the next day.
On the morning of October 6, they called to say the scheduled ceremony
had been postponed. The Democratic sally had infuriated the White
House and had caused them to alter their plans. It also seemed to harden
their attitude toward the senator from Indiana—reminding them as it
did of the bipartisan origins of the bill. Although they had, at first,
invited Quayle to the festivities, they seemed no longer interested. "We
had a dozen Indiana media people cleared for the ceremony, plus the
staff, plus some of Dan's friends," recounted an aide. "But we said it [the
postponement] was all right with us. We told them that Dan could not
make it either Tuesday or Wednesday of next week, but that any other
time was fine. Dan had been scheduled for weeks to be back in Indiana
and to go to some out-of-state fund raisers in Michigan." The White
House scheduled the ceremony anyway, for the next Tuesday at noon.
And the Quayle staff scrambled to reschedule their senator's trip,
finding stand-ins, asking for rain-checks, changing flights to get him to
the ceremony on time.

On Monday, the day before the ceremony, the White House called
to tell them that the signing had been changed from noon to prime time
in the evening. It was further evidence of the importance they now
attached to the bill. "I called Dan to tell him about the change, and he
said, 'Screw it, they can go ahead without me,' " recounted a staffer.

> It seemed obvious to us that they didn't care whether he was
> there or not. I had to reschedule Dan back to his original plan.
> And they held the ceremony, with some Job Corps trainees
> watching and with Donovan and Angrisani standing in the
> background. What an irony.

In a major and deliberate departure from accepted practice, not a single member of Congress was present. The Associated Press description of the TV event said that twenty or so job trainees provided the backdrop while "a cheering section of invited guests and White House employees mingled with reporters to provide loud applause." [40] And S 2036 became Public Law 97-300. Reagan hailed JTPA as "an important step forward for America [that] would make a difference on Main Street." And he claimed that it would train one million people. "The administration," AP summed up, "is touting the legislation as the centerpiece in its effort to counter unemployment." [41] Not once did the president so much as mention the name of the Republican who wrote and managed the bill he now so ardently embraced. From the perspective of the subcommittee chairman, a fairer summary of the proceedings would be this: that the administration, deserving of a minor share of the credit for the bill, had stolen all of it for themselves—in broad daylight and on prime-time national television. And for the rest of 1982 the president and the Labor Department displayed it prominently as their accomplishment. [42]

In the strategic sweep of things, however, Dan Quayle was reaping the harvest he had sown earlier by introducing a bipartisan bill, and by putting it on a fast track—thereby taking and keeping the policy initiative away from the administration. After all, the signing ceremony was the first time the administration had gained control of the process. And even then, despite many modifications, it was S 2036, the Quayle-Kennedy bill, that had to be swallowed by the administration and signed by the president. One could hardly have expected them to welcome the Massachusetts senator to the White House for the ceremony. And surely that legacy of frustration and hostility helps to explain the cavalier treatment of the stalwart Republican conservative to whom they were so deeply indebted for the legislation they wished to acclaim.

Quayle took the unusual slight without a murmur. On National Public Radio he contented himself by saying it was to be expected that many people would want to claim credit for such an important bill. [43] His Democratic cosponsor, however, exhibited no such restraining loyalties. "The record will show," said Kennedy, "that this important legislation was delayed for months . . . because of White House intransigence and repeated veto threats." [44] And he added, "I share the concern of others in Congress about the President's decision to exclude us from the White House ceremony to sign our bill." [45] Surely, in this last sentiment, the senator from Massachusetts spoke for the senator from Indiana.

Quayle's absence from the signing of his own bill was not yet the final insult he would absorb from the administration in the matter. From the beginning, job training legislation had been a low-salience issue. It had not been well covered or much covered by the national media. With a prime-time presidential signing in the offing, therefore, the Quayle office was suddenly inundated with inquiries about the bill—its aims, its history, its contents, its relation to other bills, its proponents and opponents, and so forth. It fell to the press secretary to handle these inquiries. "The main question they asked," he recalled,

> was, "When did President Reagan support the bill?" They were trying to stir up trouble. My answer was, "Senator Quayle believes that when the president came on board is not as important as the fact that he now supports the bill completely and that we are happy he will sign it."

Only one reporter ever used that careful comment. Instead, they used another comment of his—one intended only as "background." In the course of a long conversation with one reporter, on the day of the ceremony, explained the press secretary, "I made the honest statement that 'the Labor Department threw roadblocks in our path all the way.'" That comment worked its way quickly through the journalistic community and thence to the White House.

Kenneth Duberstein called Quayle in Indiana and asked him to ask his press secretary to ask the White House correspondents to keep the offensive "backgrounder" out of their commentary on the signing ceremony. Said Quayle to his aide, "I'm not telling you what to do, but I just wanted you to know the situation." The press secretary called the key scorekeepers, but to no avail. He recalls what happened.

> I turned on the evening news. On CBS, there was a picture of Dan on the screen and below it they printed, "An aide to Senator Dan Quayle said, 'The administration threw road blocks in our way.'" "The administration," not the Labor Department. NBC was even worse. They showed a picture of Dan and beneath it an aide to Senator Dan Quayle said, "The White House threw road blocks in our way." The White House! Not the Labor Department, not even the administration. As soon as it was over, Duberstein called. He was livid. He wanted Dan to hold a press conference to set the record straight. He wanted a letter of apology.

The senator did not respond to that request. So, the administration extracted one more piece of flesh in retaliation.

When he returned from Indiana, Quayle asked the White House to have his picture taken with the president. He wanted some visual, usable recognition of his authorship. He also requested that his wife and children be allowed to accompany him to the White House. He was told that he could not bring his wife and children and that he would have to come in unannounced through the side gate. As the staffer who made the arrangements put it: "They said, 'After all you've done, you've got nerve to ask if you can bring your kids. You can come, but no wife or children.' They ended up sneaking him in and sneaking him out." To the bitter end, they had kept from him the full measure of credit he had earned. The politics of credit, it appears, is only partially predictable from the politics of passage.

The passage of JTPA was a substantial legislative accomplishment. Ample confirmation of its importance lay in the eagerness of the president and his colleagues to praise it, publicize it, and take credit for it. On January 25, 1983, in his State of the Union message, the president said, "We must offer both short term help and long term hope for our unemployed. I hope we can work together on this, as we did last year in enacting the landmark Job Training Partnership Act." Contained in that comment is a large, albeit hidden, compliment to the subcommittee chairman. For while the politics of credit kept obscuring his efforts, the politics of passage just as surely clarified his contribution. In what was, of course, a collective endeavor, Dan Quayle was the leader; and the passage of "landmark" legislation is solid evidence, therefore, of his ability to govern. If, in his first year, he had learned something about getting involved, in his second year he had learned something about making public policy. It was a quantum leap upward to a more complex and more consequential senatorial activity.

Whether or not the president, the White House staff, or the Labor Department gave the subcommittee chairman credit for his governing accomplishment was far less important to the achievement of his personal goals than was the reaction he would receive inside the Senate. His chief desire was to accomplish something in the Senate and earn a reputation there as an effective senator. At year's end, reflecting on his experience with JTPA, he was unprepared to say that he had achieved those goals; but he felt he had made progress. Talking about gaining credit among insiders, he was hesitant but positive.

> Only the senators and the job training community know what I've done. So it's very limited here. I think the senators know. But it's hard to know what they think. It's hard for me to judge that. Baker did ask me to be in a group of four senators to think about the whole problem of jobs legislation. . . . John Chafee [R-R.I.] came up to me and thanked me for helping him in his reelection campaign. . . . He said it [JTPA] was the main thing he had to talk about. . . . It helped other people in similar campaigns. So they know. And before the recess, Baker asked

me to lead the fight against the Byrd-Kennedy public jobs bill. Logically, they should have had Senator X do it, but they turned it over to me.

There were, in other words, small but encouraging signs.

Public collegial praise can be found in the remarks of Ted Kennedy at the time of the conference report. Even allowing for the normally exaggerated amenities of such exchanges, they still reveal a special recognition of legislative accomplishment. For example: "I point out at this time, and I think the Senator from Indiana has been entirely too reluctant to do so, that this legislation would not be before the Senate if it had not been for the efforts and energies of the Senator from Indiana." Or, "I think this legislation as much as anything that has come out of our Labor and Human Resources has been really the result of the tireless efforts of the Senator from Indiana . . . and his very effective work." [46]

Senator Hawkins called Quayle "the chief architect of this legislation." [47] A bit more formally, perhaps, in his 1982 year-end summary of legislative highlights, Majority Leader Baker listed fifth among the "several important legislative accomplishments" of that year "an important new law . . . to create job training, S 2036, introduced by the distinguished senator from Indiana, Mr. Quayle." [48] Only four other senators were mentioned by name in the report. It was about as official a recognition of his achievement as his peers were likely to bestow.

A senator's inside reputation is a very unofficial and informal attachment deriving from a gradual accumulation of anecdote and accomplishment, of trial-and-error experience, of evaluation and re-evaluation. One natural center for communication and judgment on such matters is the office of the party leader. On the day S 2036 passed the Senate, I asked one of Howard Baker's most trusted aides to grade the performance of the subcommittee chairman. "B-minus," he answered. "The reason I grade it down is because I think it could have been handled better in the early period. It didn't need to be confrontational. But this one was confrontational from the word go." This was the judgment of a man whose job was to keep peace in the family, to avoid "a pissing match," and who was feeling most acutely the denouement of Quayle's running feud with the administration. But, he added, "That's what comes from being green. It was a good learning experience for Quayle." It was a very mixed judgment.

Six months later, with JTPA signed into law and with everyone connected with it claiming credit for Quayle's accomplishment, I returned to the same man with the same question about Dan Quayle and the other fifteen freshman Republicans. Now, his judgment was decidedly less mixed. Looking first at the entire group of first-termers, he

said, "There are three or four real good ones in the group"—_____,
Quayle, _____, and maybe _____. About Quayle specifically, he said,

> Quayle is loud; he's boisterous; he says what he thinks; he
> won't follow any one person for very long. But he's learning
> that there is a reason for having the [party] leadership. He's got
> a lot of potential. He did one hell of a job to get that job
> training bill passed. He took on the administration. He took on
> a wild committee chairman. He took on some tough interest
> groups. He had to work things out with the other party. He had
> to work things out with the other house. I don't think many
> people know what a hell of a job he did. He has the potential to
> mature in the process. Right now, he's a rough-cut diamond.
> He's got a lot of fire in his belly. He wants to do things. He can
> become one very fine senator.

Again, this is a judgment from the leadership's perspective—about
someone with a mind of his own who is not yet predictably cooperative
but who has marked legislative ability. It is not the picture of a Senate
star. But it is the picture of a very promising, and already effective,
senator. And the inspiration for the picture is JTPA.

If, in his first year, he had gotten involved, in his fashion, in his second year he had made policy, in his fashion. The governing style he exhibited in his JTPA activity was an extension of that which he displayed
in his AWACS activity. As such, it added to the development of a
distinctive, "results-oriented" governing style. Above all, there was the
desire to get something done together with an optimism about the
chances of doing so. That is why he so valued, and never regretted, the
alliance with Kennedy. "You've asked me all along whether I thought
Kennedy was a help or a hindrance," he reflected in December. "He was
a help. Once his name was on the bill, everyone knew there would be a
bill. . . . And he kept saying all the way through, 'We've got to have a
bill.'" That was what Quayle most wanted, to get a bill.

As he went about getting it, he displayed the same enthusiasm that
was evident in his first year—the "go-get-'em," "fix-it-up, fix-it-up"
spirit that led him to want to set the legislative pace. Later, when he was
involved in another issue on another committee, he said,

> I'm frustrated about this issue. I have been too much on the
> defensive, and I don't like that. I'd rather be out front. So I'm try-
> ing to devise a comprehensive plan so that other people will
> have to treat my plan. As it is, I have some little things and other
> people have some little things. So I trade "my little things for
> your little things." I don't like that. But so far I can't put
> anything together to take the lead. . . . I can't get hold of it. It's
> frustrating.

His desire to be out front, on the offensive, leading, was as much a matter of stylistic preference as it was a matter of strategic calculation. His decision to seize the policy initiative, like his decision to embrace bipartisanship, grew out of a combination of strategy and instinct.

Other elements of his governing style, too, were exhibited and strengthened in the fight for JTPA. In his work with Kennedy, he showed what we earlier called his instrumental independence, a willingness to entertain, even welcome, alternative approaches to a problem. Kennedy captured this characteristic, too, in his September comments. "I have found . . . the Senator from Indiana to be open to ideas and suggestions and . . . tireless in attempting to try and find ways so that those of us who might have approached this in a somewhat different way could get behind legislation. . . . He worked with us to fashion this legislation." [49] This statement describes an open-mindedness about approaches to problems that had been in evidence since Quayle's earliest days in the House. And with it went an ease in working with others to get something done—be it AWACS or JTPA.

Throughout his coalition-building efforts on JTPA, he displayed another stylistic element—an exuberance that was hard to contain. Sometimes it was contagious—as with his staff. Sometimes it spilled over into impatience, coupled with a lack of awareness of how that impatience might be affecting others—like his committee chairman or the administration's emissaries.

Related both to his exuberance and his desire to be out front was his stylistic preference for straight talk in dealing with others. It is a frankness in political thinking and political maneuver that I first observed on the campaign trail—and, which, incidentally, made my observation much easier. It is as if, in his drive to get something done, he does not have time for circumlocution or mystery or deviousness. "When he's thought about something," said a staffer, "he's always willing to step out front and say what he thinks, straight out. Sometimes, he's the first to say it. We on the staff are always saying to each other, 'I hope he's right.' " Saying what you think sometimes breeds difficulty. But, more often, straightforwardness about your opinions and your agenda facilitates negotiations with colleagues. And JTPA proved him to be a successful negotiator.

When it was over, he remained very much the self-confident kid. But, it appears, he was a wiser one. For he learned that working the legislative process was not all fun and success, that it entailed uncertainty and punishment as well. "It was fun to push it through," he said at year's end. "But you have so many ups and downs, highs and lows, so much anguish and you lose so much sleep. It's kinda nice to just sit back now and talk about it." By way of summing up, it could be said that, in piloting JTPA into enactment, he had displayed a broadly political, coalition-building interest and some talent to match. He had strengthened a governing style that was not tied to any one substantive policy area. If he could lead in one instance, he could lead in others.

In December I accompanied him to his featured presentation on JTPA at an American Enterprise Institute public policy seminar. He spoke to a group of thirty-two invited guests—a large segment of the Washington "job training community," the issue network involved in his legislation. I asked the subcommittee chairman how many of the thirty-two he knew. His surprising answer was: "Two." But in light of his own talent and predispositions, it was not so surprising.

On the way back from the forum, where he had been introduced as "the mover and shaker" behind the training bill and praised by another featured speaker for being "as responsible as anybody in the country for the bill," [50] I asked him if he felt like the father of JTPA. "A little bit, I do," he answered. "It was our bill and we put it together—the political part of it." It was an appropriate comment about his style, akin to his comment about AWACS that his interest lay in "broad concepts," not "fine print." A staffer put it this way. "Some senators like to do the intellectual work of drafting legislation. Others like to get to know the other senators and build support for the legislation. Dan is one of the latter. Not many of them are good at it. Dan is." JTPA provided more evidence in support of that judgment.

By the end of 1982 Quayle's initial period of adjustment to the Senate had ended. And his JTPA activity had made an enormous difference in that respect, because it made him feel like a senator. When I asked him whether his work on JTPA had not given him more self-confidence and made him feel more comfortable, he discussed his adjustment to his job and his development on the job. "There's a difference between being confident and being comfortable," he answered.

> I've always been confident. But I don't think I felt comfortable till I'd been through a lot of the process. When I first held hearings in Indiana and in Washington, I had never done that before. You don't know how a thing is going to work till you actually do it. It's a growing experience. You make mistakes, but you learn. I was uncomfortable even at the end [of JTPA] when I thought we might lose the bill. I kept saying to myself, "They can't veto the bill—not with 10.1 percent unemployment." But then I couldn't be sure. Meese was very serious, "all or nothing." You see, I hadn't had enough experience to know what they would do. That's when Hatch was so important. He said, "I need it," and he was up for reelection. They would do something for him that they wouldn't do for me.

Once you've been through the whole process, you feel more comfortable. With the $50 million dislocated worker program, I've just gone ahead with it on my own. When I started the jobs bill, I knew I had to have help, so I asked Kennedy. With the dislocated worker bill, I didn't ask anybody. I didn't feel I needed anybody. Maybe if I started in on a jobs bill now, I could do it all by myself. You feel more comfortable once you've been all the way through the process. I don't know how you could feel comfortable in the Senate without going through the process once. I'd say I probably got to feel comfortable some time last summer. It's gradual. I don't know whether you ever feel completely comfortable.

The young senator from Indiana had, by his own accounting, learned and grown in the Senate. JTPA had been a major agent of his development. It had been gradual. It was incomplete. And it would continue.

NOTES

1. Subcommittee members were Dan Quayle, R-Ind., chairman; Orrin Hatch, R-Utah; Don Nickles, R-Okla.; Paula Hawkins, R-Fla.; Howard Metzenbaum, D-Ohio; Edward Kennedy, D-Mass.; Claiborne Pell, D-R.I. Their meeting on the youth employment legislation had been pro forma.
2. Quayle press release, "Opening Statement, Markup of S 2036, Training for Jobs Act," (no date); Press release, "Statement of Senator Edward M. Kennedy at the Employment Subcommittee Executive Session on Job Training Legislation," April 22, 1982.
3. All quotations from the markup session are taken from the "Senate Jobs Training Markup Manuscript," Senate Committee on Labor and Human Resources, and/or from my own notes taken at the meeting. See also Drew Von Bergen, "Bipartisan Job Training Bill Advances," *Washington Post*, April 23, 1982.
4. For example, see Alan Ehrenhalt, "In the Senate of the '80s, Team Spirit Has Given Way to the Rule of Individuals," *Congressional Quarterly Weekly Report*, September 4, 1982; James Miller, "Running in Place: Inside the Senate" (New York: Simon and Schuster, 1986), 160-162; Lawrence Evans, "Influence in Senate Committees" (Ph.D. dissertation, University of Rochester, 1987).
5. For example, see *Congressional Record*, July 1, 1982, S7820; September 30, 1982, S12712.
6. Memorandum from Kris Iverson and Bob Guttman to Orrin Hatch and Dan Quayle, April 29, 1982.
7. On Donovan's problems and his blowup with Hatch, see the 1982 series of articles by George Lardner, Jr., in the *Washington Post* on May 1, 4, 5, 12, 16, 19, 22, 27, and June 15, 17, 22. Hatch's suggestion that Donovan resign is detailed in George Lardner, Jr., "Hatch Urges Donovan to Consider Quitting," *Washington Post*, June 17, 1982. Donovan's reply is contained in George

Lardner, Jr., "No Intention of Resigning, Says Donovan," *Washington Post,* June 22, 1982. On Donovan's effectiveness, see Lou Cannon, "Donovan Seen as Irreparably Damaged Even If Inquiry Formally Clears Him," *Washington Post,* June 22, 1982.

8. Memorandum from Kris Iverson and Bob Guttman to Orrin Hatch and Dan Quayle, May 18, 1982.
9. Draft letter from Raymond Donovan to Orrin Hatch, circa May 14, 1982.
10. Memorandum from Albert Angrisani to James Baker, Ed Meese, David Stockman, Ray Donovan, and Kenneth Duberstein.
11. Memorandum from Dan Quayle to James A. Baker, May 21, 1982.
12. "Memorandum of Understanding," from Ken Duberstein to Dan Quayle, June 1, 1982.
13. Ibid. David Stockman also pledged administration support for S 2036, provided that six specified amendments, with specified language, were adopted. Letter from David Stockman to Dan Quayle, May 26, 1982.
14. They began transacting business in room S-324 of the Capitol at 3:45 P.M., finished at 5:25, and took fifteen minutes out for a Senate vote.
15. All quotations from the meeting are taken from the transcript, "Training for Jobs Markup," Senate Committee on Labor and Human Resources, and/or from my own notes of the meeting.
16. He made the same argument at length when the bill reached the floor. See *Congressional Record,* July 1, 1982, S7828.
17. Letter from Dan Quayle to Howard Baker, June 10, 1982.
18. *Congressional Record,* June 22, 1981, S7254.
19. Letter from David Stockman to Dan Quayle, June 18, 1982.
20. Letter from Dan Quayle to David Stockman, June 23, 1982.
21. *Congressional Record,* June 29, 1982, S7537-S7538.
22. Letter from Don Shasteen to Orrin Hatch, with attached "Amendments," July 1, 1982.
23. *Congressional Record,* July 1, 1982, S7820-7821.
24. *Congressional Record,* July 1, 1982, S7822-S7823; S7852.
25. On the Kennedy amendment, see *Congressional Record,* July 1, 1982, S7828-S7829; on the Metzenbaum amendment, see *Congressional Record,* July 1, 1982, S7836.
26. *Congressional Record,* July 1, 1982, S7849.
27. On Duberstein, see Steven Weisman, "Reagan's 'Invisible' Link to Congress," *New York Times,* August 19, 1982.
28. For an article on department liaison officers under Reagan, including Shasteen, see Bill Keller, "Executive Agency Lobbyists Mastering the Difficult Art of 'Congress and Liaison,'" *Congressional Quarterly Weekly Report,* December 5, 1981.
29. Harrison Donnelly, "New Job Training Legislation Awaits Senate, House Action," *Congressional Quarterly Weekly Report,* June 12, 1982.
30. Public Law 97-300, Section 108d; Section 101 (a)(4)(A)(iii).
31. *Congressional Quarterly Weekly Report,* April 17, 1976, 922.
32. As quoted in Lawrence Longley and Walter Oleszek, *Bicameral Politics: House-Senate Conference Committee Interaction* (New Haven, Conn.: Yale University Press, forthcoming 1989), Chapter 9, as quoted from *Los Angeles Times,* June 25, 1984.
33. As quoted in Longley and Oleszek, *Bicameral Politics,* Chapter 1, as quoted from *Roll Call,* June 2, 1983.
34. "Conferees Settle Aspects Stalling Job-Training Bill," *Wall Street Journal,*

September 24, 1982; "Senate OK's $3.8 Billion Jobs Bill," *Boston Globe*, October 1, 1982.

35. *Congressional Record*, September 30, 1982, S12711-S12718, S12731; *Congressional Record*, October 1, 1982, H8447-H8456.

36. Television News Index and Abstracts, Vanderbilt University Television News Archive, September 28, 1982.

37. "President's News Conference," *New York Times*, September 29, 1982.

38. Ibid.

39. Rich Jaroslovsky, "Job-Training Bill Gives the Democrats Political Mileage," *Wall Street Journal*, October 6, 1982.

40. Wire services, "Optimistic Reagan Says Let's Stay on Course," *Minneapolis Star Tribune*, October 14, 1982.

41. Associated Press, "President Signs Job Training Bill," *Minneapolis Star-Tribune*, October 13, 1982.

42. For example, see Seth King, "Donovan Dinner Dais: No Reagan, No Bush," *New York Times*, October 31, 1982; "Text of President Reagan's Press Conference," *Congressional Quarterly Weekly Report*, November 13, 1982; John Byczkowski, "Chamber Just Misses Out on Talk with Reagan," *Rochester Democrat and Chronicle*, November 20, 1982.

43. "All Things Considered," National Public Radio, October 13, 1982.

44. Associated Press, "President Signs Job Training Bill."

45. Otis Pike, "Reagan Skilled Politician," *Fargo Forum*, October 17, 1982.

46. *Congressional Record*, September 30, 1982, S12713.

47. *Congressional Record*, September 30, 1982, S12715.

48. *Congressional Record*, December 23, 1982, S16114-S16116.

49. *Congressional Record*, September 30, 1982, S12713.

50. The speaker was the undersecretary of labor, Mac Lovell, with whom Quayle had had no contact during the passage of JTPA.

Seasons of Campaigning

CAMPAIGNING AS EXPLANATION

Every senator spends his or her life moving between two contexts, Washington and home, and between two activities, governing and campaigning. There is an intertwining of the two contexts and of the two activities. Senators come to the business of governing heavily influenced by their prior campaign experience. Their early interpretation of their election, as in Dan Quayle's case, provides an especially visible linkage between campaigning and governing. When senators return to the business of campaigning, they are heavily influenced by their governing experience in Washington. An especially influential link is their explanation at home of what they have been doing in Washington.

From an objective point of view, the explanatory linkage is a requirement of the representational relationship. It is an accounting, by the representative, of his or her performance in office to the people who sent him or her there, that they can use in deciding whether to send the representative back. From the perspective of the individual representative, however, explanation is largely a matter of strategic manipulation. That is, the officeholder exploits the explanatory process to demonstrate that his governing activity makes him deserving of continuing electoral support at home. While the idea of accountability sets a requirement that there be explanation, it does not specify what kind of explanation must occur. Least of all does it specify the kind of in-depth, educational justification of one's governing activity that extreme ideas of accountability might require. Subject to the effectiveness of the challenger in forcing extensive explanation, the process is very much in the control of the officeholder. In the incumbent's hands, explanation tends to be thin on justification and thick with advertising, credit claiming, and persuasion. This explanatory exploitation, at home, of one's governing activity in Washington is a large part of what every incumbent senator's campaign is all about.

The six-year senatorial cycle means that the explanatory linkage between governing and campaigning has time to develop long before "The Campaign" is thought to begin. Typically, our analysis of campaigns begins when the opposing candidate can be identified and compared. But this focus may overlook the beginnings of the incumbent's explanatory activity and hence the earliest linkages between governing and campaigning. It is not clear whether the description of these early linkages will add to our understanding of the governing/campaigning sequence or of election outcomes. But we will not know until we try. That is what we propose to do here.

We shall examine some of Dan Quayle's explanations, in Indiana, of his major second-year governing achievement in Washington—the Job Training Partnership Act. We shall examine his JTPA-based explanations, interpretations, and persuasions from their beginnings in 1982 to their culmination in 1986. We shall trace their development and their impact—if there was any—on Quayle's campaigning. We shall take our tracings in the season before he had an opponent and in the season when he had one.

My interest in the early explanation of Washington activity to constituents began with a visit to Indiana in the late summer of 1982. The trip was undertaken primarily to see how the young senator was doing after almost two years in office. My one previous visit to his home state, in October of 1980, had left me with some impression of him as a candidate and as a campaigner, but without much sense of his support patterns or of his developed home style or of his durability. I wanted to take these soundings—as a counterpoint to my observations in Washington—in the middle of the electoral cycle. When Quayle agreed to let me come, he put the home visit in a cyclical perspective, too.

> I'll be helping local candidates. But I'll be keeping a low profile. After the [1982] election, I'll pick up some, but I won't really go hard till 1985. Some people campaign all the time. I would just burn out doing that. And I don't want to burn out.

It was a good description of the early phases of campaigning and it contained no hint of a conscious intent to exploit his Washington accomplishment.

The intention on my part was to look for traces of S 2036 only as they might, like anything else, appear in the setting Quayle had described. In mid-June I had asked Quayle how S 2036 had played during his most recent trip home. But his reply revealed nothing to stimulate my interest. "It comes up," he had said.

> People are interested. I told them the bill had passed in committee. But they are much more interested in my tax simplification scheme. They are more interested in big new ideas than they are in my slogging through the mud back here trying to pass a bill.

What I found in Indiana, however, altered the focus of my attention. For, while S 2036 was still a distinctly minor theme of his visit, it took on a far broader presence in Indiana than I had ever imagined. Indeed, its presence seemed far more significant than Quayle's own description had implied. Because of my immersion in its Washington progress, my attention was immediately drawn to its incarnation locally. And it was not long before the effect of Quayle's job training bill performance in Washington on his performance at home had emerged as the most fascinating aspect of the trip—fascinating enough to change my angle of vision on the entire campaigning process.

In Washington, job training legislation was certainly a little-publicized issue. Its deepest conflicts lay beneath the surface at each point of passage, and no point of passage drew much media attention. The best-covered event was the introductory press conference with Kennedy; but none of the major national TV networks came. And none of them paid any attention to the bill until the president signed it. By any standard, press coverage was negligible. When Senate floor debate on the bill began, there were four reporters sitting in the press gallery; in mid debate, the number rose to a high of six; and during the roll call only two remained.

The next day, news of the bill's passage in the *Washington Post* was buried in five paragraphs in the middle of a story headlined: "Congress Leaves for Holiday With Money Tangle Unsolved." [1] The *New York Times* carried a short UPI dispatch on page A11. [2] During the latter part of the debate and the roll call on the House bill, only two reporters sat in the press gallery in that chamber. The next day, there was no mention of the bill's passage in the *Washington Post*. The *New York Times* story carried a byline and a headline, "House Approves Job Training Bill to Replace Expiring CETA Plan"; but it was placed on page B9 and only half the story was devoted to it. [3] If, therefore, the news of Dan Quayle's governing achievement was to get back to Indiana, the Washington press corps and the national television networks would not be the ones to do it.

We have made no effort to accurately gauge media interest in Indiana. But such clues as are available indicate that it, too, was minimal.

One measure, letters to Quayle from home on the subject, shows an average of twenty-three letters a week from January 1, 1981, through August 31, 1982. It ranked tenth in volume of mail generated during that period, accounting for about 1 percent (747 letters) out of the total of 56,184 letters. It ranked far behind abortion, taxes, entitlements, environment, and defense by this measure.[4] I asked Quayle's press secretary if any Indiana reporter had followed the bill closely and knew what the subcommittee chairman had gone through in the course of it. He said, "No." When it was over, Quayle said he told the reporters from his home state that

> "You missed one of the great stories of the Congress—JTPA." They said, "We know it." I said, "All Reagan was interested in was budget and taxes, and that's all you wrote about. But the one bill we did pass was JTPA. I don't know how you missed it." I kept asking [my press secretary], "How come they aren't writing about it?"

My own observation, throughout, had been that Quayle was less concerned about credit than I thought he would be or should be. He never mentioned it without prodding. I was around his staff a great deal and I never heard of any effort to garner publicity for his efforts. He told his closest advisers afterward that "We had a hell of a fight to get that passed. But we didn't do as good a job as we could have in publicizing it. We just said, 'The bill passed the committee.' " So one answer to his own question is simply that he did not push anybody to write about JTPA, and no one else took the lead. The entire Quayle enterprise was remarkably unaggressive about credit claiming. In this respect, my experience ran totally counter to the proposition that senators are perpetually preoccupied with credit-taking publicity.

When I suggested that Quayle did not seem to care about credit, his press secretary demurred, "He has as big an ego and wants as much credit as anybody else." But he added, "He just played this one very quietly." Why he did so remains a matter of speculation. Perhaps he was too embattled to think about how it was playing elsewhere until it was over. Perhaps he believed his efforts might bring negative publicity, in the light of his fight with the administration. Or perhaps it was the oversight of an inexperienced senator and an inexperienced staff.

When, however, he discussed credit taking in general—much later, in 1986—he did express a distinct lack of intensity about it. "I believe in getting my fair share of the credit," he said,

> but who gets the credit is not one of my concerns. A lot of these guys spend all their time working to see who goes first. I don't worry about the billing. I worry about getting something done. I want my share, but I don't get all upset if it doesn't happen.

On the one occasion in 1982 when I raised credit claiming with respect to S 2036, he did, indeed, follow these sentiments. S 2036 had been officially reported to the Senate "by Senator Hatch on behalf of Senator Quayle," so I asked him what he thought about what seemed to be a reversal of a tradition. He agreed that it was a committee tradition that each subcommittee chairman reported his own bills.

> It's his staff that was the problem. I heard that at one point they decided to call it the Hatch bill. They decided that he should take political credit at home for passing this great piece of legislation. . . . It sounds like something that a bunch of clowns over there would do. . . . The only people who will ever know who reported the bill are Supreme Court justices trying to interpret legislative intentions. That won't make any difference. It's my bill.

It was one of the few times I ever heard him refer to it as "my bill." And it came in the context of a direct challenge. Otherwise he was just not aggressive about it. I concluded that he did not think about it much, but that when he did he felt fully confident of his ability to claim credit when it became necessary to do so.

The saga of S 2036 was underplayed, if not ignored, in the media. So, of course, was Dan Quayle's part in it. Thus his effort to convert governing success into support at home began without the initial momentum imparted by prior publicity and on a baseline near zero in terms of extra-Senate recognition. His was a standing-start, self-help explanatory operation. For that reason, it proceeded very slowly and very slowly gathered strength as it went along.

OBSERVATIONS AND REFLECTIONS: INDIANA, AUGUST-SEPTEMBER 1982

When we got together on August 30 in Indiana, the job training bill was in its early House-Senate conference stages. The conferees had met only once, to settle on a means of proceeding. "We worked it around," explained Quayle,

> to where there was agreement that [Chairman Augustus] Hawkins and I would sit down and see what we could agree to and then bring it back to the group. That means Bob Guttman and Susan Grayson [Hawkins's staff chief] will see what they can work out. It took us three hours to agree to that much. . . . We'll work things around on a few issues and then I'll have to stop and see what the administration wants. It may take me some time to get to Jim Baker, so I don't know how soon we can finish.

The conferees planned to meet again when he returned to Washington. They had not yet reached their impasse. He expressed the confident view that he expected the conferees to agree and the president to sign the bill. But whatever explanatory success he would have, on that trip, would have to be based on Senate passage of S 2036 alone and not on a final legislative product. JTPA had not yet come into being.

Given, then, the lack of a media sendoff and given the incompleteness of his task, it is striking how much political benefit could be derived from his job training activity. By "much" I do not mean the conclusive weight of the benefit. I mean the constituency-wide scope of the benefit. Neither by word nor by deed was there any indication that Quayle planned to exploit his Washington activity on that trip. But the opportunity to mention it or to respond to others' mention of it was widespread. And any mention at all meant favorable mention. Only rarely was job training legislation uppermost in anyone's thinking. But the presence of S 2036 could be observed nearly *everywhere.*

In four full days, the senator gave five speeches to civic clubs and/or business groups, spoke at five fund-raising events, participated in seven press conferences and/or interviews, and held three informal meetings with special groups.[5] These twenty talking appearances took place in eight Indiana communities and in six media markets. Job training legislation was mentioned in fifteen of those appearances, in seven of the eight communities, and in all of the media markets. (See Table 4-1.) What follows is a descriptive account of the fifteen instances. It was the cumulative impact of these small occurrences that forcefully focused the attention of this observer. So an effort will be made to simulate for the reader the scope and cumulative impact of these instances. The following running account has been taken from notes written at the time, together with some later reflections.

Quayle's fund-raiser on August 30 has nothing whatever to do with JTPA. But it is my first solid contact with his primary constituency. And it sets a mood for this week. The event is a golf tournament at the Orchard Ridge Country Club in Fort Wayne. It is a gathering of upper middle-class Republicans—a couple of House members, large financial donors, local party leaders, volunteers and staffers from his first campaign, local business people, golfing friends. There is talk of his early campaigns, talk that he is "coming along," talk about his becoming president. It is typical of talk among a politician's strongest supporters. Quayle's first obligation is to stand on the tenth tee of the golf course and hit a drive with each foursome as it comes along. He is a fine, seven-handicap golfer, and it has been a major athletic, social, and even political diversion for him since he was a youth. So the event is very comfortable for him. "He's out there complaining that he doesn't get to

TABLE 4-1   Dan Quayle Speaking Events, August 30-September 3, 1982

Date, place, event	Job Training Bill mentioned (S 2036)	Mentioned first by Quayle
AUGUST 30		
Fort Wayne		
Fund-raiser for Quayle	no	—
AUGUST 31		
Fort Wayne		
Speech—Lincoln National Life		
Insurance	yes	yes
Press conference	no	—
Lafayette		
Speech—Lincoln Club	no	—
Press conference with local candidate	yes	no
Interview with reporter	yes	yes
Kokomo		
Fund-raiser for local candidates	yes	yes
Press conference	yes	yes
Speech—Jaycees	yes	no
SEPTEMBER 1		
Indianapolis		
Interview—radio talk show	yes	no
Fund-raiser for congressional candidate	yes	no
Press conference	no	—
Meeting—Quayle Productivity		
Advisory Group	yes	yes
Meeting—black civic leaders	yes	no
Seymour		
Fund-raiser for congressional candidate	no	—
SEPTEMBER 2		
Anderson		
Speech—Chamber of Commerce	yes	yes
Interview with reporter	yes	no
Muncie		
Fund-raiser for congressional candidate	yes	no
Indianapolis		
Meeting—Quayle Executive Committee	yes	?
SEPTEMBER 3		
Valparaiso		
Speech—Pfizer Corporation	yes	yes

putt," laughed a staffer. "He says, 'I'm not playing golf. I'm just shaking hands.' He's not happy. He's so competitive."

His second obligation is to say a few words after dinner. Much of the talk is given over to kidding the two members of Congress and to good-natured bantering with the audience. He says they are his "political family," and he tells them that families share values and philosophies. He talks a little about the economic situation. He ends with a benediction "my grandfather used to say at his newspaper family picnics":

> Happy have we met.
> Happy have we been.
> Happy shall we be.
> Till we meet again.

It is a perfect expression of his own outlook on life, and a nice reminder of the person I will be travelling with. "It was pretty relaxed wasn't it?" he says afterward. "It's good to be home with family."

The next morning, Quayle gives a breakfast speech to a large audience of Lincoln National Life Insurance Company employees in Fort Wayne. It is essentially the same talk he will give again to civic clubs in Lafayette, Kokomo, and Anderson. It covers economic progress during the Reagan administration; prospects for reduced interest rates and unemployment; problems of trade, of regulation, and of the budget; and relations between Congress and the executive on matters of spending. It is "The Speech" for this trip. He will perfect it as he goes along; and it will reach final polished form in Anderson. ("It takes me four days to get warmed up," he says.)

Two aspects of "The Speech" are noteworthy from my perspective. First, the tone and his message are upbeat, conveying, again, his congenital optimism. Despite a continuing recession and 13 percent unemployment in Indiana, his emphasis throughout is on "the positive trend lines," "the bright signs," and "a different picture than has been given by the critics and the columnists." "We are laying the foundation for an economic upturn and recovery," he says. And he sums up with comments like, "I'm far more optimistic than the average person; the future is far brighter than the doomsayers predict; next year will be better than last year." "The Speech" reveals the same upbeat conservative presentation I have observed since 1980.

The second noteworthy aspect of "The Speech" lies in what it does not convey. It does not convey anything about Dan Quayle's job training bill. It contains no hint that, as a senator, he has been doing something to alleviate the economic situation he describes. In short, "The Speech" contains no credit claiming. Yet it is the one presentation he has planned for and thought about. The total absence of S 2036 from his prepared remarks tends to confirm what I have felt all along in Washington—that the young senator has not yet, for whatever reason, recognized the political capital that might be made out of his governing accomplishment. The other possibility, of course, is that he recognizes its potential but is deliberately husbanding it, in keeping with his cyclical view of campaigning, until such time as he needs it. At this stage, I incline toward the former view. In either case, however, the fact is that he has not yet integrated his Washington performance with his presentation of self at home. Every indication is, therefore, that the development of S 2036 as a campaign asset—if such there will be—is in its earliest stages.

The senator is, of course, not oblivious to what he has done. And, when prodded, he will respond. In the question-and-answer period after his Fort Wayne speech, the sixth question (out of nine) asks for his opinion of the president's "new federalism" ideas. He answers,

> The best example of new federalism is the job training legislation I am pushing. It combines a number of categorical programs into one program. It gives more power to the governor and to business and industry. . . . That, to me, is what new federalism is all about. . . . We are taking power from the Department of Labor and giving it to the states and private industry. If it passes in its Senate version, it will be at least a model of what other new federalism programs should look like. It is the only program I think we will get in this Congress.

It is an easy, natural way to discuss job training and to indicate that he had some part in it. It is an unobtrusive way to associate his work with the beneficial trends and the future improvements he has been discussing.

After "The Speech" is given to a luncheon group in Lafayette the next day, the Q-and-A period produces no mention at all of S 2036. But later, after a tour of the local Caterpillar Tractor plant, at a press conference to endorse a Republican candidate for the Indiana state Senate, Quayle's job training bill becomes a major part of the dialogue. It is not Quayle, however, but the local candidate who initiates it. He says, "I am happy to have the author of the jobs bill—which passed 95-0—here with me." And he proceeds to stress the need for jobs and the importance of training. Quayle responds, "He put his finger on the problem—jobs, training, growth." He says that the job training legislation is important to Lafayette and to Indiana as they diversify their industry. "Job training will provide a talent pool to match the engines Caterpillar expects to come off the assembly line."

The local candidate chimes in that "the secret of success in job training is local coordination, and as state senator I will be best suited to do that coordination." Quayle agrees.

> The old training program did not work because it spent too much on income maintenance. The new program will train for jobs, along the line of the new federalism. Decisions will not be made in the Labor Department but in Lafayette, Indiana. The businessmen in Lafayette know where the new jobs will come from. Do you think some bureaucrat in Washington knows where new jobs will come from? No. Your state senator, your local businessmen know where the new jobs will come from.

Reporters for five newspapers and one TV station hear the exchange. The appeal of job training legislation is not just that it addresses an urgent national problem or that it involves a new and better intergovernmental relationship, but that it has a direct local application. The local candidate senses that, picks up on it, and piggybacks on the Washington work of his United States senator.

Later that day, following another plant tour, a sixth reporter catches up with Quayle for an interview that focuses on the difference between his minority status as a House member and his majority status in the Senate. "In the Senate the majority has control of the gavel," he says.

> We're able to establish policy, we're able to initiate legislation and see it get through. For example, just on my Subcommittee on Employment and Productivity, the jobs training legislation which hopefully will be signed by the president, probably is the most important piece of domestic legislation that this Congress will adopt. While I was running I did not expect or anticipate that I would be chairman of that committee. With the turnover, I was able . . . to get that position and all of a sudden I am in a situation where we'll have a real impact on what will happen in Indiana in job training, and in the nation as a whole.

A direct question about life inside the Senate has triggered the most personal comment he has made about his connection to job training legislation. He comes close, here, to claiming a leadership role in the Senate passage of S 2036. It is a degree of credit claiming that he does not indulge in any public setting on the trip.

In his remarks at a fund-raiser for three state legislative candidates in Kokomo, he brings up the subject himself, unaided, as an example of "the positive signs and positive declining trends in the country" that he wishes to emphasize. Kokomo is a town hit hard by the problems in the auto industry. But, "We've had bloody noses and come back before," Quayle tells the audience, "and we'll do it again." "We [Republicans] have cut $2 billion from training under the previous administration," he says, "and we've given authority not to some bureaucrat in Washington but to the people of Howard County. We are taking the lead in talking about jobs and opportunity. Let's not kid ourselves. There will have to be new industry.... We can take the leadership on that issue." Job training fits easily into the optimistic message of the trip. In the press conference afterward, he discusses the section of S 2036 dealing with dislocated workers, and he urges people in troubled industries to seek training under its provisions. "The bill's in conference. It passed the Senate 95-0 and ... will go on to be signed by the president," he adds. He does not mention his own connection with it.

In the Q-and-A period after his speech to the Kokomo Jaycees that evening, he gets a direct question on S 2036. He does mention his connection. "I'm a supporter of yours," says the questioner, "but is the benefit of the jobs bill worth the cost?" "It will be beneficial in the short run and in the long run," Quayle says.

> And it is consistent with my philosophy. When I took control of the subcommittee, we were spending $5 billion. In the first year, we cut $2 billion. Now we have instituted a program that will give power to the local business leaders right here in Howard County. We've got to have new jobs. Lots of people are not going back to their old jobs. They don't want to sit there on food stamps and welfare. We've made a serious reduction in the amount of money spent. In its heyday CETA spent $11 billion. The new program spends $3.8 billion and it will far outstrip CETA. It was a failure and we don't want a failure. If you go through it, you will find the new program is a good program at the least cost to government.

The major emphasis here is one of frugality—cost-effectiveness. And, again, the Kokomo emphasis is less on the large number of untrained poor people the bill is intended to train than on the retraining of the smaller number of workers jobless because of industrial change.

The next day's activities begin with a talk show appearance in Indianapolis. The second caller, describing herself as "an instructor in a CETA-funded project," asks, "I'd like to know the status of the Quayle-Kennedy training bill." She gives the senator a legitimate chance to talk knowledgeably and intimately about the Washington legislative scene. "The Quayle-Kennedy training bill has passed the Senate unanimously," he begins. But the host interrupts. "For people who might not know, senator, what is it?" Quayle describes the legislation as a "replacement for CETA" that "gives the power back to the local level where it belongs" and enjoys "strong bipartisan support."

It is currently in the conference committee. We had our first meeting; we'll have our second meeting on September 8. I am convinced that by the end of the month we will put it on the president's desk and I am optimistic that he will sign it. . . . I think it'll probably be the most significant piece of domestic legislation to be passed by the Congress.

The listener asks for a more detailed description of who will control the money locally, and what difference it would make in Indianapolis. He answers that the existing Indianapolis program has done "an outstanding job," is "a model" for others, and that "I do not envision any change in the relationships here in Indianapolis." This particular opportunity is the only one during the visit that—with its "Quayle-Kennedy" description—sounds suspiciously like a friendly "plant." Quayle takes advantage of it to give a knowledgeable commentary on an important bill and on its local ramifications. Again, he tailors the reply to the audience. For the only time during the trip—with a large undifferentiated listening audience—he mentions bipartisanship.

Across town at a breakfast fund-raiser for a Republican congressional challenger, the political appeal of S 2036 is in evidence again. "The number-one issue is jobs," says the candidate. And he adds, "I've come out in favor of some of the bills Dan Quayle has sponsored in Washington. One of the most important is the job training bill." When he introduces Quayle he calls him "a leader in Congress" and says "his legislative leadership has been phenomenal." "I can't remember a bill," he continues, "unless it meant nothing to anybody, that passed the Senate 95-0. [It was] remarkable to get administration cooperation, and Democratic cooperation, to get a bill through that was sponsored with Senator Kennedy."

During his brief remarks, Quayle expounds on the virtues of his legislation in terms of Republican philosophy and his own upbeat brand of conservatism. "We are the ones who are talking about jobs and job training," he tells the contributors.

We are the ones who are out there doing things, not just criticizing. I get a little bit distressed sometimes when I hear so much that is negative. There are a lot of positive signs. We are training people for jobs, giving them new skills. We aren't just sitting on the sidelines. There's an old saying, "Don't give people fish. Teach them how to fish." That's what we are doing.

It is the second time in two days that a political candidate has found Dan Quayle's legislative record appealing enough to want to ride his coattails. Republican party people, it seems, are in the vanguard in learning about and applauding their junior senator's legislative work in Washington.

In his Indianapolis office that afternoon, the senator meets with two groups, both of them for the first time. The first is his "Productivity Advisory Group," which he has set up to help him think about the second charge of his Subcommittee on Employment and Productivity. It is "happenstance," he tells them, that he chairs this subcommittee. Seven bankers, business people, lawyers, and professors engage in a freewheeling, wide-ranging discussion of matters relating to productivity—especially the proper role of government and, most particularly, the incentives and disincentives, stability and instability of the tax system. At one point, someone mentions that high taxes are forcing companies to cut back on their "human resources budget because you can tolerate it in the short run." And that includes training. Briefly they discuss some alternatives—let government do it or give a tax incentive for training. Quayle jumps in to mention his bill and its goal of training people that private industry will not touch. But it is a small eddy in the flow of the conversation. Quayle's other current legislative interest is his tax simplification program; and that is the subject matter of the day. Nonetheless, job training is present in this conversation with a group of seven widely influential business-oriented people in Indiana.

Quayle's second meeting stands in the sharpest contrast to the first one. Thirteen leaders of Indianapolis's black community have come to talk about their problems. They are about as far from Dan Quayle culturally as a group could be; they are strongly predisposed to oppose Quayle politically; they are not an advisory group to him. But the matter of job training is of central importance to them. And, to a degree not met by any other group that he will talk to during this visit, they have an idea of what he has been doing in this area.

He had talked with some of them by telephone when he supported the voting rights bill. He begins with that entree. "We're here," he says, "to continue the dialogue we began with the voting rights bill." And he tells them that "There ain't going to be anyone who agrees with you more on civil rights than I do." Twice he says this. His use of "ain't," my notes say, "was studied, strange, and revealed a certain uncomfortableness. But he plunged ahead ... with expressions of openness and dialogue." "Whatever your views were before the election," he tells them, "I want you to know that I want to help. I wasn't in there before. I'm a new senator; and I want you to know that I believe in representative democracy." He says that he wants to "put everything up front" and "put my cards on the table." "Dan Quayle is accessible. My door is always open." But also he tells them that "I have been disappointed and disillusioned by the lack of input from the black community." A priori, the group was not the most likely one with whom to have a constructive dialogue. But, surprisingly, Quayle's job training bill makes one possible.

The first man to speak, a minister, asks what the role of community-based organizations will be in the job training program in the light of business domination of the PICs in S 2036. Quayle assures him that the participation of such organizations has been written into the bill. Then the minister asks how much flexibility there is in the idea of "supportive services." Quayle recounts the battle over that provision and says there is flexibility in the bill. He adds further assurance. "I'm telling you in private, but I won't say it publicly, that the Senate is going to give away a lot of the inflexibility over allowances in our bill when we get to conference." He states his firm opposition, however, to wages. The minister talks about the need for payments to "kids who need a break." And he ends on a cautiously complimentary note. "Understand," he says, "I'm not criticizing you for what you did. I'm praising you for what you have done. I know you had trouble with the administration. I know you didn't have to do what you did. You're the only one we've got."

The next speaker, from the Urban League, says that while he too has praise for what Quayle has done he is worried that people will think S 2036 is the panacea for all unemployment problems. He asks Quayle if he doesn't think job training is being oversold as "the answer" when, in reality, it is "a drop in the bucket." Quayle replies that unemployment is "unacceptable." He continues,

> I don't think this bill will solve all our problems. I just say, it will help. A lot of training is being done by private enter-prise—$2 billion a year. But there are folk that private industry just will not touch, whose skills are not close enough so that industry feels it is worth their while to train. Those are the folk we are aiming our bill at—people who need help but can't get it anywhere else. And the new category of dislocated worker.

It is a different emphasis—and a different audience—than Kokomo. The Urban League leader seems satisfied.

The subject of job training has opened up the meeting on grounds most favorable to Quayle. And the conversation moves to other subjects. Several members describe the difficulty minority businesses have had in getting their fair share of government business, even that to which they are guaranteed. Quayle expresses surprise and says he will mention it to the governor the next morning. A second minister warms to the exchange. "Our problem is that there is nobody on our side," he says.

> We need somebody who will cry foul. You're all we've got. As you grow in the job, you will learn other things. For you to just say out loud that you are surprised at what you have heard would be a great help to us. Of course, that would put you out on front street.

He knows Dan Quayle is not about to get out "on front street." But he is encouraged. When the meeting breaks up, he says to a colleague, "He may not do all the right things. But he'll listen."

They talk about high-level government jobs. A fourth man says, "You said you were disillusioned with the lack of input. I understand what you are saying. But let's look at it both ways. We are on the outside. You are on the inside. You can tell us when appointments are coming up that we might be interested in." Quayle indicates that he could do that. Other subjects are touched upon. Finally, the Urban League leader asks Quayle if he would be willing to set up an advisory group of black leaders. Quayle enthusiastically agrees. "Let's go at it," he says, and shakes hands around the table as the meeting breaks up. It seems to have been a good meeting, a step forward in relating to the most distant of his constituents. And without his work on S 2036, it would not have been possible.

Or so it seemed to me. Afterward, I asked the Quayle staffer who set up the meeting, an assistant state director and a black man, how he thought the meeting had gone. He pronounced it "a big success." "The purpose was to open up a dialogue," he said.

> It was extremely important to the black leaders that here was a man who had really done something. It gave him credibility with them. They knew he didn't have to do what he did on job training. They were aware that he was opposed by the administration. So they knew he was not just a guy saying what he would do. They knew of his support of the voting rights bill. But the jobs bill was extremely important, almost essential to the success of the meeting. And it was a big success. That last sentence was the evidence—the suggestion of a minority advisory committee. Two years ago, there was no way those men would ever have thought of such a thing. They didn't think Dan Quayle could be of any help to them, or listen to them, or relate to them. Now they know he will listen. They know he won't do a lot of things they want. But they know he has worked hard to do something that helps them.

There were no illusions on either side. They had begun to talk across a wide gulf; Quayle's civil rights vote plus his job training bill had provided the essential bridge.

The next morning, Quayle is introduced at the Anderson Chamber of Commerce with the comment that "He has recently authored a job training bill and introduced a flat tax bill." The meeting runs until the last minute, however, before the job training bill is mentioned. The very last questioner asks him what can be done for skilled workers, such as machinists and tool and die makers who are among the unemployed. "That's one of the ingredients of the job training bill I have moving through the Congress," he answers. "It is in the conference committee right now and hopefully will be signed by the president in September. It will provide training for young people and for people in the labor surplus (like tool and die makers and machinists) for new jobs coming in the future." Afterward a radio reporter picks up on the last question and inquires about the status of the job training bill. "I can see the end of the tunnel," he says. And, for the first and only time on the trip, he calls it "the Quayle job training bill." That is what his press releases have called it.[6] It is an outright claim for credit that, apparently, does not yet come naturally to him.

From Anderson, he travels to Muncie to endorse another congressional candidate—who also associates himself with Quayle's governing achievement. "I've watched his career as a senator . . . and some of the things Senator Quayle has been able to accomplish," says the candidate by way of introduction. "His job training bill is particularly important in the time we are in, and it certainly demonstrated the Senate's approval of that. . . . The vote was 95-0." He notes that he and Quayle had met a retrained worker in these plant tours earlier that day. "A retraining program is what we need," he says. "It's a positive step and not just a handout for someone to buy votes." [7]

Again, the 95-0 vote seems to have impressed a candidate. And another group of Republican stalwarts has learned, perhaps, to associate their junior senator with a specific legislative accomplishment. The last day, speaking to the executives of the Pfizer Corporation, the same message reaches a group in the far northwest corner of the state. The facility where he speaks is new, and so he leads off by recognizing Pfizer's good fortune at creating new jobs in contrast to old facilities where jobs are declining. And this provides a quick, easy transition to a couple of comments about his work in Washington. "One of the pieces of legislation I've been associated with," he says, "is training for jobs in a society that is in transition. People are losing jobs that they aren't going to be able to go back to." It's a problem, he continues, "that I've worked very hard on—reorienting and redirecting labor. . . . Jobs are what we are all trying to develop." And then to other subjects. It is more testimony to the ease with which job training fits into a great range of policy discussions without dominating them.

On his next to last day, the senator has dinner at a lakeside retreat with his Executive Committee, eight friends who advised him during his 1980 campaign and with whom he meets every few months to discuss his current political situation. They are the innermost core of his political support. They are the people—along with his wife—whose only interest is the nurturing and the promotion of his career. They are mostly people he met when he worked in the governor's office or in law school. They are all from Indianapolis. "The state is run from Indianapolis," he says. None of them advised him when he was a House member. "It's strictly through friendship that the group was formed," the senator explains.

> I had an advisory group when I was in the House, but it was completely different. . . . We had to have someone from each of the party factions. Each member represented a distinct group and would report back to that group. You had to do that because . . . everybody knew everybody. You couldn't keep any one group out. I didn't know any one of them when we began. It was a smaller group—four people. They kept me in touch with the party factions. But they were not my friends. In a Senate campaign, nobody knows or cares who is on the advisory committee. You can do it strictly by friendship.

The Executive Committee is joined by four principal members of the Washington staff—the administrative assistant, the chief legislative assistant, the press secretary, and the top constituency liaison person. They represent the Washington end of the political axis; and they, too, are strongly devoted (currently at least) to the promotion of Dan Quayle's career in public life. They are, however, mostly silent partners during the meeting.

Everyone at this gathering knows something about Quayle's job training success. But no more than in any other of his appearances this week does it dominate the proceedings. Still, it seems to me to be the unstated premise on which the discussion rests. The senator poses the central question: "What do I do in 1983?" He tells the group that he has spent two years learning the business, concentrating on the legislative job, gaining the respect of his peers, getting a Washington reputation. But he wonders what he ought to do in what he calls "my last uncluttered year," before he has to start running for reelection. They agree with his premise that 1983 will not be a campaign year. They talk about raising between $100,000 and $250,000 in seed money during 1983. Their plan is to have their organization in place by the time the 1984 elections are over and to begin campaigning in earnest at that time. They urge Dan to be "more visible at home" in 1983. But they agree when one of them tells Quayle, as a consensus opinion, that "1983 should be another year in which you concentrate on your reputation in Washington—a Washington reputation year."

The discussion makes it amply clear that his friends are pleased with the reputation he has gained for himself. "In the beginning, remember," says one, we worried a lot about whether you had the qualifications to be a senator. Were you too young to be a senator? Would people take you seriously as a senator? Could you gain the respect of your peers in Washington? Were you smart enough to be a senator? All that is behind us now. We know you have the qualities to be a good United States senator. That's been proven. It's the foundation on which we will build for the next four years.

The comment is one more measure—from the uncertainty to the confidence of his closest political friends—of how much the lightly regarded House member has grown into a bona fide senator in two years.

At one point, Quayle indicates his assessment of S 2036 in summing up the record of the Ninety-seventh Congress. "We've passed the two budgets, the two tax bills, and the voting rights bill. Add the job training bill and that's just about it for this Congress." And there is little doubt that the passage of S 2036 underlies their confidence in him. Still, however, only one explicit exchange on job training occurs during the meeting. During the discussion of visibility, one member picks up on what he heard at the breakfast fund-raiser in Indianapolis the day before. "When [a congressional candidate] stands up and says he can't remember when anyone got a bill like this through 95-0, that's the kind of publicity we want. I never dreamed you could get that kind of mileage out of CETA, or 'Son of CETA.' We should milk it for as long as we can and in every way we can."

Quayle says that he made a mistake in not playing up each stage of the bill and admits that he is not adept at getting publicity. One of his Washington staffers interjects that "There isn't much news in 7-0, 9-0, 95-0." But Quayle persists. "We had a hell of a fight to get that passed. But we didn't do as good a job as we could in publicizing it. We just said, 'The bill passed the committee.' " [8] For a moment, members of the committee join in suggesting ways to capitalize on his accomplishment, such as presenting the governor with the first training check or visiting training facilities. "Don't hide your light under a bushel," admonishes one member in conclusion.

That is all the direct discussion there is of S 2036. Still, it is the one specific issue they discuss in terms of marketing. Shortly thereafter they turn more generally to the problem of marketing—the problem most central to their concern. "We've talked about the pipeline from Washington to Indiana," one group member begins,

but we haven't talked about what we are going to send through the pipeline. Who is Dan Quayle? What are we going to market? Bowen is the country doctor. Lugar is the intellectual.

What is Dan Quayle? What is the theme that we will use to package the candidate? We ought to think about that so all of us can start pushing that theme—in legislation, in press releases, in warding off the opposition.

Quayle's Washington staff has prepared, for the meeting, a "Report of Legislative Activities, Ninety-seventh Congress." And they, too, have posed the very same question for the group. "The staff needs," they say on page one of their memo,

> a fairly precise definition of the personal identity desired for the Senator and the themes to be developed for the remainder of the first term. This includes a determination of the issues to be emphasized, preferred committee assignments, and the "personal style" to be employed in pursuing these objectives.

These two sets of questions frame the discussion that follows.

It is a rambling and totally inconclusive discussion. Poll results showing a drop in name identification lead to a discussion of newsletters and other mailings. There is more urging that Quayle become more "visible" at home. There are discussions on possible committee changes (to Finance), on possible opponents (House members Lee Hamilton and Phil Sharp), on staff arrangements in Indiana (relations on the joint Quayle-Lugar staff), on voting groups to target (farmers), and on various of Quayle's issue positions to date (price supports, taxes, Israel). The desultory issue discussions make it clear that the concern of this group is not with issues per se but with the marketing of issues. Their input is entirely on the way each issue is playing in Indiana. They are not searching for a winning issue. And it occurs to me that if they did not have S 2036, they might be. Referring to the seven-page issue review brought by the Washington staff, one member jokes, "Can I put it in my car and read it later?" And another says, "That's your business. If we can help, let us know."

Drawing inferences from some poll results, suggestions come from around the room that Quayle could be identified as "activist" or "populist" or "a fighter." None produces a whiff of agreement. The marketing discussion comes full circle when Quayle returns to the original question and the group chimes in with a series of humorous responses. (See Chapter 1, pp. 4-5.) That is where it ends.

It is interesting to me that no one suggests "leader" or "effective senator" or anything that plays off his legislative accomplishment. It seems that, despite their satisfaction with Quayle's Washington reputation and their confidence in his senatorial stature, his Executive Committee members do not yet fully understand the political potential of his job training achievement. They—except perhaps the one who had been at the breakfast—do not yet recognize what I have observed during my visit in terms of the widespread appeal of S 2036. But, then, neither has the candidate himself. Or, if he has, he remains markedly backward about exploiting it. Until Quayle, his advisers, and his Washington staff move more aggressively to associate the senator, at home, with his Senate accomplishments in Washington, Dan Quayle's political persona will remain incomplete and his electoral potential unrealized.

During my four-day visit to Indiana, I had found talk about Dan Quayle's governing achievement to be omnipresent in his home setting. Sometimes he broached the subject; sometimes others did. They were not dominating but his comments had a broad and versatile reach. And they had a positive thrust. They allowed him to explain his Washington activity to every element of his constituency—geographic, reelection, primary, and personal. The subject matter of S 2036—jobs, training, employment—had even gained him entree to one of the most distant elements of his geographic constituency, leaders of the black community. The local government-cum-business philosophy behind S 2036 allowed him to use it as an example of a less-government brand of conservatism that appealed to the civic and business groups that made up a large part of his reelection constituency. Senate passage of S 2036 by 95-0 was appealing to a group with a special interest in problem-solving leadership: Republican candidates and their partisans—a group that made up the bulk of his primary constituency. And, for members of his Executive Committee—his personal constituency—his success with S 2036 underlay a wholly new level of confidence in the senatorial capacity of the young man they would work to reelect.

Altogether, Dan Quayle and S 2036 combined to display impressive political potential. And, clearly, it was only beginning to be tapped and only beginning to reverberate. It was still only a presence not a theme. But the gradual, even inadvertent, conversion of a Washington governing accomplishment into an Indiana campaign success was under way.

While the young senator is not yet prepared to present himself to any of his constituents as an effective legislator, he does come across on this visit—as he had in 1980—as an effective campaigner. He is not yet a particularly articulate or persuasive or, altogether, powerful speaker—though he is a knowledgeable one. But in face-to-face encounters he is bright-eyed, attentive, and informed. He uses exaggerated body language effectively to convey both his feelings and his unbuttoned approach to others—staggering under the burden of a flowery introduction, slumping at the thought of a vexing problem, waving both arms in oratorical flight, lighting up his face at a turn in the conversation, putting his fingers to his head when in thought, holding hands and slapping backs as he meets people.

"You saw him at his best yesterday," said a staffer on September 1. "He loves to jump from group to group, take off his coat, roll up his sleeves, shake hands, and talk to people." He is always in motion. And he is—as in Washington—characteristically impatient. "Just get me there," he says when his driver worries about directions. "Don't show me a gap in the schedule," he tells his staffers, "or I'll fill it. When you guys get me out here on the campaign trail, I'm like a thoroughbred ready to run." As a stylistic matter, he conveys youthful enthusiasm, curiosity, and vigor. It is a comfortable match with the optimistic upbeat outlook he brings to his discussions of policy.

Obviously the Indiana senator enjoys campaigning. His staffers, however, fret constantly about the low payoff from his campaign-like pace and style. Their worries provide a running counterpoint to whatever he does on the trip. As always, they say, he had intervened to fight the schedule. Several of them call him "temperamental" about it. "He wants to go 100 percent all the time," says one. "If he isn't, he thinks he's not being productive. Then, when we do go 100 percent, he says, 'Stop and give me a break.' I'm resigned to the fact that he's a habitual complainer. . . . But he's the chairman of the board. He has at least 51 percent of the control over what he does here." "The one recommendation coming out of the last [Executive Committee] meeting," says another,

> was that Dan get out of his campaigning style on his home visits and that he go instead for quality events that promise a big payoff. There was a consensus among everybody that this was his number-one problem. So we worked out two schedules [for this trip] that followed that pattern. But then he began changing them and filling in all these little things that crowd up the schedule and don't do us any good. It's gone down hill ever since.

"This is a typical Dan Quayle schedule," says a third staffer. "It is packed. But he doesn't do enough that is substantive or constructive." It is not clear, however, what it is that they wanted him to do. "We don't think he has to go to every little knot-hole in Indiana and shake hands," says one. "We think he should do things that are more constructive, that he should be more interested in quality than quantity. He has done a lot of constructive things in Washington that he could talk about." If this concerned staffer has S 2036 in mind, he does not say so. Nor does any other member of the half-dozen staffers I meet and travel with. Not one.

The tension I observe between senator and staff flows ultimately from a difference in perspective between the person who must perform and be judged in public and people who do not. To the candidate, a moment not spent campaigning or a trip home without a lot of one-on-one campaigning is time wasted. During this trip, I also observe tension between the senator and his advisers. One manifestation is his desire for usable advice and their tendency to be discursive. At the end of his meeting with his Productivity Advisory Group, he says to them, "I'll be rewriting the tax bill, and before we do we want your comments—and, again, specific suggestions." On the way out when asked how he thought it went, he says, "Fine, but we've got to get them to be more specific." Similarly, on the way home from the Executive Committee meeting he expresses reservations. "The one message I got was, 'Come home more.' That's all they ever tell me, every time we meet." Given their perspective, however, this is the advice one would expect to hear.

If a broader perspective on Quayle's job is to be found, it is most likely to come from the senator himself. It is he who is on the firing line. At several points in the Executive Committee meeting this difference in perspective becomes visible. Commenting on his endorsement of Republican candidates during the visit, one member calls it "hand holding"; but Quayle demurs and calls it "a time to see the party faithful . . . a beneficial time." In the discussion on targeting the farmers, one member calls them "a tiny minority"; but Quayle interrupts to say, "Yes, but a lot of people are sensitive to agriculture." And on the issues. When a couple of members express skepticism about his amendment to decrease price supports on sugar, he tells them, "We've gone too far now to think of turning back. If I'm the only one standing on the floor, I'll be there by myself for two days fighting for the amendment."

When several of them voice their disapproval of his vote for a tax increase with its interest-withholding provisions, he tells them that "I took the high road on the tax bill." He explains that "If I had wanted to please my constituency I would have voted against it" and that "the withholding provision was hard for me to swallow." "But," he says, "everybody had some part of it he didn't like. You had to vote for the package. It was a good bill." Finally, when several of them criticize Israel for its bombing of Lebanon, he says, "I have not changed my position of absolute support for Israel one iota. My support is ironclad." In all these cases, Quayle's view of the matter is conclusive. In all cases, it is the view of the person who must decide and act—and accept responsibility.

The answer to the question I had posed at the end of my 1980 trip to Indiana—"Will he grow?"—seems clear, now, at the end of my second trip. Yes he has. And he has brought evidence of that growth with him to the Executive Committee meeting. For his perspective in that meeting has greater breadth and reflects a greater richness of experience than that of his closest advisers. His Washington activity, and their acceptance of it, leaves no doubt who is in charge of the Quayle enterprise. It is not possible to measure the impact of his S 2036 experience on his growth. Doubtless the change has been gradual. But the heart of his experience has been legislative in nature and S 2036 has been, without competition, his most thoroughgoing legislative experience.

In his interview with the reporter in Lafayette, he articulates the effect of his Senate legislative experience on his view of his job. It is, perhaps, the best subjective measure of his growth. He is asked about the change from House member to senator. "Has your outlook changed?" "From being in the minority in the House of Representatives to majority in the United States Senate is quite a transition," Quayle begins.

> When you are in the minority you can be much more pure, with your philosophical and ideological viewpoints. In other words, you can always be on the attack, can always criticize, and you can say, "Any slight deviation from these principles is not going to get my support." When you're in the majority you have to govern. And when you have to govern, you've got to be far more responsible. You don't deviate from basic tenets, basic principles that are near and dear to you; but as those principles advance in the legislative process, there is going to be compromise.
>
> Furthermore, you've got to take into consideration a lot more people rather than just the narrow base that you originally started with when you were in the minority. You're no longer the minority. You're no longer the opposition. You're the people of responsibility. And with that goes a far greater challenge, a far greater degree of complexity in dealing with these issues. It's something that one relishes and enjoys, but it is quite a change. It's very easy to be on the critical side and say, "Well, here's what you ought to do," and maybe go down a narrow path and be very narrow in your ideology—particularly in a campaign as you are going against somebody.
>
> But as you're in there and responsible for what goes on, you've got to be in a position to take those principles and mold them into a policy that's going to be conducive to getting things done. I mean you're not going to get things done if you're a simple ideologue.... What you do is take goals, but what you have to look for are results. You've got to be able to achieve those goals. The only way you're going to do that is through interaction with your fellow colleagues or president or the constituency you represent. That is ... the biggest change as far as I am concerned between the House and the Senate.

It is hard to believe that his frame of reference for this answer is anything but S 2036. His comment is a distillation of his approach to that bill and the lessons learned in guiding it through. But whether or not that is the case, the view he expresses comes from a maturing legislator.

Expressions of responsibility and complexity and institutional self-consciousness have replaced the irresponsible, simplistic, Congress-baiting posture of his days in the House. He may still be something of a kid. He has also become something of a political leader. And that change can be seen—by someone who is looking for it—in Indiana as well as in Washington.

AN INTERIM: SEPTEMBER 1982-OCTOBER 1985

I did not return to Indiana until the fall of 1985, when Quayle's reelection effort was under way. My sole purpose, on that and subsequent visits, was to examine the campaign usage of S 2036—now officially the Job Training Partnership Act. I had no first-hand knowledge of what had happened during the three intervening years. The senator had, predictably, moved on to other issues—principally Senate reform, as chairman of the Temporary Select Committee to Study the Senate Committee System, and military procurement, as chairman of an Armed Services Committee Task Force on Selected Defense Procurement Matters. Each of these assignments, incidentally, could be read as a vote of confidence by leaders inside the Senate.

There were other complimentary signs, too. A veteran *New York Times* reporter wrote in late 1984 that "Quayle has emerged as a leader among the 16 Republicans elected in 1980." [9] And in mid-1985 Washington's influential *Congressional Quarterly Weekly Report* wrote that Quayle "has built a reputation as a pragmatic, thoughtful senator with an interest in finding ways to make the Senate work more efficiently." [10]

I did not know, however, whether he planned to capitalize heavily on the passage of JTPA. I had never heard him talk about doing so. But I also knew he had self-consciously refrained from getting into a campaigning posture till the last two years of his term. Assuming—as I did—that he would sooner or later exploit JTPA in his campaign, two conditions would probably have to be met. First, he would have to continue, somehow, to reap favorable publicity from his association with JTPA and the jobs issue in general. He could not, in other words, let his work drop from sight. Second, JTPA would have to work. Or, at least, it had to avoid becoming a disaster. As far as I could tell, looking back from the vantage point of October 1985, both conditions had been met in the interim.

For one thing, Quayle had kept his hand in the subject matter from the very moment JTPA passed and congressional attention turned, amid rising unemployment, to a jobs creation bill. First, he helped the Republicans ward off a late 1983 Democratic public employment bill.

Then he held hearings in his own subcommittee on the advisability of a job creation bill. Shortly thereafter, he proposed his own $2 billion public service employment bill; and, later, he joined a similar bipartisan effort that passed in early 1984.[11] This continuation of his JTPA interests earned him his first bit of national media attention since his January 1981 profile, "The Charmed Life of Indiana's Golden Boy."[12] This time a *New York Times* profile by a top congressional reporter was headlined, "A Conservative Shows His Liberal Bent: Indiana's Quayle Seeks More Money for Jobs, Less for Defense." Quayle, wrote the author, "has taken the lead in championing the cause of the structurally unemployed— those who have been eliminated from the job market by a lack of training or education."[13] The difference in the two treatments by the media was another measure of his growth as a legislator—one that matched the view from my own vantage point.

Nevertheless, the behavior of the Quayle enterprise in late 1983 indicated strongly that they had as yet no plan for capitalizing on his association with JTPA. October 1, 1983, marked the official beginning of the new program. President Reagan devoted his weekly radio message on that day to praise of JTPA as "an historic and bold program."[14] Five days later the president went down to the Labor Department "to celebrate the start of the government's new job training program." There, he showered more praise on the program.[15]

From the Quayle office, however, came not a word to signal the start of the program, no effort to associate Dan Quayle with the milestone he, more than any other person, had created. The contrast is striking—celebratory public embraces by the people who had dragged their feet most of the way and silence from the program's architect and shepherd. At a time when the senator is saying privately that "I never got one iota of support from the Labor Department," the secretary of labor is taking bows for the achievement. Later, a Quayle staffer called it "a missed opportunity" to garner favorable publicity. And he said further, "I don't think the Quayle people understood what they had—an unusual accomplishment from one of the sixteen Republican freshmen." In retrospect, it seems as though Quayle and his staff were no more aggressive about credit claiming in the fall of 1983 than they had been in the fall of 1982.

Or, not much more. The middle of November did bring the first outward sign of special attention by the enterprise to JTPA. An entire newsletter, widely distributed in Indiana, was devoted to "JTPA: Teaching Job Skills for a Lifetime."[16] Mostly a description of the program, it predicted that 26,000 unemployed Hoosiers would participate in the first three months. Its closing paragraph said that "As the principal Senate sponsor of JTPA . . . I will be closely monitoring . . . this new job training program which President Reagan has called 'bold and historic.' " Not only did Quayle promote himself in the newsletter, he demoted Edward Kennedy. He spoke of JTPA as something "I sponsored with Senators Kennedy, Hatch, Hawkins, and Pell." Both phrasings reflect a definite sensitivity to electoral concerns.

Shortly thereafter an even greater sensitivity emerged. On a November orientation trip to Indiana, Quayle's new press secretary paid a courtesy visit to his counterpart in the governor's office. He recalled,

> When I introduced myself, he said, "I know. You work for Senator Quayle of the Kennedy-Quayle bill." I got the message. He was telling me that what was getting through back home was Kennedy, not Quayle. So I set out to cut Kennedy from every mention of JTPA. You will not see the word "Kennedy" in anything that came out of that office after that day. In our releases, we always call Dan "the principal Senate sponsor of JTPA."

So far as I can tell, he succeeded. The spirit was even caught by the subcommittee staff, whose official "Primer on JTPA," published on October 1, 1985, says the act was "introduced" by Quayle and "originally cosponsored by U.S. Senators . . . Hatch, Hawkins, Kennedy and Pell." [17] The Massachusetts senator's demotion, ostracism, and overall publicity fadeout—as administered by the Quayle camp—was among the early indications that a serious electoral effort to capitalize on JTPA was in the offing.

Beginning in 1984, the Quayle office stepped up its attention to JTPA. The new press secretary took it as his mission "to see Dan Quayle through the next election." He was determined, he said, "to make sure that everything that could be related to Quayle and JTPA was related" and "to capitalize on every opportunity to remind people" of the relationship. One of his early changes was a revision of the senator's widely distributed biographical sheet. He took Quayle's JTPA achievement out of the eighth paragraph where it had been languishing and moved it into the first sentence of the first paragraph. The biography itself was enlarged from twelve paragraphs to thirty-six paragraphs, with most of the added material devoted to Quayle's legislative activity.

Another sign of the press secretary's effort was a regular stream of press releases touting the benefits of JTPA for the state of Indiana and for elements of that constituency. For example, April 2, 1984, "Quayle: Indiana Receiving 'Full Share of Federal Funds' Under JTPA for Training of Dislocated Workers." In this release Quayle says that Indiana received more than a proportionate share of these monies "under the distribution formula I wrote into Title III of the Act." Or, May 7, 1984, "Quayle Explains How JTPA Is Designed to Serve Women's Needs."

Here Quayle, "principal Senate author of JTPA," speaks to a women's workshop in Indianapolis. Or, June 20, 1984, "$718,462 In Discretionary JTPA Funds Awarded for Retraining Laid-Off GE Workers in Fort Wayne." Or, July 6, 1984, "JTPA Begins First Full Year: Goal to Tackle Youth Unemployment." Here, Quayle, "author of JTPA," talks to Indiana Black Expo. Or, August 15, 1984, "Quayle Recommends Summers 2000 As a Model Summer Youth Program Under the Job Training Partnership Act." Here, Quayle speaks in Indianapolis about that city's summer programs. Or, November 1, 1984, "La Porte Awarded $1 Million in Discretionary JTPA Funds for Retraining of Unemployed Auto Related Production Workers, Quayle Announces." With this set of press releases, Quayle has been able to associate himself with the interests of a wide range of groups in the state—women, blacks, dislocated workers, unemployed youth, and residents of certain geographical regions.[18]

His September 1984 newsletter featured a section headed "Indiana Leads the Way Under JTPA." And, in his December 1984 newsletter, Quayle's "Progress Report on JTPA" says: "I sponsored [JTPA].... More than 35,000 Hoosiers participated in JTPA during the first nine months.... For [this] program year our state will receive $92 million.... I'll keep working to make sure our state gets its full fair share of federal JTPA funds." One newspaper analysis of federal funds flowing into Indiana says that "The only kind of grants on which Indiana did better than average was in the job training program. Senator Dan Quayle (R. Ind.) wrote the act setting up the program." [19] The extent to which the Indiana media picked up on this stream of press releases is unknown. Surely, it produced some favorable publicity. In any event, it signalled a new credit-claiming aggressiveness on the part of the Quayle enterprise.

July 1, 1985, was the anniversary of JTPA's first fully funded year. This time, the Quayle people did not miss the opportunity to garner credit-claiming publicity. They decided to hold a series of oversight hearings in Indiana "to determine whether JTPA is meeting Indiana's substantial training and retraining needs." [20] The hearings were timed to coincide with the anniversary and designed to reap widespread notice at home. The staff tested the water with a "discussion forum" and "site visit" in Kokomo in April, and another in Columbus in June.[21]

Quayle then presided over six subcommittee hearings—kickoff hearings on July 1 in Indianapolis and Evansville, followed by hearings in South Bend and Gary on July 2 and in Lafayette and Fort Wayne in August. The kickoff date featured an Indianapolis luncheon speech and an Evansville fund-raiser appearance by the new secretary of labor, Bill Brock.[22] Altogether 221 people, representing all seventeen of Indiana's service-delivery areas, participated in the six hearings and five staff-directed discussion forums.[23] These 1985 oversight hearings were the most home-oriented, and hence the most electorally oriented, of several sets of oversight hearings conducted by the subcommittee chairman during his six-year tenure. In 1986, moreover, he sponsored—as "the result of oversight activities that have taken place since JTPA was enacted"—the "Job Training Partnership Act Amendments of 1986." On October 1, his symbolic attentiveness to JTPA was legitimized by congressional passage of the amendments.[24]

As for the success of JTPA, an objective and/or definitive judgment is difficult to make. And certainly not after one or two years of operation. In a politically realistic sense, therefore, *some* evidence of success is all that would be needed to undergird Quayle's credit claiming at home. Or to put it another way, only a certifiable disaster could dim the luster of legislative accomplishment in time to adversely affect the Quayle campaign in 1985-1986.

There was criticism of the program. But the criticism was directed at the limitations of the program, not to its failure. Thus, Nicholas Lemann's description of JTPA as "a program that is quite small . . . and that is oriented in the job training business to what is called 'creaming,'" and not geared "to dead end kids" or "the multiple problem individual."[25] Or the *New York Times* story headlined, "U.S. Jobs Program Supplanting CETA Aids the More Able."[26] But Lemann called JTPA "the Reagan administration's one new social program."[27] And the *Times* article said that "the program has made a great deal of difference in the lives of those who have been trained."[28] So criticism was typically balanced by an "OK-as-far-as-it-goes" judgment. The *Washington Post* editorialized that JTPA "seems to be performing reasonably well" and "apparently [is] serving a useful function."[29] In short, despite criticism, no disaster occurred. Congress's Office of Technology Assessment concluded in a report on the displaced worker part of the program that "judgments should be made cautiously at this point," and that "it's still too early to assess the program's effectiveness."[30] That was a favorable enough judgment for the senator from Indiana.

There was also sufficient offsetting praise for the program to keep the balance—temporarily at least—clearly on the positive side. There was extravagant praise, ironically, from the administration. In July 1984 Secretary Donovan called JTPA "one of the greatest achievements in the history of government social policy" and claimed it would train a million people in that year.[31] And in his 1985 State of the Union address the president repeated his 1983 praise of JTPA. He said, "We will continue to support the Job Training Partnership Act, which has a nearly two-thirds job placement rate."[32] In Indiana there was more praise than criticism. The governor reported in July 1984 that "The vision of Senator Dan Quayle, who co-authored the legislation, has become a reality.... In Indiana, the program is working."[33] In the Fort Wayne area considerable success was reported, and its Northeast Service Delivery Area won public recognition from the National Alliance of Business as one of fourteen outstanding programs nationally.[34] The Hoosier Falls Area in southeast Indiana won special public praise from the Labor Department.[35] Without a doubt, the program in practice provided a solid enough base for the candidate to run on. And, as his campaign unfolded, the intention of the Quayle enterprise to do so finally became clear.

OBSERVATIONS AND REFLECTIONS: INDIANA, OCTOBER 1985

In October 1985 I went to Indiana for a quick day-and-a-half peek-in at Quayle's reelection activity. There were plenty of signs of a campaign in progress. His statewide organization was in place, and his forty county coordinators had met with his Executive Committee early in December 1984 to get started.[36] Four people were now on a campaign payroll, working out of the state Republican headquarters. Fund raising had been under way since early 1985 and had produced $800,000. One campaign newsletter had been circulated. "The Campaign," however, had not yet begun. Quayle had not formally announced. And, more important, he had no certain opponent. One person was most frequently mentioned, but he had done very little. So there was only half an assumption that this person would be the challenger. (As it turned out, he was not.) Quayle himself was not yet in a campaign mode, setting a more leisurely pace than when I had last seen him in 1982. In his three public appearances, he boosted Republican political achievements in general. He never mentioned any of his own. But, unlike 1982, he now expressed privately a clear appreciation of the importance of JTPA to his reelection prospects. And so did those around him.

The day's centerpiece was the "Kickoff Luncheon" for the state Republican campaign at which Quayle was the speaker. He was introduced by the lieutenant governor of Indiana, who left no doubt as to what he considered to be the highlight of the senator's five-year career. "The number-one issue in our state is still jobs," he said. More than half of his remarks were devoted to JTPA, and to the need to spread the word about Quayle's authorship. "The trouble," John Mutz began,

> is that people still know him as the man who beat an unbeat-able three-term incumbent senator. They don't know what an outstandingly successful senator he is. One of the best legisla-tive success stories in America is the Job Training Partnership

Act crafted by our junior senator.... It was a new concept ... but now it has achieved universal acceptance. I know how successful it has been because I was with the Department of Commerce when it became law and I have worked on economic development as lieutenant governor. He brought together the most liberal and the most conservative people—a great legislative achievement and a sign of the great ability he brings to public life.... These are things the public should know about him.

On the long table outside the dining room was a booklet containing the Indiana state Republican platform for 1986. In its preamble the platform lauded JTPA, "written" by Dan Quayle. Its text described, endorsed, and adopted "Quayle's JTPA" as a major economic development plank.[37] As they had in 1982, Indiana's Republicans were associating themselves with Quayle's legislative achievements wherever possible. Their actions gave evidence that his thinking was in close harmony with theirs.

In the Mutz introduction, an ingredient above and beyond the substantive merits of JTPA also came through. It was that Quayle's legislative effectiveness, his political leadership, was gaining him a reputation in Washington as a very good senator. Mutz presented his judgment of "great legislative achievement" not simply as his opinion, but as the opinion of seasoned national observers, too. "The national media said he was a superior member of the Senate who had not yet received credit," said Mutz. "He has a record acclaimed by the national media who watch day to day in that body." It was the same accolade that had long since been absorbed by Quayle's Executive Committee, but now it was being heard more widely.

The special bit of recent evidence supporting this message was a September 1985 judgment by the editor of *Politics in America* that Quayle was one of "the twelve most effective but underrated" members of Congress. Few accolades could be more complimentary to a first-term legislator. The editor's selection criteria were that the legislators be "unpretentious, rarely partisan legislative professionals who are candid, well informed and not prone to self-promotion."[38] It was a good description of the legislative style we have watched develop in the course of JTPA—without which he never would have made the list. In his speech the editor called Quayle "an iconoclast without being a maverick"—a notion similar to that of "instrumental independence" used in this study.

The editor of *Politics in America* is one of Washington's most knowledgeable and respected students of Congress. His judgment was published in all the major papers covering Indiana and in many of the smaller ones—the *Indianapolis Star*, the *Cincinnati Enquirer*, the *Chicago Tribune*, the *Fort Wayne Journal Gazette*, the *Louisville Courier-Journal*, the *Lafayette Journal and Courier*, the *Madison Courier*, the *Kokomo Tribune*, the *Hartford City News Times*, the *Huntington Herald Press*, the *Goshen News*, and the *Dearborn County Journal Press*, among others. The idea that Dan Quayle might just be an especially good senator was beginning to reverberate around the home territory. It was an idea rooted in his JTPA accomplishment.

In a familiar pattern, national media judgments were being picked up and propagated by the local media. In this case the judgments gave the media an appealing story line. A young man, favored in life and without accomplishment, had gone to Washington tagged as a lightweight and in five years had become nationally recognized as a praiseworthy United States senator.

In fact, that story line had begun to surface locally with the first campaign analyses. And it was bringing Dan Quayle favorable notice. For example, "In 1980, Quayle rode the Ronald Reagan tide to upset Birch Bayh. . . . Democrats considered that outcome a fluke and Quayle a lightweight. Yet Quayle has worked to shake that image and to a considerable degree, he has been successful." [39] Or, "During the 1980 campaign and in his first months in Washington, Quayle was rapped by Democrats who questioned whether he was intelligent enough to function in the Senate . . . now they grudgingly grant Quayle respect for his legislative accomplishments." [40] In an article headlined "Indiana's Freshman Senator Wins Praise as 'Young and Rising Star,' " the author reminded readers that "It wasn't long ago that Quayle . . . had been drawing much less than favorable comments from the media." [41] All of these articles cited his work on JTPA.

Later in the year, the story line was given additional impetus from Washington, where another one of Washington's top congressional reporters wrote in *National Journal* that "Contrary to predictions made in 1981, Quayle has been a Senate success story." Citing JTPA, the author wrote that "his legislative record is among the most productive of the 1980 class." *National Journal* named him one of three (of sixteen) freshmen Republicans who were "potential Senate leaders." [42] The author quoted an Indiana Democratic House member to the effect that "Quayle has performed legislatively and politically higher than the general expectations in 1980." And he ended with the judgment that "He may not be in the top rank of Senators in power or skill, but he has clearly made himself a force to be reckoned with. Some who have watched him believe that his potential is unbounded." [43] Three months later came the judgment in the *Congressional Quarterly Weekly Report* that "Dan Quayle did not attract much attention in the two

House terms he served ...," but that he had "built a reputation as a pragmatic, thoughtful senator...." [44]

The story line found its way, eventually, into editorial endorsements. For example, "Six years ago ... the prevailing opinion was that he ... was a 'lightweight.' ... [He] has spent the subsequent six years proving that assumption ... wrong. Dan Quayle has been a good senator." [45] It is a classic case of low expectations confounded and success thereby magnified. It was a made-to-order story line, and it matured both nationally and locally in time to become a major theme of campaign commentary. At the heart of it all, indispensably, was JTPA.

My sole intention, on this 1985 visit, was to focus on the impact of JTPA. So, I had talked beforehand to Quayle's press secretary. He was unequivocal about the intentions of the Quayle campaigners. "It's a godsend," he said of JTPA.

> We can use it in a hundred ways. Mostly, it enables us to portray Dan as a genuine conservative, but a conservative with a heart. It also allows us to present him as an effective senator. It's the biggest weapon in our arsenal.

In Indiana, his campaign manager was equally convinced of its value. We talked before the Republican luncheon about the appeal and the problems of publicizing JTPA. "It's the job of the campaign to get the message across to people in the state," she said.

> It's funny. People don't know about the jobs bill. They connect him with jobs, but not with JTPA. It seems too technical. Maybe it takes time. You have to wait till the grants actually get made.... Now, with the third anniversary and all, it's proven to be a bona fide bill, and we can do something about it. I just finished talking to our county leaders' meeting. I told them, "We have a real legislator here and we have to tell everybody about him." And I used the jobs bill as the example. I talk about the jobs bill all the time.

The assumption behind these comments was, of course, that the new job training program was working—that is, having some recognizable payoff at least in Indiana.

When I raised this question with Quayle, he asserted that it was. "It's working very well," he replied.

> People come up to me and talk about it. They compare it to CETA. It's doing especially well in Indiana. We found out the other day that 73,000 trainees have gotten jobs. The key is the domination of the Private Industry Councils by business. That was the key provision in the bill. We got that from Hawkins in the conference, and it has worked the way we thought it would. ...

> We held hearings on it around the state this year. It gave people a chance to come in and praise the program. Most of them have—especially the business community. They are strongly behind it.... The program is criticized for what is called "creaming"—that we are training the unemployed, but the easiest of the unemployed, that we don't reach down to help the hard-core unemployed. I'm not sure whether that is the case or not.

It seemed to me that he was convinced it was working well enough to support a credit-claiming campaign; that he had a measure—73,000 trainees—of its success; that the constituency of greatest interest to him philosophically and politically, the business community, was satisfied with it; and that he was not in any mood to dig more deeply to engage the most serious criticisms—not, at least, during the remainder of his campaign effort.

He, like his campaigners, had every intention of relying heavily on his JTPA accomplishment when the campaign got under way. "It's important to me," he said.

> And it will be important in the campaign. It's especially important in a state like Indiana. Jobs is still the big issue— even though unemployment is down, from a high of 14 percent to 8 percent. For a Republican, it's a good issue. It deals with a big problem and it shows we can handle it better. The business people are strongly behind it. We are doing it at one-third the cost, so we can demonstrate fiscal responsibility, too. When I formally announce, I'll go around to some job training centers and use them as backdrop. That will remind people of what I did. It was the only major piece of domestic social legislation passed by this administration. It's a building block that allows you to talk about lots of other things—jobs, education, economic development. You can take it almost anywhere you want to.

It was the most straightforward acknowledgment I had heard from the candidate himself of the immense versatility of the issue as I had observed it in 1982. Thus, although JTPA was very little in evidence, it had become widely and clearly assumed that Dan Quayle's reelection campaign would be a JTPA-centered campaign. Its central strategic premise would be that a Washington accomplishment would anchor an election victory at home.

The senator and his manager possessed June 1985 poll results showing that 27 percent of Indiana's voters had read about or heard about Quayle's sponsorship of JTPA. And, like his campaign manager, the senator believed that number was far lower than it might be. But he also believed that an important segment in the state did know of his accomplishment. "The people who followed it know about it—the media, business leaders," he said.

> They are what I call the echo chamber, the knowledgeable people. They know what I did. And, of course, there are the constituents of the program—the trainees, the members of the PICs—they know about it. But people in general do not know about it. We will talk about it in the campaign every chance we get. There will be lots of chances because it is such a broad subject. And we will have campaign advertising.

On a base of "the knowledgeable people," he planned to inform an ever-larger fraction of the electorate.

In the fall of 1985 his election prospects seemed bright. Indeed, an operative of the Republican National Committee said to me, "This seat is safe. But I tell people, 'For God's sake, keep it safe.'" In the June 1985 poll, Quayle's name recognition stood at 94 percent. The number of Indiana voters who had favorable opinions of him stood at 68 percent, with those having unfavorable opinions standing at 12 percent. On the question of whether he deserved reelection, 55 percent answered favorably. All these numbers were unusually favorable for a Senate candidate. "It looks very good," he said.

> [But] it's a funny situation for me. I'm used to being twenty points behind. I've always been behind—against Roush, against Bayh. So I know how my opponents will feel. But I caught up. That could happen to me, too.

Of course, he had no definite opponent. And "there is not a lot of interest in my race." The problem he worried about, therefore, was "the arrogance of the party." "The Republicans have had things so good for so long in Indiana that they might not think they have to work for it." His campaign, however, was insulated somewhat from any lassitude on the part of the organizational party. Of his forty county coordinators, only two also chaired the party in their county. Only half of the coordinators were holdovers from the 1980 campaign.

During my 1985 visit the senator was, as usual, upbeat in his presentations. He was buoyed, that week, by the capture of the *Achille Lauro* hijackers several days earlier. That event produced for him the only applause line he would get in each of his two speeches that day. In the luncheon speech, it was: "Talking to people and listening to what they have to say, I think we should all say, 'Hip, hip, hooray for Ronald Reagan and the U.S. military.'" In his evening speech to Hendricks County Republicans it was: "We, as Americans and as Republicans, have to be darn proud of President Ronald Reagan and the way he handled that situation."

Both were typically positive and sunny speeches in praise of administration accomplishments. With one exception. In the evening, he devoted one-third of his talk to "the farm situation," a subject I had not heard him emphasize before. "Believe me," he told the audience, "I know the farm problem is there." He talked at length about the family farm, as "the heartbeat of our state," and about the ripple effects of low farm income and high farm debt. He offered suggestions, but no panaceas. Afterward, he said it was the electoral problem that worried him the most. "It is a difficult issue," he said.

> You don't know how it will go, but you know it's the one issue that can come up and bite you. It affects everybody. I've learned a lot about agriculture and I mention it wherever I go as I did this evening. I talk a lot about it to show I'm sympathetic. But I'm afraid the solution will not be easy to take in the short run. Fewer people will be farming. Still we've got to help them.

As I left, the farm problem was the only discernible cloud on his campaign horizon.

"THE CAMPAIGN" FOR REELECTION

By the time I returned, in October of 1986, "The Campaign" for the U.S. Senate in Indiana was over. Indeed, it was over before it began. No national media person ever came to take a look at it. The most likely Democratic challenger withdrew from consideration, for health reasons, in December. Dan Quayle formally announced in February. By this time, a once-promising list of Democratic possibilities had dwindled to zero.[46] Throughout 1985 Quayle had spent a lot of time showing the flag to prospective opponents. "When the mayor of Fort Wayne was thinking of running," he recalled,

> we went into Fort Wayne and held a big fund-raiser right under his nose. When the mayor of Evansville was thinking of running, we held JTPA hearings there and invited him to come as a witness. We made him help us. When Congressman Phil Sharp was thinking of running we held Lincoln Day dinners in Anderson, Muncie, and Richmond—all in his district. We were saying to all of them, "Come on, take me on. We're ready for you." And none of them wanted any part of that kind of tough race. They all backed off.

Everywhere he went, he talked of a $4 million campaign budget. Whether or not these strategic forays helped convince likely opponents to withdraw, it did express Quayle's enormous self-confidence and his own appetite for a tough race. "I want an opponent. I'm ready. I'm well organized," he would tell reporters. "We're prepared to do battle with the best person that they can put forward. . . . I'm at a good point in my career, and I think my political career would be enhanced by running against a strong Democratic candidate." [47] None appeared.[48]

In April a desperate state Democratic party announced that anyone who wished to do so could apply for their endorsement. And they held auditions for the several applicants. The winner was Valparaiso University Professor and Valparaiso City Councilwoman Jill Long. She had already declared her candidacy for Congress and was running far behind in that primary. She was unknown. As the party's designee, she won the May Senate primary. But their endorsement was about all she got from her party. As a top Indiana Republican put it, "The party recruited her and then dumped her." She raised only $100,000 (compared with Quayle's $2 million) and she was not able to buy a minute of statewide television. In June a top reporter described the Long effort as "a disaster . . . so far behind Quayle that it is scary." [49] In July another top reporter wrote that

> Jill Long has yet to make it past the "who's that" stage with In-
> diana voters much less challenge Quayle's lead. Even if she
> does mount a credible challenge, Ms. Long will be battling one
> of the most formidable political figures in the state.[50]

It was a classic instance of a sacrificial weak challenger against an incumbent who had been steadily gaining political strength in his own right.

After the May primary, with both candidates formally nominated, the Quayle campaign took its last complete poll. It found Quayle far ahead, favorably regarded, and enveloped by a friendly environment. He was leading Long 64 percent to 27 percent among Indiana's voters; he was perceived favorably by 73 percent and unfavorably by 10 percent; his job performance rating was 70 percent approval and 14 percent disapproval. Beyond that, 54 percent of the state's voters expressed satisfaction with the way things were going nationally and 62 percent of them were satisfied with the way things were going in Indiana. Quayle's name recognition stood at 95 percent, Long's at 33 percent. His pollster's review only confirmed what Quayle's campaigners already knew—that he would "easily defeat Jill Long" and that he would have "a painless reelection." [51]

With reelection assured, the Quayle people set three extra goals: Save money wherever possible, make as few mistakes as possible, and win by the largest margin possible. It was the third extra goal that drove "The Campaign." As Quayle's pollsters put it in the June report,

Because winning itself is not a serious concern, the central question is how to engineer an overwhelming victory. A vote share of 60 percent or more in November would be unprecedented, as this mark has not been achieved by any senatorial or gubernatorial candidate since World War II.[52]

Their target became the 58.8 percent record vote by which Richard Lugar won election to the Senate in 1976. Indiana political reporters, and Quayle himself, took the view that rock-bottom support for both parties was 40 percent and that 55 percent should be considered a landslide.[53]

A "generic senatorial ballot" in the June poll—that is, would you prefer to vote for a Republican or a Democrat for the Senate?—produced a 42 percent-40 percent Republican margin. "That confirmed my belief," said Quayle, "that the basic split is 40-40, that each party has 40 percent of the vote, and we fight over the rest." Shortly before the election, he discussed his expectations. "I have to get 55 percent," he said. "I'm counting on that. If I didn't get 55 percent, I don't know what I'd do. Anything between 55 percent and 60 percent is adequate. I can't complain. Anything over 60 percent would be great."

There is no evidence that the appearance of a weak challenger and the 60 percent goal had any effect on his strategic plan. Certainly nothing changed the campaign's intention to exploit JTPA in every way and at every opportunity. Poll results indicated that plenty of room remained for such exploitation and Quayle's pollster advocated it. The 1985 survey showed that 27 percent of the state's voters had "read or heard about Senator Quayle's sponsorship of JTPA." The 1986 survey found that the number had risen to 45 percent and that "this large increase reflects positive shifts in almost all demographic subgroups." Further, they found that recognition meant favorable judgments. "Seventy-three percent of voters who have read or heard of the Job Training Partnership Act believe that it has been helpful to people in the state. Only 14 percent feel that it has been ineffective."

These results were obtained by feeding people the name of the Act. When called upon to mention JTPA on their own, as a Quayle achievement, however, almost none did. So there remained plenty of room to increase recognition and a universe of room to increase recall. The polling report's main substantive recommendation was, indeed, that Quayle should continue to emphasize JTPA. It read:

> Open ended questions about problems facing Indiana and the nation gave ample evidence that unemployment is on the minds of many voters as it has been for years. Quayle's sponsorship of the [JTPA] must be conveyed to more voters. Knowledge of Quayle's work on this legislation has increased since June 1985, but the electorate is far from saturated. Those

voters who are familiar with JTPA have a highly favorable opinion of it. Further use of the program should only be dangerous if the opposition can convince voters that it has not worked. The tie between legislative activity and a job creation program also can enhance Quayle's image as an effective U.S. Senator and public servant for Indiana.[54]

Well before they received this advice, the Quayle campaigners had decided upon a campaign top-heavy with JTPA "explanations."

Consider, for example, his campaign advertising. The first sentence of every campaign "bio sheet" called the senator "a respected national leader" or "an accomplished legislator," and it was followed up immediately with the job training example. No longer was he reluctant to claim credit. All qualifiers—of sponsorship, authorship, chamber, and session—were now gone. His "bio" read, "In 1982, Quayle authored and won unanimous passage of [JTPA], widely considered the most significant piece of domestic legislation enacted during the Reagan Administration." [55]

The cover of his campaign brochure displayed his campaign theme: "Effective Leadership for Indiana." Inside, two of his five pictures were devoted to JTPA. One showed Quayle and two others with JTPA hats on. The centerpiece of the brochure was a picture of Ronald Reagan writing and Dan Quayle looking over his shoulder. It was the picture the senator had bought with the price of humiliation. It was entitled, "1982: President Reagan Signs Quayle's JTPA into Law." Beneath it was a description of the program and of its 94,000 Indiana participants. One page of the brochure was devoted to four testimonials. One based its praise explicitly on his JTPA achievement. And the *Politics in America* editor's judgment—based heavily on JTPA—was highlighted. Thus, in his most widely distributed piece of campaign literature, JTPA was, again, everywhere.

The senator's television advertising began immediately after the May primary and ran for two weeks. It began again in mid-October and ran for the final three weeks. It consisted of a sixty-second spot and five thirty-second spots. The long one was an all-purpose spot summarizing both his Washington accomplishments and his ties to home and family and God. It opened this way:

> Remember back in 1980. Things were in bad shape. Then we elected a new generation of leadership, a leader like Dan Quayle. Dan Quayle wrote the nation's Job Training Partnership Act and today tens of thousands of Hoosiers are learning better skills for new jobs.

One of the thirty-second spots described four of Quayle's accomplishments. It opened this way:

> We elected Dan Quayle to the Senate six years ago. Let's look at just part of what he's done. Dan Quayle wrote the nation's JTPA and today millions of Americans are learning better skills for new jobs.

During both of these leadoff statements, pictures flow across the screen of Quayle alone at his desk writing, of a carpenter, a computer operator, machinist at work, and of Quayle shaking hands with a worker. On the governing-and-explanation side of his televised message, JTPA is given both top billing substantively and a strongly positive tone. Visually the link is forged between Dan Quayle's legislation and real help for real people.

Another thirty-second spot hits the viewer between the eyes with the same positive, people-oriented JTPA message. It is devoted entirely to the testimony of one JTPA trainee, "Peggy." A series of pictures shows her driving to work, getting out of the car, walking along the street, talking into the camera, answering the phone, running the mail through a stamp meter, working at a computer console, showing papers to people, shaking hands at a counter with Quayle, and, finally, standing beside Quayle as a voice says, "Senator Dan Quayle" and "Effective Leadership for Indiana" flashes on the screen. "Peggy" says,

> I was without a job. I was without marketable skills. I felt like I was a failure. Couldn't get a job. Can't support myself. I was a burden on society.
>
> [Voice: Peggy turned to Senator Dan Quayle's Job Training Partnership Act.]
>
> The Job Training Partnership Act gave me good usable skills. I got a job before I even completed the training program. Dan Quayle's jobs program made it possible for me to get a good job and start my life over again.

Peggy Pate was a real trainee, who wrote to Quayle thanking him for his help. Her appealing earnestness and her "stream-of-consciousness" sentiments earned her his campaign's praise as "the academy award winner." The Peggy ad ran heavily during the May period and again from the fourteenth to the thirty-first of October—as did the other two already mentioned.

In these and other ads, there is a strong dosage of Quayle's cheerful, touch-heavy campaign style—shaking hands, patting arms, hugging shoulders. The style is encapsulated in the thirty-second spot that ran most heavily in the last week of the campaign. It is a flashing collage of smiles and good times, which the producers called "Bandwagon." It has no talking, only a happy, snappy, musical theme together with glimpses of the senator walking in parades, playing basketball with his boys, sitting with his daughter and her dog, walking with his wife in a county fair, embracing the elderly, cooing at babies, and, always, shaking hands. By sound and sight, it evokes the optimism that is the hallmark of his campaign style—and of his policy stance as well.

Just as clearly as his advertising campaign, Quayle's talking campaign left no doubt about the primacy of his governing accomplishment. "JTPA is almost always the first thing I talk about," he said when we met in October.

> I did several radio interviews today. Their first question was: "Why should people reelect Dan Quayle?" I began with "effective leadership" and swung right into JTPA. It's right there. It's about jobs, which is our number-one problem and the catalyst for all economic development. After all, economic development is what it's all about—except for war and peace.

So far as I could tell, he had followed that prescription from the beginning of "The Campaign."

In his formal announcement in February he said that "I am proud to be the primary author of the Job Training Partnership Act . . . which has been roundly acclaimed as one of the most important pieces of domestic legislation enacted during the Reagan administration . . . [and under which] Indiana has been allocated $223 million . . . and more than 94,000 Hoosiers participated." [56] When the state's reporters began writing about his campaign, they would report his heavy emphasis on JTPA. For example, "Asked what he considers the highlight of his first term, Quayle cited passage of JTPA." [57] Or, "He points with pride to his performance in the Senate, including his sponsorship of the Job Training Partnership Act." [58] Or, "He touts what he considers the highlight of his years in the Senate, the Job Training Partnership Act." [59]

His JTPA-centered talking campaign had the all-purpose effect he had predicted for it years earlier. When I asked him what he would have talked about had he not had JTPA so handy, he commented,

> I would have had to talk more about trade. That's a tough issue because it's so easy to demagogue on the other [protectionist] side. We have a trade policy, but it's not popular. With JTPA I can focus on jobs instead of trade. After all, what's the purpose of trade except jobs? With jobs you can go in almost any direction. You can use it to lead into any subject. That's the beauty of it.

On the campaign trail, JTPA enveloped, preempted, and subsumed a large number of other issues where upbeat talk might have been more difficult.

In light of our two long chapters on Quayle's efforts to guide JTPA through a difficult passage, it is interesting to note what the reporters never asked him about—how he did it. In all of my travels, I never heard anyone, anywhere ask him to describe or explain the governing process in Washington. The only relevant comment I ever saw reported in the press was Quayle's comment that "Legislative accomplishments are measured in inches and seconds, and it took a lot of inches and seconds to get that one passed." [60] But it was not a response to a process-oriented question.

Most interesting is the total absence of any reference to Quayle's prolonged battle with the administration—unless one reflects on the anomalous, two-person signing ceremony depicted in his campaign brochure. Quite to the contrary, the president took the occasion of Quayle's campaign to thank him—finally—for his leadership on JTPA. In early October, the senator held an anniversary celebration luncheon in Indianapolis—to which the president sent a congratulatory letter. "I want to thank you," he wrote,

> for the leadership that you displayed in guiding the Act from introduction to enactment. It may not be called the Quayle Act—but without Dan Quayle I know we would not have a Job Training Partnership Act.[61]

The letter added legitimacy to his claim to be an effective leader. But he already had legitimacy enough. So the letter was not material to the election.

The picture of harmony the letter presented, along with the absence of any hint of the earlier conflict, is a measure of the separation between the governing and campaigning processes. In Washington, how it is done affects the legislator's reputation. Indirectly, therefore, and in the form of a capsule judgment, the legislator's Washington behavior will reach people back home. And if it is favorable—as it was in Quayle's case—it buttresses the legitimacy of the legislator's claim of success in governing. But people at home will not ordinarily look behind that summary judgment to inquire, for themselves, into the evidence for accomplishment and the legitimacy of the claim. It would require more information than they want and a finer judgment than they need.

Thus, interest in what really happened in Washington remains in Washington. And the legislator has every incentive to keep it there. Explaining his conflict with the administration or his alliance with Kennedy back home could only have brought unpleasantness to Dan Quayle. If challenged, however, Quayle would have superior command of the evidence and the detail and the favorable Washington judgments. So the challenger, too, lacks incentive to demand process-related explanations. A rare challenger under rare circumstances might force the incumbent to make such explanations involving the governing process.

If it happened, it would be a sign that the incumbent was in trouble. But it is not likely.

Certainly, it did not happen in Indiana. The most diagnostic event—and perhaps the only noteworthy event—of "The Campaign" was the one Dan Quayle-Jill Long debate, on September 7. The earliest moments of the debate were taken up with questions of foreign policy and defense. But at the first mention of the domestic economic situation, Quayle "swung right into JTPA." "One of the real prides [*sic*] of my career thus far," he said,

> has been in the introduction and passage of the Job Training Partnership Act—to get people involved in the system to give people the opportunity to go to work. Thus far, under JTPA, we have trained 150,000 Hoosiers. JTPA has used economic development, education, community-based organizations, business, and labor to create an environment of opportunity.

And in his prepared three-minute closing statement, JTPA received top billing. As usual, the trademark of his comments was their tone of optimism. "I believe the future is very, very bright for the people of this state and for the nation," he said.

> Indiana is at an all-time high for the number of people holding jobs. Two point eight million Hoosiers are working today. There are a lot of smiling faces out there. Oh, sure, we've got problems, problems out on the farm, problems with the trade deficit, problems with the budget deficit; we've got problems with arms control. But we can beat those problems! But people are generally optimistic—and they ought to be. Interest rates are down, inflation is down, things are moving ahead, so the future is very, very bright and it offers a lot of hope, a lot of opportunity, a lot of success.

After a brief discussion of the importance of the family and of freedom, he got down to cases. And cases meant, overwhelmingly, JTPA. "Now I've worked hard for the five and a half years I've been in the Senate and I'm proud of my record," he began.

> I've worked hard and I'm proud I was the author of the Job Training Partnership Act—the Job Training Partnership Act that has allowed 150,000 people of Indiana to go through and get a job and an opportunity. That Job Training Partnership Act sees labor working with business. It sees the private sector working with the public sector. The Job Training Partnership Act is working! It's helping out dislocated farmers; it's helping out our dislocated steel workers, our dislocated auto workers, and those economically structurally unemployed.

These closing remarks were his best opportunity to sum up what he believed his campaign was all about. Not surprisingly to a student of his career thus far, he chose to emphasize his optimism and his accomplishment.

The debate pointed up the large number of issues on which the candidates differed and the depth of those differences.[62] Not, however, on the value of JTPA. But the debate pointed up, also, something about the challenger that ensured "The Campaign" would be neither close nor interesting. Long was intelligent, articulate, well organized, and decent. But she displayed no competitiveness. She did not hit hard or press her openings or try to put Quayle on the defensive. She stated her views on all the questions put to her—thoughtfully, calmly, rationally.

She was more teacher than combatant. She used only one and a half minutes of her allotted three minutes for a prepared closing statement. And when the moderator reminded her that she still had a minute and a half remaining, she said simply, "I'll give my remaining time to Senator Quayle." To most actively engaged politicians, such a concession would be incomprehensible. "Can you imagine any politician giving up a minute and a half of free statewide exposure?" exclaimed a top Quayle campaigner afterward. "It was worth $12,000!" And it was donated by a candidate who never did raise enough money to buy statewide television. After the debate, Long said she wanted more debates. But as the Quayle campaigner put it, "She should have been hitting us on that from day one. . . . Now, when she issues a call for debates, the reporters don't even call us. No one pays attention." As the campaign progressed, she found it hard to command attention for anything she said.[63]

Jill Long's debate performance reflected perfectly the kind of campaign she wanted to conduct—a positive campaign and a campaign on the issues. From the outset to the end of "The Campaign," she declared her intention not to conduct a negative campaign. Immediately after her endorsement, she said, "It won't be a negative campaign against Senator Quayle. It will be a positive campaign about me." [64] Party leaders urged her to "get tough," "kick him in the ass," "take the gloves off," "force him to confront the issues," or "draw him out." But to every such suggestion, she would reply, "I want to avoid criticizing Quayle." [65] Or, "I am still going to take what I call the high road. I am not going to attack Dan Quayle." [66] Or, "I can tell you—I will not run a negative campaign." [67] Or, "[I'm] not running for Godfather of the Mafia. . . . [I prefer] a gentlemanly manner." [68] To the end, she remained both resolute and unruffled in this stance.[69] It was a civics book stance, one in which she never sought advantage but only exposition. She issued about a dozen press releases, several of which were handcrafted policy papers, and most of which did not even mention Quayle's name.

One consequence of her decision was that her behavior tended to confirm the view that she had no chance.

From a pollster's perspective, another consequence was that the incumbent's reputation, which normally declines during a campaign, did not. In mid-October Quayle's pollster said privately,

> His favorable-unfavorable ratio is 71-11. What's amazing about that is not the 71 percent favorable but the 11 percent unfavorable. No matter how popular a senator is, the unfavorables are in the 20s. But no one has said anything unfavorable about him during the campaign. Lots of politicians start as low as Quayle, but no one stays that low.

It was the numerical result of Jill Long's campaign strategy.

From an observer's perspective, the challenger's lack of aggressiveness meant that the incumbent's explanation of his Washington performance needed to go no farther and no deeper than he wished it to. It meant he could control the campaign agenda and frame the campaign questions. Campaigns can be mechanisms for forcing incumbents to explain. In Indiana, the challenger's campaign did not work that way. Courtesy of his opponent, Dan Quayle was left free to explain in the manner most congenial to him—upbeat and optimistic, without personal discomfort, or defensive detours. "We're out there every day creating sunshine, organization, and votes," he replied when asked, "How's it going?" in October. "My opponent has to go into a lot of detail in describing the problems she's talking about," he said later.

> We don't. We just say everything is rosy, more jobs, more people working. All the reporters ask me about my failures. Are they kidding? There are no failures. Failure? Failure isn't in my vocabulary.

He was still the self-confident campaigner he had always been. And, now, he had a proven record to go with it. Still, his opponent's "positive campaign" allowed him to campaign with this kind of hyperbolic optimism and an unchallenged philosophical conservatism, to play up his "favorables" without enlarging his "unfavorables."

None of this is to shortchange his abilities as a campaigner. They would have been potent protectors of his incumbency no matter how stiff a challenge he had received. On a par with the person-to-person skills we have described, he displays good political instincts. And they underpin his strategic decisions about campaigning just as they undergird his strategic decisions in his JTPA efforts.

For example, Quayle's judgment set the pace of his campaign much as his judgment set the pace of JTPA. Except that in the Washington case he speeded things up and in the Indiana case he slowed things down. In the matter of timing, the 1986 campaign was Quayle's campaign. There was his oft-stated view of the electoral cycle, in which the last two years would be reserved for campaigning in earnest. But his Executive Committee wished to advance the cycle and persisted from the beginning that he come home more often and do more to increase his visibility than his view warranted. Early in 1985 Indiana Republicans complained about the slow pace of his fund raising.[70] In the summer of 1986 his consultants complained about the slow pace of his television advertising.[71] In all three instances he set his own pace in accordance with his own judgment. "I feel I have a good instinct on these things," he said at one point. "[It's] not the conventional, political, professional thinking, but my instinct tells me not to [speed up]." [72]

His instincts had served him well, and he had confidence in them. In October I heard him advise a congressional candidate to alter his campaign tactics. "I'm telling you," he said, pointing vigorously to his stomach and thrusting his hands beneath his belt,

> I feel it in my gut, deep down in my gut. Trust old dad. It's my instinct. I don't care what your polls tell you. I'm listening to people on the street. You have to trust your instincts.

Respect for those instincts and, hence, for his prowess as a campaigner was growing in the state—as respect for his instincts (on bipartisanship and timing) had grown in Washington. After watching Quayle campaign several times, a statewide reporter pronounced him "the hottest political property in Indiana . . . a potent political package . . . [with] a little extra that makes him stand out in a state filled with attractive Republican politicians: the common touch." He went on to explain: "He has deep Indiana roots and thinks Indiana thoughts. And his politics are Indiana politics. . . . Dan Quayle's greatest strength [is] his understanding of Indiana voters." [73] It is a ringing tribute to Dan Quayle's political instincts.

To the outside observer, Quayle neither exudes nor articulates a strong sense of identity with Indiana—with the specialness of its places or its people or its past. He does not seem steeped in any of its lore. Yet he seems to have a proven instinct or "feel" for the sum total of all that—for what is distinctive and what is not, for what is expected and what is not, for what is acceptable and what is not, for what is admired and what is not—in Indiana. And it makes him an especially astute campaigner there.

The campaign I observed in October was a relaxed form of time-serving. In a close contest, he would have been pushing very hard at that time. "I'm not working as hard in 1986, as I did in 1985," he admitted. "Home was more important then. I assume we're doing well.

It certainly is different from 1980." Four days before my mid-October visit, Quayle had announced that he was stopping all fund-raising activity for himself and working only for other candidates.[74] It was described as "a move unprecedented in Indiana politics." [75] A day after that the Quayle camp had sent to the press their complete poll, taken in early October, as proof of their "lead of historic proportions." [76] This move, too, was described as a "never-before" move—"the first time Republicans released copies of a poll report to the media during a campaign." [77] But not once did he utter a word in disrespect or disparagement of his opponent or her campaign. In private conversation he remained scrupulously complimentary. In public he simply went about his business and ignored Long completely. When it was over, he congratulated her. "We showed the state of Indiana . . . that you can, in fact, conduct a positive U.S. Senate campaign and stick to the issues." [78]

In two October visits, I caught a few glimpses of his desultory campaign—enough to satisfy my curiosity about the usage and effects of JTPA.

On a day when he had to remain in Washington, I listened to him speak to the Indiana Broadcasters Association by telephone hookup. His first substantive comment was: "We've got to continue to focus on human resources, education, training for the development of skills. Our priority now has to be people. That's top priority with me." And he continued, "My JTPA has trained 163,000 people—83 percent of those trained found jobs and 60 percent find jobs with skills." As we have traced his campaigning, we have seen the number of Indiana trainees he has been able to cite grow steadily—from 26,000 to 35,000, to 73,000, to 94,000, to 150,000, and now, at campaign's end to 163,000. These are electorally beneficial numbers. They gave the most concrete expression to his theme of "effective leadership for Indiana."

Later that day, I saw the expression of a longer-run theme flow from his JTPA association. Quayle spoke by satellite hookup to a Symposium on the Future—a convocation of several hundred top high school students, convened by the Hudson Institute, an Indianapolis think tank. "I'm very optimistic about the future," he told the students. "I'm one of those people who are going forward. I'm not afraid of the future. . . . My Job Training Partnership Act, which the governor has implemented in Indiana, may soon be training people 65-70 or over. We need to start thinking about education, training, and jobs for the elderly."

At a press conference afterward with Gov. Robert Orr, the director of the Hudson Institute played off Quayle's comments to discuss his success as a senator. "There are two types of people in the world—Type A and Type B," he said.

> Type A people welcome change and see it as an opportunity when it comes. Type B people resist change and ignore it when it comes.... You have to have guts to do what Senator Quayle did with his JTPA, to challenge the conventional wisdom and challenge the view of the administration. He's a leader whom you might have thought would be Type B who turned out to be Type A.

Privately, he said, "Everyone thought he would be conservative and not very bright. It's just the opposite. He's bright and he's not conservative in the sense that he likes to examine new ideas and he's open to change. He's the archetype A." His comments were another version of a familiar story line, as it was being expressed by the "knowledgeable people" in Indiana's "echo chamber."

On a late October day on the road in northern Indiana, we toured an establishment that cleaned uniforms of all sorts—the Eagle Uniform and Linen Service in Goshen. Twelve of its employees had been hired through the Elkhart job training program. And all twelve had remained with the company—some for as long as two and a half years. Quayle talked with individual workers, with the owner, and with Elkhart JTPA officials about program details. It was a small-scale JTPA success story. It produced smiling pictures of Senate author, company owner, employees, and local JTPA officials. And it helped generate an Elkhart press release headlined "Quayle Pledges to Continue Working for Indiana's Economic Development." [79] It was the final press release of his campaign. It was my first encounter with trainees and an ideal event to round out the remarkable variety of Indiana contexts in which the impact of Quayle's governing accomplishment could be felt and talked about.

In November, Dan Quayle was reelected with 61 percent of the vote. His campaigners had met their goal—the largest percentage margin ever received by an Indiana candidate for the U.S. Senate. The argument of this chapter would be that his governing accomplishment with JTPA was indispensable and essential and necessary to this success at home. That cannot be proven. But in support of that judgment we have provided copious evidence of the clear intentions to use JTPA, of the widespread usage of it, and of the multiple positive effects flowing from that usage. In his early fifth-year campaigning and in "The Campaign," Quayle exploited his JTPA achievement in every way imaginable. It overwhelmed every other aspect of his record and of a campaign conducted on his record.

Quayle's campaign manager can have the last word in this regard. When I asked her, in October, to describe the effects of JTPA on the campaign, she answered,

JTPA is the whole campaign. It's everything. It's the first thing
he talks about almost everywhere he goes. All our opinion polls
tell us that jobs is still the number-one issue in this state. He
can talk jobs like nobody else can, because he did something
about it. When he goes someplace he can tell people how many
jobs were created there and exactly how many dollars went into
the area. He can name companies that laid off workers and
point to companies that hired trainees. So it's pure gold. And it
sews everything together. He brings home the bacon; he is a
national leader; and the program embodies his philosophy of
private/public partnership. It becomes a model for other programs. And it is exemplified by the partnership that is rebuild-
ing places like Indianapolis. JTPA is his suit of armor.

Nearly all of the campaign potential I had first observed in 1982 and followed since then is contained within the scope of that commentary. If
campaigns affect election results, then JTPA affected Dan Quayle's
reelection. To the degree that it did, it provides us with an example of a
home payoff for a Washington performance. More specifically, perhaps,
it provides us with an example of how a campaigning legislator can
manipulate the explanatory process so as to extract reelection benefits
from governing accomplishments.

CONCLUSION

Six years of intermittent attention to Dan Quayle's political activity have
yielded two stories. One is the sequential campaigning-to-governing-to-
campaigning story. It is driven by the demands of the cyclical "master
sequence" of senatorial life. It traces Quayle's activity from his election
through his most important legislative effort to his reelection. Its
emphasis is on the 1982-1986, governing-to-campaigning part of the
sequence. Its theme is the strategic manipulation of his governing
activity in Washington to help him win reelection in Indiana. The
second story is one of individual growth and accomplishment. It is
driven by the interaction of personal attributes and opportunity. It traces
Quayle's activity from his earliest electoral efforts to his achievements as
a subcommittee chairman in the United States Senate. Its emphasis is on
his activity during his first two years in that body. Its theme is the
growth of a lightly regarded politician of no legislative consequence
into a highly regarded politician of considerable legislative consequence. In both stories, the pivotal event is Quayle's activity during the
enactment of the Job Training Partnership Act of 1982. Hence, the
central place it occupies in our discussion.

Taken together, the two stories trace the career development of Dan Quayle as an elected politician and as a legislator. It had been, by late 1986, a remarkable development. Shortly before his reelection, Quayle reflected that

> I haven't had many failures. So I just keep going on the theory that when you're hot you're hot. Now what will happen when the roof caves in on me, I don't know. It hasn't yet. And I never think of it doing so. . . . I've risen very fast—first office, Congress; two terms; then the Senate. I never earned my spurs, as they say. And I guess I'm still flying high.

He retained the self-confidence and the optimistic outlook with which he began in politics—and to which he had since added a proven capacity to get things done. In six years in the Senate he had, indeed, earned his spurs—legislatively and electorally. He had achieved his two stated goals—a reputation as an effective legislator and a reelection of historic proportions.

He had done so—according to the stories presented here—by taking the fullest advantage of a legislative opportunity. His continued career development would, similarly, depend on the situations in which he subsequently found himself—different situation, different career direction. As he thought about life after reelection, he speculated about three such prospective situations, each of which would present a new opportunity.

"Anything over 60 percent [of the vote] would be great," he said in contemplation of his electoral margin. "It would bring a lot of national attention. Whether I would behave any differently, I don't know. I tend to doubt it. But I honestly don't know. It would depend on the circumstances." But he said moments later that he was about to hire a speechwriter. "I'm doing it all out of my head now," he said.

> It limits what I can do. My staff gives me notes and then I get up and put them all together myself. I need more help so that I can take part more on the floor, write some op-ed pieces for papers and magazines, and give more in-depth speeches on subjects that interest me.

He was thinking about reaching larger, broader, more substantively interested audiences. "What I really enjoy is to talk about . . . JTPA or SDI [the Strategic Defense Initiative] . . . to large audiences. I like to be able to get below the surface, two or three levels down in the argument. It's not as easy as shaking hands but it's more fun." He recognized that his JTPA success could not be duplicated automatically in other areas, and that a different kind of preparation might be called for elsewhere. "I was a coalition builder on JTPA," he said.

> I worked to put together the votes, working in a bipartisan manner. But defense is a little different. I've been struggling there. People stake out positions of a more theoretical nature and then gradually things coalesce and a compromise is reached. It's different from JTPA. No one is going around asking people what they are interested in and putting together a coalition. In defense, I stake out a position and wait for others to come to me. I don't have anything to do with putting it all together, but sometimes my position gets used. Or I work with a couple of others to stake out some position. Do you see the difference? Defense is less of a coalition-building thing.

He seemed to be preparing himself for a new kind of intellectual effort, one that would be required to take advantage of any opportunity that might develop out of increased national attention.

The two other potential opportunities depended upon the overall results of the 1986 elections as they affected partisan control of the Senate. If the Republicans kept their majority, the most likely change of chairmanships would make Quayle chairman of the Labor and Human Resources Committee. Clearly, he had thought about that possibility. He talked some about it.

> It would be a hard committee to run. But I would try to work with Kennedy. He controls that side of the committee. I'd go to Kennedy first. If I couldn't get Kennedy, I'd try to pick off some other Democrat. . . . On my side, I'd have to deal with Weicker. But I can do that. . . . Kennedy and Weicker are pretty close and they work together a lot. When they do, they can control the committee. Under Hatch, they run the committee most of the time. The Democrats love Hatch because they can roll right over him.
> If they tried that with me—and they would—I'd try to beat them in committee. If I couldn't, I'd vote their bill out of committee and tell them I intended to put my bill in on the floor and beat them there. I'd argue, on the floor, that the committee is not representative of the Senate, that the committee bill is not representative of Senate thinking, and offer my substitute. And I'd beat them. I'd have to prove to them that they no longer controlled the committee agenda, that I could and would take them on on the floor, and that they would have to compromise on my terms inside the committee. I know I'd have to do that sooner or later. I'd probably start with an education bill. But it would be a very hard committee to manage.

This seems like a comment grounded in experience. It is also a comment that presumes a strong effort at leadership. An opportunity to lead the full committee would present a more severe, more complex test of Quayle's legislative abilities and instincts than he had yet faced. But it would not require a much longer leap than the one he had already made. Predictably, he would relish the new challenge and would attack it with open-mindedness, straight talk, and high spirits.

The third possibility came from a contemplation of Democratic control of the Senate. That eventually would deprive Quayle of both his subcommittee and full committee leadership opportunities. For him, thinking about this situation produced the most puzzlement over how he might prepare for such a circumstance and how he might act if it occurred. "I don't know what I'll do if the Democrats take over the Senate," he said.

> I only know that I will hate it. I'll hate it. What I like about this job is being able to set the agenda, get my teeth into things, and have an impact. I want to affect the results. If I can't, I'm not interested. My staff gets very nervous thinking about me being in the minority. They remember that in the House if I couldn't affect something, I ignored it. I'm not happy going off making speeches somewhere if I can't influence the results. I suppose the minority can do more in the Senate. It will be interesting to see what I do. But I know I'll go crazy.

As it turned out, this was the new situation that did develop. And with it went a new opportunity for him. It was not new in the sense that he had already experienced minority status in the House—a status that bored and disabled him. But now he was in the minority in a different institution and he was a different politician at a very different stage in his career. So he would never revert to his earlier impotence. He was, moreover, still a very young man of thirty-nine when he won reelection.

So what, then, would he make of this new opportunity? What turn would his career take in the years after 1986? Would he develop a more national role for himself? Would he alter the elements of his governing style? Would he find a different kind of effectiveness inside the Senate? What effect would such activities have on his standing in Indiana? These are the questions with which we are left. They can only be answered by another large set of observations.

EPILOGUE

When these last lines were written, in the summer of 1987, there was no evidence in sight that the opportunity for "another large set of observations" would so forcefully or so soon present itself, as it did exactly one year later.

There exists, now, a greater incentive than ever to pursue the twin themes of accomplishment and growth still further, and to follow a new set of contexts and sequences in the public life of the vice president.

As a closing thought, one can only express the hope that this will be done and that, when it is done, this book will have helped to frame the challenge.

NOTES

1. William Chapman, "Congress Leaves for Holiday with Money Tangle Unsolved," *Washington Post,* July 2, 1982.
2. United Press International, "Senate Passes Bill for New Job Training Plan," *New York Times,* July 2, 1982.
3. David Shribman, "House Approves Job Training Bill to Replace Expiring CETA Plan," *New York Times,* August 5, 1982.
4. Office of Senator Dan Quayle, "Report of Legislative Activities 97th Congress, January 1981-August 1982," September 2, 1982.
5. He also toured several small-sized industrial plants in between speaking engagements and introduced the secretary of the navy at a procurement conference luncheon. "Navy Secretary Urges Increasing Defense Funds," *Indianapolis Star,* September 2, 1982.
6. Press release, "Quayle Training Bill Clears Committee," May 26, 1982; press release, "Quayle Training Bill Clears Senate," July 1, 1982.
7. Press release, Van Natta Campaign Committee, "Van Natta Receives Quayle Endorsement," September 2, 1982.
8. See note number six.
9. Hedrick Smith, "Senate Republicans See Obstacles for Reagan," *New York Times,* November 28, 1984.
10. Rob Gurwitt, "GOP Aims to Elude Senate Takeover Bid in '86," *Congressional Quarterly Weekly Report,* July 20, 1985. On Senate reform, see Marjorie Hunter, "Turning the Senate Away from Trivial Pursuits," *New York Times,* September 21, 1984; Dan Quayle, "The New Senate: Two Steps Backward," *Congressional Record,* January 13, 1987, S689-S690; "Summary of Hearings Held July 31, 1984, and August 2, 1984," "The Temporary Select Committee to Study the Senate Committee System," July 31, 1984.
11. *Congressional Record,* December 14, 1982, S14674-S14678; press release, "Quayle Schedules Hearings on Jobs Creation Programs," November 24, 1982; Howard Kurtz and Helen Dewar, "Jobs Bill Pressure Increases," *Washington Post,* January 28, 1983; Helen Dewar, "Democrats Sway President, But Lose Political Advantage," *Washington Post,* February 22, 1983; Margot Hornblower, "House Democrats Are Feeling Feisty as 1984 Approaches," *Washington Post,* March 5, 1983; *Congressional Record,* March 7, 1983, S2174-S2177; Helen Dewar, "Reagan and Hill Ruling by Consensus," *Washington Post,* March 26, 1983.
12. Elizabeth Bumiller, "The Charmed Life of Indiana's Golden Boy," *Washington Post,* January 11, 1981.
13. Martin Tolchin, "A Conservative Shows His Liberal Bent," *New York Times,* February 20, 1987.

14. Seth King, "Framework of New U.S. Job Program Is in Place," *New York Times*, October 2, 1983.
15. David Hoffman, "Inaugural of Jobs Program Features Barbs at Democrats," *Washington Post*, October 6, 1983. See also Kathy Sawyer, "Angrisani Quits Training Post at Labor Department," *Washington Post*, October 15, 1983.
16. The Quayle Report, "JTPA: Teaching Job Skills for a Lifetime," November 1983.
17. "A Primer on the Job Training Partnership Act," *Congressional Record*, October 1, 1985, S12391–S12392.
18. An internal staff memo on March 13, 1985, noted, "We've highlighted how JTPA serves many of its constituencies—dislocated workers, summer youth, women—and now . . . we need to find sites where we can showcase how it also serves those 55 or older. . . . What about an oversight hearing later this year. . . ?"
19. John Reiter, "Indiana's Bigger Share of Federal Spending Still Is Small," *Evansville Press*, March 29, 1985.
20. "Report on Oversight of the Job Training Partnership Act in Indiana," *Congressional Record*, October 1, 1985, S12386–S12395.
21. Ibid.; press release, "Quayle Staff to Conduct Public Forum in Kokomo on April 2 on Operations of Job Training Partnership Act in Cass, Fulton, Howard, Miami, Tipton and Wabash Counties," March 12, 1985.
22. On March 16, 1985, Secretary Donovan resigned. See James Dickenson, "Donovan Swept Under by Charges," *Rochester Democrat and Chronicle*, March 17, 1985.
23. "Report on Oversight of the Job Training Partnership Act in Indiana." The staff forums were held in Kokomo, Columbus, Salem, Marion, and Muncie.
24. *Congressional Record*, June 13, 1986, S7509–S7511; press release, "Congress Approves Quayle Initiated JTPA Amendments: Bill Makes Unemployed Farmers Eligible for Retraining," October 1, 1986.
25. Nicholas Lemann, "The Culture of Poverty," *Atlantic Monthly*, September 1984.
26. David Rosenbaum, "U.S. Jobs Program Supplanting CETA Aids the Most Able," *New York Times*, July 22, 1984. See also Paul Maryniak, "Real Help Elusive in Job Training Partnership," *Pittsburgh Press*, April 13, 1986, and succeeding article as reprinted in *Congressional Record*, April 28, 1986, S4924–S4926.
27. Nicholas Lemann, "The Odd Conversion of Donald Regan," *Washington Post Weekly*, December 7, 1983.
28. Rosenbaum, "U.S. Jobs Program Supplanting CETA." A similar postelection assessment is Karen Blumenthal, "Job-Training Effort, Critics Say, Fails Many Who Need Help Most; Federal Program Is Accused of Shunning Hard Cases in Seeking Quick Results; But It Scores Some Successes," *Wall Street Journal*, February 9, 1987.
29. "What's Left of the Job Programs?" *Washington Post*, March 14, 1985.
30. "Displaced Worker Programs," *Congressional Record*, April 28, 1986, S4923–S4924; Peter Behr, "Wanted: Job Training that Makes Sense," *Washington Post Weekly*, March 3, 1986.
31. Rosenbaum, "U.S. Jobs Program"; Kathy Sawyer, "Job Training Program Draws Donovan Praise," *Washington Post*, July 27, 1984. See also "A Real Jobs Program," *Wall Street Journal*, September 24, 1984.
32. Keith Harriston, "Quayle and Lugar Praise 'Upbeat' Speech," *Louisville Courier-Journal*, February 2, 1985.

33. Press release, Office of the Governor, "State Receives Nearly $47 Million in Job Training Funds: Orr," June 29, 1984.
34. "Outstanding JTPA Programs," *Congressional Record,* September 28, 1985, S12289-S12291; Bill Zlatos, "Job Training Plan Earns High Marks," *Fort Wayne News-Sentinel,* January 3, 1985.
35. Clay Rice, "Officials Say Job Training Program Is Working," *Louisville Times,* August 16, 1984.
36. Tom Loftus, "Quayle Off and Running Before Foe Can Get Set," *Louisville Courier-Journal,* December 16, 1984.
37. "Let's Talk Politics," Indiana Chamber of Commerce, 1986, 24-25.
38. Alan Ehrenhalt, as quoted in Chuck Conconi, "Personalities," *Washington Post,* September 10, 1985; "The Underrated," *New York Times,* September 10, 1985.
39. Loftus, "Quayle Off and Running."
40. Associated Press, "Quayle Preparing for 1986 Bid on Reelection to the Senate," *New Albany Tribune,* December 10, 1984.
41. Keith Harriston, "Indiana's Freshman Senator Wins Praise As 'Young and Rising Star,'" *Louisville Courier-Journal,* December 16, 1984.
42. Richard Cohen, "Dan Quayle," *National Journal,* April 12, 1986; "Top—and Bottom—of the Class," *National Journal,* April 12, 1986.
43. Cohen, "Dan Quayle." The same story line is featured in Michael Barone, ed., *The Almanac of American Politics: 1988,* 393-394.
44. Gurwitt, "GOP Aims to Elude Senate Takeover Bid in '86."
45. "Retain Quayle as U.S. Senator," *Bloomington Herald-Telephone,* October 20, 1986. See also "U.S. Senate—Quayle," *Bedford Times-Mail,* October 26, 1986.
46. For the "possibilities," see Loftus, "Quayle Off and Running."
47. *Louisville Courier-Journal,* December 24, 1985; David Gourevitch, "Quayle Hoping for Some Competition," *Louisville Times,* circa December 24, 1985.
48. "Indiana Question Mark," *National Journal,* December 7, 1985.
49. Tom Loftus, "Democrats' Once Bubbly Optimism Is Going Flat," *Louisville Courier-Journal,* June 15, 1986.
50. John Krull, "Senator Dan Quayle Rides High," *Indianapolis News,* July 1, 1986.
51. "Overview," Dan Quayle Election Survey, Market Opinion Research, June 1986, 27, 56. All June 1986 poll figures are from this document.
52. Ibid., 27.
53. Patrick J. Traub, "Quayle's Lead May Influence All Races," *Indianapolis Star,* October 12, 1986.
54. "Overview," Market Opinion Research, 57.
55. "Biography of U.S. Senator Dan Quayle"; "U.S. Senator Dan Quayle: His Biography and Record"; "U.S. Senator Dan Quayle: Effective Leadership for Indiana."
56. Press release, "Statement of U.S. Senator Dan Quayle in Announcing His Candidacy for Reelection," February 17, 1986.
57. Kurt Van der Dussen, "Quayle Gears Up for '86 Campaign," *Bloomington Herald Times,* December 15, 1985.
58. Linda Graham Caleca, "Quayle Proud of His Votes Supporting Reagan," *Indianapolis Star,* April 13, 1986.
59. Krull, "Senator Dan Quayle Rides High."
60. Ibid.
61. Press release, "Quayle Honors Hoosier JTPA Entities on Fourth Anniversary of Act's Signing; Reagan, in Letter, Commends Quayle for Leadership in

Guiding JTPA into Law," October 13, 1986; letter from Ronald Reagan to Dan Quayle, October 2, 1986.

62. Gerry LaFollete, "Long, Quayle Both Score in Debate," *Indianapolis News,* September 8, 1986; "Debate: Long, Quayle Open Senate Campaign," *Franklin Daily Journal,* September 8, 1986.

63. "Jill Long, desperately needing TV exposure in her uphill race, came to South Bend yesterday for a news conference and got no TV coverage," Jack Cowell, "TV Snubs Long's Trip to Area," *South Bend Tribune,* October 2, 1986.

64. Doug Richardson, "Democrat Jill Long Builds Recognition in Senate Race," *Evansville Courier,* April 8, 1986.

65. Doug Richardson, "Long to Center on Differences: 'I Want to Avoid Criticizing Quayle,'" *South Bend Tribune,* August 24, 1986.

66. *Indianapolis News,* September 1, 1986.

67. Douglas Davidoff, "Demos Urge Long to Confront Quayle," *Indianapolis News,* circa September 1986.

68. Jeff Owen, "Good Candidate, Bad Politician," *Franklin Daily Journal,* September 9, 1986.

69. Bob Schneider, "Defeated Long Still 'Pleased' With 40 Percent Share of Vote," *Indianapolis Star,* November 5, 1986.

70. *Indianapolis Star,* September 1, 1985.

71. Associated Press, "Quayle Presses Reelection Campaign," *New Castle Courier Times,* July 7, 1986.

72. Ibid.

73. Krull, "Senator Dan Quayle Rides High." See also John Krull, "A Battle Cruiser and a Lifeboat," *Indianapolis News,* October 30, 1986.

74. Press release, "Quayle Will Schedule No Additional Fund Raising Activities Between Now and Election Day," October 14, 1986.

75. James G. Newland, "Quayle Scores Lopsided Senate Victory Over Long," November 5, 1986.

76. Traub, "Quayle's Lead May Influence All Races."

77. Ibid.

78. "Quayle Buries Long in Winning Second Term in Senate," *Louisville Courier-Journal,* November 5, 1986.

79. Letter from Richard Nymeyer, Elkhart County START Center, October 30, 1986; press release, "Quayle Pledges to Continue Working for Indiana's Economic Development," October 30, 1986.

Index